THE THEORY OF ECONOMIC PROGRESS

C. E. AYRES

THE THEORY OF ECONOMIC PROGRESS

A STUDY OF THE FUNDAMENTALS OF ECONOMIC DEVELOPMENT AND CULTURAL CHANGE

Second Edition

SCHOCKEN BOOKS · NEW YORK

First SCHOCKEN PAPERBACK edition 1962
Second Printing 1965
This edition is published by arrangement with
The University of North Carolina Press

Library of Congress Catalog Card No. 62-18158

Manufactured in the United States of America

Foreword—1962

THE THEME of this book is a very simple one. It is that human progress consists in finding out how to do things, finding out how to do more things, and finding out how to do all things better. If the question is asked whether some things are not better left unlearned, the answer is No; and the reason is, all things are related—causally related. Learning to kill people might perhaps be thought of as a lesson better left unlearned. But not only is the art of killing people exactly the same as the art of killing animals for food (an activity which goes back not only to the dawn of human culture but even to our zoölogical predecessors); the art of killing people is indissociable from the art of keeping people alive. Doctors know best how to kill people, unless perhaps physicists know even better.

In using such comparatives as "more" and "better" it may seem as though I am prejudging the whole matter. What do "more" and "better" mean? The answer is, the meaning of such terms is implicit in the process. In both cases it is a processual, or operational, meaning. The meaning "more" is implicit in the meaning "amount," whatever may be quantified. Any quantity implies moreness and lessness; and the same is true of "better." This is an activity word.

Any and every doing implies betterness and worseness, and in every doing the significance of "better" and "worse" is implicit in what is being done.

Moreover, all these meanings are aggregative—and this is the most important point of all. They are so because that is the way the world is. Everything anyone does affects his other doings and also the doings of other people. The temptation is strong to think of certain things and acts as intrinsically good, and of others as intrinsically bad, as though each were suffused with good magic or bad magic. Indeed, the inveterate addiction of mankind to belief in magic is the source of our temptation. But the simple truth is that nothing exists by itself. No act is performed by itself. All are causally related, and can be known and judged only as aggregates.

Thus progress is an aggregative term. There can be small aggregates as well as large ones, of course. We can speak intelligibly of a single individual's progress in learning to swim, or of a whole community's progress in physical fitness. By the same token, we can speak of human progress in general, meaning the broadest possible aggregate of all human activities.

At this point, however, a serious difficulty arises. Are all human activities alike in the sense of being parts of the same aggregate? The answer to this question assuredly is No. All are alike in the sense of being human. But through all human activities there runs a deep cleavage—or perhaps it would be better to say a sort of polarity, since at all times we are to some degree subject to opposing influences. Two forces seem to be present in all human behavior in all ages: one progressive, dynamic, productive of cumulative change; the other counter-progressive, static, inhibitory of change.

Our common tongue contains no satisfactory terms with which to designate these forces. The terms used in this book —technology and ceremonialism—derive from Thorstein

Veblen, who pioneered the study of the interaction of these forces. Each must be understood as being used in a very broad and also a very special sense. Thus "technology" must be understood to include all human activities involving the use of tools—all sorts of tools: the simplest striking stones of primeval man as well as the atom-splitting bevatrons of present-day physicists; written language, books, and the symbols mathematicians manipulate, as well as marks in the sand, notches on a stick, or the fire built around the trunk of a tree to fell it.

But tools are not technology. The two commonest mistakes people make with regard to technology are (1) thinking of it as non-human tools, and (2) thinking of it as human skill. Both misconceptions make it impossible to understand how technology develops. The former leads to the presumption that technology is a feature of the setting in which human beings carry on their activities, part of the physical environment of mankind; and this suggests that it is static and inert. But the other conception of technology as human skill likewise fails us, since we know that human beings are no brighter, no more apt, today than a hundred thousand years ago.

This dilemma can be resolved and the technological process can be understood only by recognizing that human skills and the tools by which and on which they are exercised are logically inseparable. Skills *always* employ tools, and tools are such *always* by virtue of being employed in acts of skill by human beings. Once the dual character of the technological process is understood, the explanation of its dynamism is obvious. Technology advances by virtue of inventions and discoveries being made—by men, of course. But all inventions and discoveries result from the combining of hitherto separate tools, instruments, materials, and the like. These are capable of combination by virtue of their physical existence. The combining is of course performed by man, and especially by bright and restless men. But no one ever made a combination without there being something to combine. Furthermore, the more there is to combine in any given situation the more likely inventions and discoveries become—unless the inveterate restlessness of human hands and brains is severely curbed.

It is what Veblen called ceremonialism that provides the curb. This type or mode of behavior manifests itself in various ways, particularly these five ways. For one thing, the social stratification which seems to occur in all societies is such a manifestation. Second, this stratification (or hierarchy, or status system) is defined and sustained by a system of conventions which delimit and prescribe the behavior that is proper to persons of every social rank. These are commonly known as mores. Third, both status and mores are further sustained by an ideology, or system of tribal beliefs, which purport to explain the magic potency which distinguishes people of higher ranks and the awful consequences which are believed to follow infractions of the mores. Fourth, the members of every community are emotionally conditioned to acceptance of the beliefs in question, observance of the mores, and respect for lines of caste and status by systems of indoctrination which begin in infancy. And fifth, all these patterns of behavior are defined, codified, and intensified in mystic rites and ceremonies. It is by virtue of sacred ceremonies that persons of various ranks have imparted to them the mysterious powers—the "ceremonial adequacy," as Veblen called it—of their particular ranks; the ceremonies define the mores; they re-enact what people believe to be their tribal history; and they are above all solemn, awe-inspiring, fear-inducing, and generally emotion-conditioning.

This system of behavior is static and inhibitory of change, such as technological activities promote, for a very obvious reason. In all its manifestations the ceremonial system is past-binding. The ceremonies are re-enactments of what is presumed to be tribal history—the more ancient the better; hence their emotional impact. Tribal beliefs resist change because they are presumed to have been laid down in the remote past, and the same is true of mores and status systems. Sacred commandments do not change, nor does the authority of ceremonially invested rank. The over-all effect of this whole system of behavior is to keep things as they are —and, presumably, always have been.

Thus what happens to any society is determined jointly by the forward urging of its technology and the backward pressure of its ceremonial system. A well known study of social change in a great number of primitive societies has established a positive correlation between change and movement. When peoples move around they come in contact with other peoples, and changes result from those contacts. This raises a further question. Why do peoples move around? The answer to this question would seem to be: people move when they have the technical means of doing so, if they are not prevented by recognized authority, moral law, and emotional attachments.

The question may still be asked, What motivates such movement? In all cases the answer is the same. People climb a mountain to see what is on the other side—or, in the words of a celebrated mountain climber who lost his life on Mount Everest: "Because it's there." These very words are being quoted today by astronauts. In short, the motive is implicit in the process. This is true of both processes. Ancestor worshippers do not decide to oppose change. They oppose change only because they hate it, and they hate it because they love "the old ways." Scientists do not seek knowledge because they are dissatisfied with the knowledge they already have. As has been said thousands of times by thousands of scientists, every discovery raises more questions than it answers. In short, the motive is implicit in the process. Mount Everest was eventually climbed by use of improved techniques for bottling oxygen in portable tanks. Thus it is literally true that what led to the climbing of Mount Everest was the bottling of oxygen.

Veblen did not schematize his basic principles quite as I have done. But he did show their applicability to all societies, including our own. Such is the import of one of his most celebrated dicta, the one I have already quoted at the end of Chapter VIII:

> . . . history records more frequent and more spectacular instances of the triumph of imbecile institutions over life and culture than of peoples who have . . . saved themselves alive out of a desperately precarious institutional situation, such, for instance, as now faces the peoples of Christendom.

These words appear in *The Instinct of Workmanship*, which was published in March, 1914: six months before the assassin of Sarajevo triggered the wars of the twentieth century. But they are even more pertinent today than when they were written. Science and technology are now advancing faster than ever. We can do things now that were not even dreamed of in 1914. And our institutional situation is more desperately precarious than ever.

2

All that I have said in the preceding pages has already been said in the body of this book. I have nevertheless repeated it here because, as I now feel, this is how the book should begin—affirmatively, with a positive statement of the basic principles with the significance of which it is concerned. This decision is based in part on the changed circumstances in which *The Theory of Economic Progress* is now being re-issued.

During the years which have passed since this book was first published the process of economic development has become the subject of a vast outpouring of books and articles. This literature is of course a product of circumstances. More than ever before, the Second World War, as it has come to be known, made non-European peoples throughout the world familiar with at least the distant view of the most advanced products of Western technology. The establishment of air fields and military depots throughout the world gave millions their first acquaintance with the Western way of life. At the same time the extensive conquests of the Japanese gave incontestible evidence that industrialization is not race-limited.

As everyone knows, these circumstances gave rise to what has become known as "a revolution of expectations" throughout the world. All the less industrialized countries are now seeking economic development, and economists have responded generously to this demand. At the present time, therefore, it is inevitable that a book bearing the title *The Theory of Economic Progress* will be assumed to be a contribution to this literature; and since the book does in fact deal with the process of economic development, this now seems clearly to be the foot it should now put forward.

But that is not how the book was originally conceived. The effort which resulted in this book was begun years earlier, and was an attempt to define the "institutionalist" way of thinking. That is why it began with a repudiation of the "classical" tradition. Even today there is no clearly defined body of principles on which institutionalists are generally agreed and by which they are known. But if there is anything that all institutionalists have in common it is dissatisfaction with "orthodox" price theory. Thus it seemed to me during the years when this book was in process of gestation that any positive statement of institutionalist principles would be unintelligible unless preceded by an explicit rejection of traditional economic theory.

But even this is not as easy as it sounds. What is it that

we object to in orthodox price theory? A poll of institutionalists would, I fear, produce a bewildering variety of answers to such a question. Indeed, I myself would answer the question differently today from the way I tried to answer it in the opening section of this book, and that is one of the principal reasons for the present Foreword. As the years have passed during which I have debated these matters with successive generations of students I have become convinced that the decisive issue is not that of price, or capital, or value, but that of our conception of the nature of the economy itself. This, I hasten to say, does not mean that I am now "taking back" anything I have said earlier about these other concepts. The point is rather that traditional ideas of the functioning of the price system are themselves incidental to an over-all conception of the economy. Our trouble—so I would now argue—all stems from a fundamental misconception of the nature of the economy itself, one to which Western society was committed by force of historic circumstances long before books began to be written on "The Principles of Political Economy."

Economics is by definition the study of the economy. But what is this "economy?" On one thing, at least, all economists agree. It is a system of interrelated activities having to do with "the ordinary business of living." So far, so good! The definition is vague enough to suit everybody. Everybody agrees that the activities in which we all engage in the ordinary business of getting a living are somehow interrelated. The decisive question is, How? The author of this ordinary-business definition was Alfred Marshall, the fountainhead of modern orthodoxy. He assumed as a matter of course that the agency by which all ordinary-business activities are organized and interrelated is "the market." He did not prove this to be the case, and nobody else has ever done so. That has simply been taken for granted. It was taken for granted centuries before Adam Smith wrote that

Magna Carta of political economy, *An Inquiry into the Nature and Causes of the Wealth of Nations,* and it was taken for granted, as it still is, for what have always seemed to be entirely convincing reasons.

What, after all, are the most conspicuous—the most public—activities in which people engage in the ordinary business of living? The answer is, of course, buying and selling. Making a living is often a lonely business. But spending it is gregarious. People make their livings in thousands of different ways. But spending is the same for all. Making a living is monotonous work. But spending it is always interesting and sometimes dramatic.

Furthermore, this has always been so. At the dawn of modern times even more than today the activities of husbandmen and craftsmen were lonely and humdrum. Such people are drudges. The community takes them and their occupations for granted, as it does housewives. But the fair was an exciting break in the humdrum of existence. Mystery and high drama suffuse the activities of merchants.

Moreover, from the dawn of modern times onward, merchants and financiers were becoming important people, more and more important as time passed. This, too, has had its effect. As I have indicated in Chapter I, our obsession with the market does not seem to me to be the result of a capitalist conspiracy. But that the importance of merchants throughout modern times has affected the common sense of the community, as Veblen used that phrase, with regard to the importance of mercantile activities seems virtually axiomatic.

At the same time, as I tried to point out in Chapter II, various challenges to statecraft which arose in early modern times had the effect of focusing attention on the market long before there was any such discipline as political economy and even before scholars had begun to think of the ordinary business of living as constituting a system of interrelated activities. One is tempted to say that the conception of a market-organized economy antedates the conception of the economy.

All this is entirely consistent with what I wrote in 1944 about our traditional obsession with the price system, and about the ambiguity of the concept of capital and the inadequacy of the pecuniary conception of value. I am now only trying to carry this reasoning to what now seems to me its ultimate conclusion, namely, that the economy itself which has all the time been the subject matter of our discipline has been completely misconceived.

Even so, the question might be raised whether it would not be wiser to ignore the misconceptions of the past and proceed at once to try to set the record straight. In some areas of human knowledge this might be wise counsel. But in this area such a simple correction of our course is impossible. It is impossible because, unlike neutrinos and polymers, supply and demand are well known to everybody. So plausible is the classical conception of the economy that everybody "knows" that the economy is the market, supply and demand, the buying-and-selling mechanism. This is what J. K. Galbraith has called "the conventional wisdom" of our society. To ignore it is to be unintelligible.

That is why it seemed to me when I wrote this book that I must make it clear at the outset that I was dissenting from the conventional wisdom. It now seems to me that I would have made this demurrer more understandable if I had said that it was the traditional conception of the economy itself from which I was proposing to dissent.

3

One major advantage which results from focusing attention upon the nature of the economy itself is that it brings economics into line with other disciplines. According to anthropologists every culture includes an economy. In a sense this is only to say that every community has some way of getting a living, which is a truism. The significant truth is that each society has its own distinctive way of getting a living. Among simple peoples some one food source is usually so important for each people's living that its economy can be meaningfully identified with that food. Thus we recognize fish cultures, taro cultures, yak cultures, and so on indefinitely. There is some evidence that the earliest known human inhabitants of Europe had a mammoth culture.

At first blush it would appear that the economies of advanced civilizations, and especially that of the modern Western world, do not lend themselves to such designation. For the more advanced a people is, the more varied is its dietary. But a moment's reflection will resolve this difficulty, and the resolution will be borne out by the facts. The truth is that every economy, however simple, is technologically based. In order for a certain article of food to have become the mainstay of any people, that people must have developed suitable tools and techniques for obtaining that food substance. The mammoth hunters who followed the retreating continental glacier, living off the huge pachyderms which fed on the vegetation of the tundra, are known to have specialized on calves. They must have developed specialized techniques for cutting the calves out of the herds and then dispatching them. They may even have used glacial ice as a ready-made deep-freeze. This is true of all food-designated economies. Each is in fact a specialized tool-and-technique economy. Indeed, whole cultures have been transformed by the introduction of new instruments. When the plains Indians of the Old West obtained horses from the Spaniards, they abandoned their ancient corn technology and commenced following the herds of bison. As identified by their principal source of food, theirs was now a bison economy. But its real foundation was horses and horsemanship.

In the same sense industrial technology is the real substance of the modern economy. This conception of the economy is not a denial of the existence of its market aspect, any more than traditional price theory is a denial of the existence of machine technology. The question is, Which is the dog and which is the tail? Granted that no exponent of the market theory has ever denied the existence of what Veblen called "the machine process"; nevertheless that theory in all its manifestations does imply that the creative principle—the economic magic of the Western economy—somehow emanates from the market, from mercantile activities, from buying and selling. Some exponents of this conception of the economy have even gone so far as to attribute all the distinctive features of modern Western civilization—not only machine technology but even science itself, and not only science but all the arts, indeed all the achievements of the human spirit—to the mercantile mentality. Absurd as such claims are, they are only an exaggeration of the concept that has been basic to our economic thinking throughout modern times. As Adam Smith put it, "As it is the power of exchanging that gives occasion to the division of labour, so the extent of this division must always be limited by the extent of that power, or, in other words, by the extent of the market."

But surely the true state of affairs is almost the exact reverse of this. Indeed, it can be stated most succinctly in these very words. As it is the state of the industrial arts that gives occasion to exchange, so the extent of the market must always be limited by the state of the industrial arts. Swapping is possible only when there is something to swap. People can indulge Adam Smith's famous "propensity to truck, barter and exchange" only to the extent that exchangeable goods exist.

Thus another and most important advantage which results from identifying our economy, like all others, by its technology is that its genesis then becomes apparent. The origin of the market-conceived economy is a profound mystery. Once the industrial revolution of the eighteenth century was accepted as a fact, sound theory required that it be preceded by a commercial revolution which might be conceived to have "made it possible." It was relatively easy for economic historians to show that buying and selling were going on, that fortunes were being made, and even that merchants were dominating the scene, long before the steam engine came into industrial use. But what brought all this about? Medieval fairs? The wealth of the monastic orders? The Protestant Reformation? All these suggestions and many more have been duly offered. But as scholars have become more and more absorbed in the effort to advise the less industrialized nations how to achieve economic development they have come to realize more and more disturbingly that none of the familiar explanations of our own economic development is entirely satisfactory. The truth is, we do not know how our own economy developed.

But if ours is an industrial economy—if its creative genius lies in its machine technology, just as that of a hunting economy lies in its bows and arrows—then the solution is obvious. Our development has been the result of a series of discoveries and inventions. Those discoveries and inventions have come about in our society just as all technological developments come about in all societies.

True, we have benefited from an extraordinary series of revolutionary technological advances, and this circumstance still requires to be explained. But when we couch the question in these terms, the answer appears quite obvious. What situation could have given rise to so vast a technological revolution? The answer calls for a unique series of combinations of technical culture traits occurring in a uniquely fluid institutional situation. If we then look back over the centuries, this is exactly what we find.

4

Although this book was written and published before the onset of the present paroxysm of economic development, it does contain, at least by implication, certain basic principles.

The first of these is that the process of economic development is indivisible and irresistible. If we consider it country by country, or invention by invention, there have already been many industrial revolutions. But in a much more significant sense all have been incidents in a general process which began in Western Europe at the dawn of modern times (thereby marking the onset of modern times) and has been spreading throughout the world ever since.

The propelling force of this vast cultural revolution has been technological. But this does not mean that institutional circumstances have not been a causal factor of equal importance. In the centuries that followed "the fall of Rome" (that is, the separation of "All Gaul" from the Empire) Western Europe manifested a unique combination of technological continuity and institutional detachment. The former meant that the technical possibility of invention and discovery was as great here as anywhere in the world, and the latter meant that Europeans enjoyed a greater freedom to bring such possibilities to fruition than did the inhabitants of any ancient center of civilization.

The "break-through" occurred during the fifteenth century. What was broken through was feudalism, the manorial-agricultural economy, the medieval world view, the absolute spiritual authority of the Roman Catholic Church, and European isolation. The forces which became manifest during this century had of course been operative for many centuries. A revolution in land transport had already been brought about by horse shoes and the horse collar, and the germs of powered machinery had been introduced in the form of windmills and water wheels and medieval clocks. The Arabic numerals and Chinese printing had been introduced, and gunpowder had been invented. By the end of the fifteenth century printing from movable types had been invented and (bibliophiles calculate) twenty million books had been printed and, for the first time in human history, were spreading literacy throughout the entire community. Ships, and the arts of navigation, had been developed to carry Europeans equipped with arms vastly superior to those of any other people to the shores of all the continents. The Copernican revolution was imminent, and cracks in the monolithic structure of the Church were beginning to appear. In short, Western Europe was launched upon a "take-off" from which there was no turning back.

The second basic principle of economic development is that the technological revolution spreads in inverse proportion to institutional resistance. The irresistible dynamism of the technological revolution which became manifest in Western Europe during the fifteenth century does not mean that no resistance was offered. Ceremonial traditions always resist change. They have done so in Western Europe from medieval times onward, though with steadily diminishing force; and they do so everywhere else, with results that still remain to be determined.

Since the technological revolution made it possible, Europeans have penetrated to all parts of the world. Their motives for doing so have been extremely various and on that account alone may be safely disregarded. The determining factor in all cases has been their ability to do so. Moreover, wherever they have gone, Europeans have taken their tools and know-how with them. Where they have encountered no effective resistance from alien cultures, technological development has continued and has even spurted ahead faster than in the mother countries, where despite all change a considerable "residue" of ancient ceremonialism still persists. That is why the United States, Canada, and Australia now stand among the most advanced industrial countries in the world today. But wherever ancient cultures prevail, and most especially among a dense population, resistance to change is correspondingly great.

Such resistance is both passive and active: passive in the sense that illiteracy is more difficult to cope with in large masses than in small ones, active in the sense that teaching people to read and write almost inevitably involves interfering with their traditional way of life and may even involve drastically modifying the language habits of a thousand years—all of which people bitterly and even violently resist. What language should the people of India be taught to read and write?

In this matter of institutional resistance the practitioners of total revolution enjoy a tremendous advantage. During the colonial period Europeans made it a matter of deliberate policy not to "interfere" with "native" cultures. They did so partly as a matter of snobbery by holding themselves aloof from the indigenous population, and partly out of respect for the human rights of the "subject" peoples as a matter of humanitarian conviction. Revolutionists scorn both these motives, and so make the extirpation of the indigenous culture their first order of business, following which the introduction of industrial technology is relatively easy. This is the secret of the astonishing rapidity with which the Soviet Union has been catching up with the West. To be sure, revolutionaries may be afflicted with traditions of their own which act as a brake on the developmental process. The compulsive collectivization of agriculture may be such an institutional liability.

Short of total revolution, what is to be the outcome of the confrontation of the irresistible force of the technological process by the seemingly immovable obstacle of a population that is vast and dense and saturated with a pre-industrial culture? Can such a mass of human beings be transformed without resort to violence? We do not know. None has been yet. But we do know the principle by which alone such a transformation must be governed.

This is the third principle of economic development: that of the creation of human capital. The nature of human capital and its significance for economic development have never been more clearly stated than by Thorstein Veblen in his two essays "On the Nature of Capital," first published in the *Quarterly Journal of Economics* in 1908, and reprinted in *The Place of Science in Modern Civilization and Other Essays* in 1919. His argument was of course based on his conception of technology. Granted that technology is human skills and know-how and the complement of tools and equipment in which such skills and know-how are embodied and through which they are exercised; the equipment is useless without the know-how. But given the skills and know-how, equipment can be reproduced. Hence the most important factor in the economic life of any people is the educational level, as we now call it, of the community. A technically sophisticated community can and will equip itself with the instrumentalities of an industrial economy. There is no instance of any such community having failed to do so. Conversely, an ignorant and unskilled community cannot advance except by acquiring knowledge and skills.

Obvious as these propositions are, they have been obscured by the "conventional wisdom." As I have tried to show in the chapters that follow, we have traditionally conceived capital both as industrial plant and as accumulated funds, and in both guises have supposed it to be indispensable to economic growth. Consequently both of these conceptions have seemed quite plausible when applied to the development of the less industrialized peoples.

Thus it seems to stand to reason that lack of funds is the

decisive impediment to economic growth, and vast efforts have been made to supply a flow of funds to regions in which such development is being fostered. This presumption is based in part on what is quite generally taken to be the actual experience of countries such as the United States in which very considerable and very rapid growth has indeed taken place. It is commonly assumed that such development was made possible by the advancement of funds by older and wealthier countries. But in a paper entitled "The Contribution of Foreign Investments: A Case Study of United States Foreign Investment History," published in the spring, 1961 issue of *Inter-American Economic Affairs,* my colleague Professor Wendell Gordon has showed conclusively that such was not the case. Using figures most carefully compiled by the National Bureau of Economic Research he shows ". . . that for the period 1790 to 1900 (or 1914) net earnings on foreign investments in the United States substantially exceeded net increase in United States indebtedness. And this relation prevailed generally throughout the whole 125-year period." In short, the hardy bands of men and women who first landed on these shores were quite capable of instituting a viable economy from the very start, and of paying for whatever imports they required with their own exports. This, and not a supply of funds from abroad, is the explanation of the growth of the American economy.

It is nevertheless true, as Professor Gordon himself remarks, that this demonstration ". . . does not question the importance of capital equipment. Capital equipment, the shipment of which is financed by outright purchase in the supplying country, may make quite a contribution." The question is, To what? Students of economic development have been much troubled in recent years by a phenomenon they speak of as "economic dualism." This is the co-existence of islands of industrial enterprise in the midst of relatively primitive economies of oceanic proportions. In some cases the industrial islands have not only been financed by foreign interests but have been built and continue to be operated by the human capital of the initiating power. In other cases the industrial islands are, or have become, largely indigenous. The industrial cities of India offer the most conspicuous example of such development. They are surrounded by rural India, where a population mass of some 350 million people live virtually untouched by the world-wide technological revolution. In short, capital equipment will work anywhere. But it will affect the lives only of those who are in direct contact with it. It does not automatically bring economic development to a whole people.

Only education can do that: hence my emphasis on the role of literacy in the "take-off" of the Western peoples. Reading and writing (and, of course, ciphering) are basic skills. As such they are even more fundamental to the process of industrialization than basic industries. To qualify for even the most "unskilled" industrial employment one must be able to "read the directions" and to keep a simple record. The industrialization of Japan dates, as everyone knows, from the Meiji revolution. What is not so widely appreciated is that the Meiji revolution not only transformed the power structure and class system of Japanese society. It was an educational revolution which brought literacy to the Japanese people and so laid a solid foundation for the industrialization that followed. The same was true of the Russian revolution. Bolshevik seizure of power was immediately followed by a massive educational effort: "Every one teach one." Without such an effort Soviet industrial achievements would have been impossible.

This is the culture-area in which the "big push" must be made. As development experts speak of it, the "big push" means setting an industrial complex going of such magnitude that its momentum will draw the whole community in its wake in an accelerating process of "sustained growth." But if it is not to be island growth—if the rest of the community is not to be left behind on "reservations," however populous, such as those of the American Indians—the big push must be applied to the entire community. Only education (by whatever name it is called) can do that.

Whether success is possible in any given case remains to be determined. No doubt Hindu priests and Mohammedan mullahs will resist the enlightenment of their people with all the wiles at their command, just as the Christian Church resisted the translation of the Bible from Latin into the various regional dialects. According to their lights, they will be right in doing so; for—we must face it—technological revolution brings its own values to fruition, to the detriment of all local and tribal value systems.

This is the fourth, and perhaps consummatory, principle of economic development. As I said at the beginning of this Foreword, and had already said in the closing chapters of this book, the values which are engendered in the technological process are universal values. Science, the intellectual aspect of technology, assumes and requires a commitment to the discovery of truth, and science prescribes its own conception of truth. It is a processual, or operational, or instrumental—tool-defined—conception of truth.

This conception of truth and of human values generally is at variance with all tribal legends and all tribal authority; and since the technological revolution is itself irresistible, the arbitrary authority and irrational values of pre-scientific, pre-industrial cultures are doomed. Three alternatives confront the partisans of tribal values and beliefs. Resistance, if sufficiently effective, though it cannot save the tribal values, can bring on total revolution. Or ineffective resistance may lead to sequestration like that of the American Indians. The only remaining alternative is that of intelligent, voluntary acceptance of the industrial way of life and all the values that go with it.

We need make no apology for recommending such a course. Industrial society is the most successful way of life mankind has ever known. Not only do our people eat better, sleep better, live in more comfortable dwellings, get around more and in far greater comfort, and—notwithstanding all the manifold dangers of the industrial way of life—live longer than men have ever done before. Our people are also better informed than ever before. In addition to listening to radio and watching television, they read more books, see more pictures, and hear more music than any previous generation or any other people ever has. At the height of the technological revolution we are now living in a golden age of scientific enlightenment and artistic achievement.

For all who achieve economic development profound cultural change is inevitable. But the rewards are considerable.

C.E.A.

Austin, Texas
April 12, 1962

Preface to First Edition

THE PURPOSE of this book is to set forth a new way of thinking about economic problems. The time will come when we shall see that the root of all our economic confusion and the cause of the intellectual impotency which has brought economics into general disrepute is the obsession of our science with price theory—the virtual identification of economics with price analysis to the almost total exclusion of what Veblen called the "life process" of mankind.

To orthodox economists such a statement of the issue must always seem unwarranted. As they still insist, what focused the attention of the founding fathers upon price was their "realization" that price equilibrium is the key to all the mysteries of economic life. Ah, sweet mystery of price!

This presumption raises a question of primary importance. On what basis does it rest? The answer which I have given in the first part of this book is neither novel nor definitive. One of the commonest criticisms of orthodox economics is that it is based on the psychology, moral philosophy, and even theology of the eighteenth century, all of which, as we know, perpetuated earlier habits of thought that are even more widely at variance with present knowledge. Economics is by no means the only science in which ancient fallacies persist, but it is unique among contemporary studies in being the only one in which eighteenth-century (and earlier) habits of thought define the prevailing tradition. All this has been said before, indeed many times, but still not often or convincingly enough—so it would seem, since the tradition still prevails. I hardly dare to hope that my indictment will prove more effective than earlier ones. But so long as the classical tradition persists, no one can neglect its challenge.

Moreover, to do so would be a mistake of the first order. For we shall not be able to go straight in economics by easy expedients, such as addressing ourselves "directly" to the "facts." Surely we ought to know by now that facts without understanding are meaningless; and understanding is a matter of perspective and pattern, that is to say theory. Does observation of the factual manifold reveal any general pattern? What are the forces that shape this pattern? In what different aspects—of production, distribution, consumption, or whatever—is the pattern manifest and what is the relation between those several aspects or functions? What sort of balance prevails among them and what is the criterion of balance and imbalance? The founders of the science owe their pre-eminence to their realization of the importance of such questions. If they were wrong in trying to elicit answers from the numerology of price, their questions still confront us.

What students of economics need today is to make a fresh start. If they would do this, they would discover almost immediately that they enjoy a very great advantage over the social philosophers of four and five generations ago. An immense quantity of water has passed over the scientific dam during the years that separate us from Adam Smith. In particular this period includes the Great Flood of 1859. The whole post-Darwinian conception of the nature of man, of the pattern of human behavior, and of social process, differs from that of the eighteenth century no less than the chemistry of the present day differs from that of Cavendish. The economist after all is a member of the scientific community, not a solitary castaway. Great sums of knowledge have already been deposited to his account by philosophers and sociologists, psychologists, historians, and anthropologists.

In this book I have tried to draw a few checks on that account. To students of the other social sciences there is nothing new about this way of thinking; and since the basic problems of social behavior are the same for all of us, what I have to say may prove to be of greater interest to them than to case-hardened economists. The problems are those which underlie the science of economics; but the ideas are drawn from a common fund, and the audience to which this statement of them is addressed is not limited by any professional barriers.

I am told that my chapters are "closely reasoned," and I hope that such is indeed the case. Does this mean that they are therefore inaccessible to non-economists or even to non-academic readers? I hope not. Stephen Leacock once remarked that there is no such thing as a book on economics for reading in a hammock, and that dictum certainly applies to the present volume. But I see no reason why anyone who is sufficiently concerned about our common fate to be willing to give close attention should be unable to follow my analysis. If such is the case, then I have failed. And the failure is a serious one, for the world cannot be saved by specialists. As I have said from the first page to the last, these ways of thinking are the result of a general social process in which the whole community participates.

Contents

There is the economic life process still in great measure awaiting theoretical formulation. —*Thorstein Veblen*

THE CLASSICAL TRADITION

Chapter I

THE SCIENCE OF PRICE

IN EVERY SCIENCE new ways of thinking are the result of a general social process in which the whole community participates. This is true even of the most specific discoveries. It is a commonplace of the history of science that no discovery is ever made that is not in some sense and to some degree anticipated by earlier work. It is also well known that discoveries which result from refinements of laboratory technique commonly depend upon refinements of tool materials and of basic machine tools which science derives from related industries and those industries from industry in general, which in turn relates to science in general. And what is true of particulars is even more obviously true of universals. The larger conceptions in terms of which science does its thinking are projections of the thinking of the whole community. Only in a community, for example, in which the idea of change had assumed paramount importance could the origin of species have come to be a problem of the highest order of significance.

In the case of economics this relationship between the thinking of the professional student and that of the community is further intensified by the fact that the ideas of economists can take effect only through the action of the community, action to which the community must in some sense or other give assent. This also is true to some degree of every science. We must not exaggerate our common ignorance. Armchair philosophers are fond of calling this an age of faith in which people trust their lives to machines they do not understand; whereas the truth is that a great many people do understand the machines they use a great deal better than the philosophers suppose—a great deal better, one suspects, than the armchair theorists themselves. Nevertheless it is true that very few of the vast army of amateur radio technicians, for example, understand the physical science of electronics; and it is not necessary to be even an amateur radio technician in order to listen to a broadcast. Scientific discoveries need to be fully understood only by a few in order to be used with comparatively slight scientific understanding by a great many. But even in such cases the whole community to some degree understands and accepts the basic scientific principles of which the new discovery is an application or extension. Basically radio is only a telephone instrument and an electric light bulb put together in a box. Even the most innocent philosopher knows that the box contains nothing occult, only a maze of wires. The community understands and accepts without reservation the principle of conduction of electricity by wires. In the case of economics it is these basic principles or elements which are in doubt, and the doubt is shared by the community at large.

Like other disciplines, economics is more than a field of inquiry; it is a way of thinking. Physics, for example, occupies a field of inquiry; but the way of thinking which characterizes modern physics is very different from the lucubrations of the ancients concerning earth, air, fire, and water. The way of economic thinking which has prevailed during the last five generations or so, follows the pattern of a system of ideas or set of principles which achieved general acceptance during the eighteenth century. The common definition of economics as the science of wealth, with the implication of money values which the term "wealth" carries in the modern world, is both an expression of this way of thinking and a corresponding identification of the world of commerce as the field of inquiry in which it prevails. Among economists this system of ideas is known as the classical tradition to distinguish it from other ways of thinking which various people have proposed from time to time both before and after the appearance of the science of wealth.

For some little time and with progressive acceleration in recent years this way of thinking has been falling into disrepute, and for obvious reasons. There was a time when the economic life of the Western world seemed to be atomistic. Whether it really was as atomistic as it seemed is very doubtful, but that is not the point. It seemed so to the community at large, to whom therefore the idea of a community of interests achieved by the canceling out of discrepant individual interests in competition made a tremendously powerful appeal. Commerce itself, the exchange of goods and services in "the market," thus acquired an extraordinary significance by virtue of which it monopolized attention to the almost total exclusion of even the most closely related industrial processes. It was of course this state of mind which gave pertinence to classical political economy. But with the passage of time the concentration of control has become increasingly extreme and therefore increasingly obvious. The community has continued to hymn the praises of competition; but the singing has become more and more perfunctory as the spectacle of the financial concentration of control of industry has become more and more obvious and inescapable. At the same time the machine has become increasingly conspicuous. Industry, as distinguished from commerce, has forced itself upon the attention of the community to a steadily increasing degree until the time has arrived when people generally have come to realize the utter dependence of modern civilization upon the efficient use of the machine. The spectacle of idle machines during the decade following 1929 has done more than all the academic criticism of the preceding generations to cloud the confidence of the community in a way of economic thinking which is so exclusively preoccupied with commerce that it scarcely ever makes mention of machines.

As a result of these developments the state of mind which now prevails throughout the community at large is one of uneasy anticipation of substantial change. This sense of the imminence of economic change is of course heightened by the contemplation of cataclysmic political changes. Whereas in years gone by senators have intoned the doom of quite trivial reforms as violations of the "eternal and inalterable laws of a beneficent nature," the present generation has seen nations maintain themselves for years and even embark on a program of world conquest without even the vestige of a gold reserve. The possibility that present world disorders may be ushering in some sort of "managerial" economy and the virtual certainty that the future will bring a steady enlargement of the economic functions of government are matters of more or less uneasy concern to thinking people everywhere.

The uneasiness people feel in the contemplation of such inevitable change is due in large part to not knowing what to think about it. The community at large is well aware of being intellectually unprepared for change, and it is the persistence of the old way of thinking which is responsible for this intellectual unpreparedness. Our confusion goes much deeper than immediate issues of economic policy. Whatever understanding of the complex pattern of the modern industrial system the community has been able to achieve has been in terms of free price adjustment in the market, the very point on which the whole process of economic change seems to pivot. The possible alternatives vary widely, having only this in common, that none of them is intelligible in terms of the classical conception of an economy of free price adjustment. However willing the community may be to adjust its thinking to the requirements of the times, it is simply unable to do so for the reason that the only general conception of the meaning of the economic organization of society is inapplicable to the forces which now seem clearly to be shaping the economic organization of the future.

The persistence of a way of thinking which somehow fails to take account of what are proving to be the basic realities of modern economic life is itself one of the great economic mysteries of our civilization, a mystery upon which many students of economics have reflected. In certain quarters the prevailing explanation has always been that of prejudice. Many circumstances contribute to this interpretation. For example, nothing could be more favorable to the growth of monopoly than the doctrine that business men must be free from governmental "interference" in order to compete. The growing dominance of business men throughout the period of ascendancy of the classical system of ideas would be enough to suggest their special interest even if they had not been all along the most ardent advocates of those ideas. But advocacy does not explain origin.

The susceptibility of social philosophers to class interest is also explicable in terms of the structure of the society from which, after all, social philosophers are drawn. The classical tradition has never been altogether uncontested. On the contrary, every generation has provided powerful arraignments not only of prevailing economic situations but of the system of ideas by which those situations were so powerfully buttressed. But the arraignments passed unnoticed and have been largely forgotten even by scholars while the traditional way of thinking has continued to persist.

This state of affairs has never been described more clearly or temperately than by Mr. J. A. Hobson in a passage which deserves a wider circulation than it has yet enjoyed.

What other conclusion can be drawn [he asks] than that the suppression of the former and the survival of the latter were due to the complexion of the Committee of Selection, that is to say, the academic, journalistic, and other intellectual advisers of the general reading public? And this Committee of Selection made its choice because it "sensed" correctly the intellectual needs and desires of the ruling and owning classes. This sense on the part of the committee of their solidarity of interests with the rich and powerful classes need not, indeed must not, ascend to the level of clear consciousness. For such clear consciousness might evoke in ordinarily honest teachers, writers, and reviewers, a hampering sense of intellectual dishonesty. The professor, or director of studies, the publisher, the editorial writer, the professional critic, librarian, or lecturer, must not believe or feel himself to be servile to outside authorities. And these authorities must take care that the pressures or other inducements they bring to bear in the selection or rejection of economic theories and opinions, are so unobtrusive that the subjects of this influence can easily be "unaware" of its exercise. Certain cruder forms of influence, no doubt, are always operative in particular cases. But the subtler, more indirect, and less conscious forces, making for the selection of safe, conservative, or otherwise convenient theories, and the rejection of disturbing and inconvenient theories, are the most formidable enemies which the "disinterested" Science of Economics has to meet....

So plain, immediate, and powerful, are the reactions upon economic practice of thought and feeling embodied in economic theory, that business practitioners must constantly desire that certain economic theories shall prevail, and must be disposed to use their influence upon the organs of public information and opinion to make them prevail....

[Thus it came about that] the main concern of a theory subservient to the new capitalism was to furnish "laws" conducive to abundant and reliable supplies of capital and labour at "reasonable" prices.[1]

[1] *Free-Thought in the Social Sciences* (London, 1926), pp. 77-80.

But this explanation of the persistence of the classical tradition is not altogether satisfactory. However powerful such prejudicial interests may have been and however much they may have determined the uses to which price theory has been put, they fail to explain the existence of the preconceived notion of which such use was made. The most striking evidence of the universality of this way of thinking is provided by the fact that even the bitterest arraignments of classical orthodoxy made use of it. Price theory is all things to all men. Mr. Hobson has himself called attention to "the looseness of structure and the discursiveness" of *The Wealth of Nations,* defects which "exposed Adam Smith's great work to grave abuses by later thinkers less imbued with his scientific spirit."

It was a "baggy" system [he continues], in that you could pick it up at various points, and it would fall into quite different shapes. For labour-men it furnishes an armoury of passages assigning labour as the original source of wealth, and condemning the excessive gains which merchants and manufacturers obtain at the expense alike of worker and consumer by their combinations to keep prices high and wages low. For radical land reformers there is a keen analysis of differential and monopoly rents, a plain admission that landlords "are the only one of the three orders whose revenue costs them neither labour nor care" and a powerful condemnation of their selfish Corn Laws and other instruments of class protection. . . .

A number of able and trenchant critics of the new capitalism, and the established landlordism, used material from the Smithian and Ricardian quarries, not only for weapons against the monopoly of land and capital, but for corner-stones in some hastily improvised system of constructive socialism.[2]

These efforts, critical and constructive, found their consummation in the work of Marx; and since Marx himself described *Das Kapital* as Ricardo in reverse, he also provides the consummatory case of the paradox of price theory. Of no other way of thinking has it ever been more com-

[2] *Ibid.,* pp. 69-76.

pletely the case that "When Me they fly, I am the wings."

The amazing persistence of the classical tradition illustrates something more than "the power of the dominant economic class to deflect a social science from its straightly rational course into supplying intellectual and moral supports for special group interests."[3] It is no less clearly a manifestation of extraordinary intellectual toughness and resiliency. How else shall we explain the demonstrated ability of this way of thinking to absorb its critics? What, after all, is the straightly rational course of economics? If, as Mr. Hobson remarks, "it must not be supposed that these early makers of Political Economy were heartless or inhumane men,"[4] and if they were not complete fools, surely some among them must have felt the force and recognized the merits of earlier criticism and must therefore have been moved to further investigation and elaboration of the points at issue; and this is even more likely to have been the case with later students. Why has the criticism not been cumulative? Why does a critic like Mr. Hobson himself, whose thoughtfulness and humanity have been so fully attested, mention Thompson, Gray, Bray, and Hodgskin as men who tried to steer economics back to its true course, and then make no further reference to their work? Have we nothing to learn from them? Is there no critical tradition by which the present generation might be guided? Apparently there is none. Anthologies of social criticism do exist, but they are chiefly distinguished by their inconsecutiveness and inconclusiveness. We have a tremendous literature of treatises and textbooks bearing witness to the consecutive character of the classical way of thinking from the middle of the eighteenth century to the present time; but on the critical side, nothing that is in any sense comparable. Such a record is not fully explained by social prejudice.

[3] *Ibid.*, p. 82.
[4] *Ibid.*, p. 84.

Furthermore the critics themselves are continually reabsorbed into economic orthodoxy, in many cases apparently without their being aware of this singular conversion. If the axioms and theorems of the classical tradition could somehow be tabulated, it would be found that there is no one of them which has not at some time or other undergone critical demolition. Even today critics of classical orthodoxy complain bitterly that it is a sort of Hydra. Classical theory presents no one head upon which a lethal blow might be delivered; instead, wherever criticism scores a stroke the particular expression that is under attack is forthwith abandoned and two more are straightway developed to virtually the same effect. But this means of course that criticism has produced no Hercules. Almost without exception attacks on the classical principles have been piecemeal efforts. Critics of the concept of utility have accepted the conventional factors of production, and critics of factorial analysis have accepted the concept of utility, and so on, with the result in each case that the effect of the criticism has been nullified.

Classical price theory has also managed to absorb the opposition. The most inclusive attack on this whole way of thinking was that of Thorstein Veblen, who dismissed price analysis altogether as a pre-Darwinian taxonomy and tried to focus the attention of students of economics upon the state of the industrial arts and the institutions of organized society. It was of course his constant emphasis on institutions as determinants of the economic pattern which resulted in his followers coming to be known as "institutionalists." But Veblen's contempt for price theory produced among his own followers a contempt for theory as such which has led them to eschew "abstract" thinking and to concentrate their efforts upon empirical studies of actual economic situations. But what are actual economic situations? Taking problems as they come means taking them in the form they habitually assume, which means in the guise of the conventional way of thinking, which means as price problems. In this fashion the "institutionalists" as a group have come to concern themselves almost altogether with empirical studies of various special types of price problems, with results which are not clearly distinguishable from the work of students who have never strayed from the classical fold, as the latter never tire of pointing out.

Meantime the orthodox insist that no one has ever denied the importance of institutions or of the state of the industrial arts. In the economic literature of the present generation there is scarcely a treatise or a textbook which fails to make some reference to institutions and the industrial arts. The prevailing opinion seems to be that whereas the classical and the institutionalist "schools" were once thought to be diametrically opposed, economists now "recognize" the difference to be only one of emphasis. "Institutionalism" is generously credited with having called attention to the importance of matters which no economist should completely overlook although they do lie outside the field of economic analysis since they are not measured by price. Needless to say, Veblen would have repudiated this interpretation. His attack on John Bates Clark, for example, affords no ground whatever for the presumption that the only difference between Clark's way of thinking and his own was one of emphasis. The easy eclecticism into which this controversy has relapsed can only mean that Veblen's criticism of the whole classical system has somehow spent itself, leaving the old way of thinking still in possession of the field.

Among professional economists the victory has been complete. When future historians of the movements of thought in the twentieth century survey the academic writings of our time they will probably designate the fourth decade as one of classical revival. At no other time has theoretical discussion been more intense or theoretical literature more profuse, and at no other time has economic thinking been more abstract—not to say abstruse—or more single-mindedly concerned with price analysis. This is true notwithstanding the flurry induced by the writings of Mr. J. M. Keynes. However disturbing may be the policies which Mr. Keynes has advocated, many students have pointed out that his "struggle of escape from habitual modes of thought and expression"[5] has been somewhat less mountainous than he seems to suppose; and his adherents (for example, Mrs. Joan Robinson) have not seemed to feel that their espousal of Keynesian doctrines involves any general repudiation of their other labors in what has certainly been commonly taken to be neoclassical price theory.

Nevertheless this victory may still prove to have been Pyrrhic, and for reasons which have little in common with directly felt class interest. History will also record a growing impatience among the rank and file of the profession, and especially among the younger men, with the outpourings of the pundits. Even on the part of those who make no pretension to knowing what to do about it, there is a growing sense of the futility of subtle mathematical analyses of wholly imaginary price situations and even more of impatience with the materials with which the profession is provided by its leaders for the instruction of the young. No one knows better than the rank and file how languidly the young respond. Publishers testify that teachers everywhere are seeking help in making a more realistic approach to the study of economic problems than that of the conventional texts.

A similar reaction may be observed throughout the community at large. Not only is the general public increasingly aware of the importance of the machine process; there is also increasing disillusionment with the dogmas of finance. The gold standard, for example, is no longer the fetich it

[5] *General Theory of Employment, Interest, and Money* (New York, 1936), p. viii.

used to be. Only a few years ago "sound" economists were assuring the world that Germany and Japan could not possibly sustain all-out war since neither had an adequate gold reserve. Not only have we seen them do so nevertheless; we have also learned that possession of the greater part of the world stock of monetary gold by no means insures victory in war. The story is being widely told of the financier who on being informed of the burning of an aluminum plant replied, "Well, it was fully covered by insurance, wasn't it?" The folly of that way of thinking is now apparent to all thoughtful people.

This general reaction goes far beyond the academic criticism of the details of classical price theory. We are approaching the middle of the century with a dawning realization that what has been wrong with economic thinking is its obsession with price. It has seemed to be axiomatic that ours is a price economy. To explain price has been accepted by virtually all economists as their appointed task. That is why the criticism of classical theory has failed. So long as economics has remained by common consent the science of price, any particular aspersion upon any particular principle could only be followed by the elaboration of other principles to substantially the same effect.

But is it a price economy? No one doubts that prices exist and play an important part in the life of the modern Western world. The question is not whether prices exist or not, nor even whether this range of phenomena is or is not extraordinarily widespread. Machines also are extraordinarily widespread. Textbook writers have fallen into the habit of inducting their readers into the study of economics by inviting them to contemplate the degree to which everyone is concerned with prices. The implication is that price is the only matter of economic significance with which everyone is thus concerned, and so the generalization seems to be justified that price is the sole agency by which the economic activities of all members of the community are related and knit up into an economy. But this is plainly false. Tools and machines and technological skills and knowledge are certainly no less widespread throughout the economy than prices and no less a matter of general concern and an agency of community organization; and the same is also true of the institutions of organized society. Surely the obsession of the modern community with price has a sounder basis than this!

It can be argued, somewhat less naïvely, that price is the central concern of economic thinking because it is only by selling their products and services in the market at a price that all members of the community make their living. But even this is true only in a very limited sense. While there are some business men who engage in virtually no other occupational activity but buying and selling, they constitute only a tiny fraction of the community. Most people devote most of their time and energy to doing other things. It would be ridiculous to say that a farmer or a physician is "primarily" a business man. However true it may be that the fortunes of farmers are affected by price movements over which they have no control, no one would argue that a farmer's market operations are more important to the community or to him than sowing and reaping. Doubtless farmers would do well to study the market, and any individual farmer who had achieved notable skill in this exercise might do better to give up farming altogether and become a broker. But a nation of brokers would raise no crops.

The range of economic studies may of course be arbitrarily limited to brokerage. However far short of the whole effort of the community to make a living the activities of buying and selling may fall, there is no reason why they should not be the object of systematic study—as, indeed, they are. Price forecasting is of course a quite legitimate occupation. Hitherto it has been regarded more as a profession than a science, since it has been a paid service rendered to clients by commercial organizations. Techniques of business forecasting have also been part of the course of training offered by schools of business administration. But however important such studies may be, they are of a very different character from what has been recognized historically as the science of economics. No one could possibly conclude from a reading of *The Wealth of Nations* that it had been written for the guidance of business men or even of common citizens in their business capacity. It is rather an exposition of the meaning which was supposed by Adam Smith to inhere in the "natural," uninstructed acts of all the members of the community. The assumptions which such an exposition makes can hardly be said to be justified by the special interests of business men, however legitimate they may be.

In recent years, to be sure, certain economists have proposed to identify the science of economics with price analysis ostensibly with full knowledge of the limitation they are imposing on the range of economic studies. They have done so avowedly in the interest of scientific precision. In effect they seem to say that however narrow may be the range of price phenomena they constitute the only economic data which are by nature quantitative and hence accessible to the precise, quantitative analysis of scientific method. The clear implication is that such a conception of economic science is dictated not by any particular way of thinking but by the fact of price, an impression which is further heightened by the lavish use of mathematical techniques. This all seems to mean that the modern "quantitative science of price analysis" is just as empirical as business forecasting, that it is engaged in analyzing data which are actually given in the operations of the market. But curiously enough this is not true at all. What the practitioners of this "science" mean by exact mathematical analysis is, first, the definition of quite imaginary price situations and then the reduction of these situations to mathematical notation in some such fashion as this: "If there were a business in which demand could be represented by a certain curve and cost by a certain other curve, then these curves would intersect at yonder point and the whole situation could be represented by the following simultaneous equations."

Nothing could be less empirical—less responsive to the supposed actualities of a price economy—than the sort of mathematical analysis with which so many contemporary economists have occupied themselves. It is, to all appearances, first-rate mathematics. But as economics it is concerned not with the analysis of empirical data but with the refinement and elaboration of theoretical devices which, as every student of the subject knows, have played the stellar role in classical theory for three-quarters of a century. As Mr. Maurice Dobb has remarked:

> . . . so long as mathematical technique retains its servitude to a particular mode of thought, the concepts which it fashions are calculated to veil rather than to reveal reality. For this mode of thought, which is enshrined in the subjective theory of value, first creates for us a realm where disembodied minds hold communion with etherialized objects of choice, and then, unmindful of the distance between this abstract world and reality, seeks to represent the relations which it finds in this realm as governing the relations which hold in actual economic society and as controlling the shape which events must have under any and every system of social institutions.[6]

That ours is in fact a price economy is not established by reiterating traditional beliefs even in the language of mathematics.

This is not to deny that important uses may be made of empirical price data, and not only by business men. The

[6] *Political Economy and Capitalism* (London, 1937), pp. 183-84.

statistical importance of price data is of course very great indeed. Since price data are numerical, and since many commercial transactions are matters of public record, or can be made so, data of this character are peculiarly accessible and peculiarly amenable to tabulation and statistical summary. No one, whatever his way of thinking, would question these facts or deprecate the efforts of statistical agencies to collect and analyze empirical price data. But facts have a way of becoming an obsession. No one would condemn parents for recording the growth of their children, since parents are not likely to fall into the habit of mistaking their children's height and weight for their intellectual and moral character. But statisticians are singularly prone to this mistake. Because price data are amenable to their analysis they find it easy to suppose that price is therefore the essential stuff of the economy.

They can even become rather impatient with theoretical inquiries which seek to raise the question what the data mean. This way of thinking has recently been stated so clearly, and by a statistician and public administrator of such eminence, that his words are worth quoting.

> It would be laughable [he writes], if it were not tragic, to watch the stream of books and articles, attempting to solve the exceptionally complex problems of present-day economics by theoretical arguments, often without a single reference to the observed facts of the situation.... There is room for two or three economic theorists in each generation, not more. Only men of transcendental powers of reasoning can be candidates for these positions. Restatements of economic theory, of which we are offered so many, are only occasionally needed, as factual knowledge advances and institutions change.
>
> The rest of us should be economic scientists, content steadily to lay stone on stone in building the structure of ordered knowledge. Instead, it seems to be the ambition of nearly every teacher of economics to put his name to a new formulation of economic theory. The result is a vast output of literature of which, it is safe to say, scarcely a syllable will be read in fifty years' time. But

the discovery of new facts, and of generalisations based on them, is work for all time.[7]

In his capacity as a statistician the author of these words might perhaps have raised the question whether the extraordinary abundance of theoretical studies may not be an indication of the rapidity and magnitude of institutional changes now going on, and even perhaps of advances of factual knowledge. Although he does not actually say so, the gist of his remarks seems to be that we have quite enough theory for present purposes. How far this is from being the case has never been shown more clearly than by the statistical studies of Mr. Colin Clark. At every point his figures indicate the presence of Veblen's "larger forces moving obscurely in the background": the incidence of technological development upon the economic life of the community, and the obstruction of economic progress by institutional rigidities, such as "the marked difficulty experienced by sons, under present laws, customs and economic stresses governing apprenticeship and education, in entering any occupation better paid than that of their fathers." Like Mr. Keynes he advocates a policy of low interest rates and reduction of the present extreme inequalities in the distribution of income. Surely he realizes how utterly repugnant such ideas must be to the way of thinking which still prevails quite generally among economists and still more in the community at large!

To what, then, is the continued prevalence of this way of thinking due? There is no a priori ground for believing and no statistical evidence to prove that our economy is of its own essential nature a price economy which therefore can be understood only in terms of price analysis. Our economic thinking has centered upon price for one reason and only one: the significance which has been imputed to the

[7] Colin Clark, *The Conditions of Economic Progress* (London, 1940), p. viii.

price system by the theories of Adam Smith and Ricardo, "the argumentative Scot and the 'stupid bothering stockbroker.'"[8] Even so we must not be too hard on the founders of the classical theory. Theirs was a tremendous task: to find meaning in "the blooming, buzzing confusion," as William James might have called it, of modern economic life. They could get little or no help from the wise men of earlier ages, since the ancient philosophers were not confronted with any such manifestation as that of the commercial age. Inevitably they had to work with the intellectual materials at their disposal, those of the seventeenth and eighteenth centuries, the inadequacy of which has long since been recognized. Small wonder their results fell short of perfection. The amazing thing is that their ideas should have been as cogent, as persistently convincing, as they are.

Classical political economy was convincing because it achieved a prodigious feat. It found meaning of a sort in the hurly-burly of modern economic life. The chaos of the economic struggle for existence, it seemed to show, is really an ordered chaos in which all things work together inadvertently for the best. This meaning still motivates the contemporary exponents of price analysis. If we ask them, "What is it that you are trying to do? You say you are simply trying to understand how prices are formed, but why should you want to know this? Why should society support you in this effort?"—there can be only one answer: "Because it is in the analysis of price that we find the meaning of the economy." The price system derives its significance from the conception of the economic life of modern times as an economy, "the economy of free private enterprise." This conception is no mere academic plaything. It is of course one of the key ideas of modern civilization, of the same order as the idea of democracy, to which indeed it is closely linked. The

[8] As Mr. Colin Clark calls them, quoting William Cobbett, an earlier heretic.—*Ibid.*, p. ix.

fate of democracy itself seems to many people indissociable from that of "the economy of free private enterprise." Neither is a simple scientific datum, an "observed fact" which emerges directly from the statistical evidence. That is why we cannot be "content steadily to lay stone on stone in building the structure of ordered knowledge." It is futile to lay stone on stone except in terms of some preconceived design. And that is why criticism of the classical design has been so completely futile. Whatever the defects of the classical design, it still remains the only over-all design we have, and will remain until another conception of the meaning of economy has taken form.

Before this can happen two conditions must be met: a new set of ideas must be found with which to make a fresh theoretical start, and the old way of thinking must be abandoned altogether, price analysis and all. Whether we are ready to meet these conditions can be determined only by trying. Reference has already been made to the tremendous advances which have been achieved since the eighteenth century in every line having to do with man, his nature, his behavior and its physical and social determinants, the nature and history of culture, the structure of society, and the process of social change. It would be strange indeed if our new knowledge were without significance for economics. But which of these materials is of most compelling economic significance? At what points does our present knowledge diverge from the ideas by which the classical tradition was conditioned?

Answers to these questions can be found only in a reconstruction of the process by which the classical tradition was originally formed. Criticism is not the object of this reconstruction. All that criticism could do has long since been done, without success. Indeed it is doubtful if intellectual liberation is ever won by criticism. What economics needs today is psychoanalysis: a rehearsal of the experiences by which the intellectual trauma came about. If we could see just how our obsession with the price system came about, we might be able to recognize it as an obsession and so free our minds for work with other and sounder materials.

It is to this effort, accordingly, that we must now address ourselves.

Chapter II

THE PRICE SYSTEM

THE CLASSICAL way of thinking in economics came into being through the combination of three ideas, each of which may be represented, with some risk of misunderstanding, by a single word: price, capital, value. These ideas developed simultaneously during the period in which feudalism was giving way to modern commercial society. Consequently it goes without saying that all three were subject to common influences. Whichever one is under immediate consideration, the student finds himself carried back to the contemplation of the larger cultural pattern which was also the matrix of the other two. Nevertheless price, capital, and value are distinct ideas, as distinct as any three ideas of the same community can ever be. Each had its origin in a different part of the common culture and is an expression of the meaning of that particular aspect. The classical concept of value derives from moral philosophy and expresses the notion of human nature and even of nature in general which came to prevail in early modern times. The notion of capital is of commercial origin in the sense of being a symbol of the structure of commercial society. The idea of the price system is also of commercial origin but in the much broader sense of a social mechanism, commercial in character, by which the whole community was variously affected and of which every element in society from king to commoner gradually became aware.

Since each of these ideas is an essential component of the classical tradition, no one can be understood except in terms of the other two. Whichever one is approached first will therefore remain incomplete until the other two have been considered. But a beginning must be made, however arbitrary, and for this purpose various considerations indicate the idea of price. It is the most general both in its origins in the minds of the whole community and in its effects as a theoretical vehicle for the other two. Furthermore, it is uniquely grounded in fact, whereas the other two are to an extraordinary degree fictitious.

Prices have existed and have had both a moral and an intellectual character in all societies though never before to any such degree as in modern commercial society. It is this difference of degree, of course, which accounts for the emergence of a doctrine of price in modern Western society as it also accounts for the development of complementary ideas. But the phenomenon is not a merely quantitative one. To understand the historic significance of price it is not enough to point out the prevalence of prices nor even the prevalence of awareness of price. Sensitive and cautious thinkers have often warned their colleagues against proceeding too casually from the particular to the general, against arguing that what is significant for individuals is likewise significant for society. In this case, however, the trouble with the reasoning which begins by noting the importance of price for individuals and their acute price-consciousness and proceeds to argue that price is therefore an important social phenomenon is a matter not of quantity but of quality. It is not enough to establish the importance of price. The question is, What is its importance? What does this so very acute and general price-consciousness signify?

The truth is that with regard to price we are conscious of different things. In particular, price has two aspects, related and yet distinct. On one hand prices exist in a pattern or system so pervasive, intricate, and subtle as to challenge understanding; and on the other hand prices have a moral quality of destiny, fate, or providence.

It is this moral quality of price of which individuals in all societies are most keenly aware and to which for this reason teachers most frequently appeal when inducting elementary students into the study of economics, usually without knowing it. Shoppers are concerned about the prices they pay, workers about the wages they receive, farmers about the prices for which they can sell. The point is their common concern. It is obviously a moral concern. The question in the minds of all is one of justice. All that life has in store for them, apparently, is determined by price. The effect of this state of mind is to short-circuit social thinking and even the feeling of social grievance. Mankind has always used the gift of rational thought with the greatest parsimony, looking always for a terminal point beyond which further reflection would be unnecessary. It is the peculiar character of price that it constitutes a terminus to economic thinking. Farmers, we often say, are not interested in sweeping social reforms or economic reconstruction; all they want is "decent prices." The same is true of organized labor: they are incorrigibly preoccupied with getting "decent wages"; while for the consuming public it is "fair prices" and the high cost of living.

In medieval society this state of mind was sublimated into a religious doctrine. The doctrine of "just price," which was the summation of medieval economic thinking, was peculiarly characteristic of the medieval mind; nevertheless, as a number of critics have pointed out only recently, this doctrine left a very deep imprint upon all subsequent economic thinking. It was after all a cost-of-production theory of price. No doubt the correlation between cost price and sale price is an obvious one. Doubtless merchants throughout the ages have countered the protests of their customers by declaring, "I'm giving it to you for just what it cost me!" —and what could be more just? But this misses the point. Throughout the ages no great social significance had ever been attached to the mumblings of merchants. By a paradox quite characteristic of medieval mentality, this society which we ordinarily think of as "other-worldly" to a unique degree nevertheless raised the merchants' plea to the level of a doctrine of the church.

Thus it was in medieval thought that price first assumed the role of a social principle. The significance of this development is apparent in the contrast between medieval and ancient economic thinking. We have given short shrift to the economic writings of the ancients, notably those of Xenophon and Aristotle. They contain scarcely any trace of a coherent theory of price; consequently, we say, they are not economics in the modern sense. To be sure, they treat the affairs of the Greek commonwealth as those of a great household and proceed to plan the economic betterment of the community in a fashion which future economic planning may perhaps identify as singularly prophetic. At all events their indifference to price stands in marked contrast to medieval thinking which in spite of all other differences has this close tie with the modern classical tradition.

Even the differences are less than they at first appear. Medieval society did not hew to the line of the just price out of "other-worldliness." All societies are other-worldly, each in its own peculiar way; and few institutions have been more intensely practical than the medieval church. The point is rather that medieval society was feudal and the doctrine of the church was feudal doctrine. But in the twelfth and thirteenth centuries when this doctrine received its final form, medieval society was already facing social revolution. A new instrument of power in the hands of a new social element was already making itself felt, and the established order did its best to strike it down. But its best fell far short of what we now call "total" action. If medieval society, speaking through the church, had interdicted commerce as such and outlawed wealth without reservation, the revolution might have been arrested. But the insidious process of economic change had already gone too far for that by the time the issue became paramount. Not even in the middle ages were men prepared to turn the clock back to medievalism. Commerce and wealth had come to stay. What the doctrine of the church attempted was a compromise, a synthesis not only of St. Augustine with Aristotle but of feudalism with the fuller life and larger horizons of world trade.

Like every compromise this one took the form, "So far shalt thou go and no farther." The merchant and his meanness, money and its power, were to be tolerated on the condition that they should not increase. The specific practices by which merchants increase their wealth and power—forestalling, engrossing, regrating—were outlawed, then as now. But chief reliance rested on the positive and all-inclusive principle of the just price and the mechanism of its enforcement. It is this mechanism which constitutes the greatest apparent contrast to later economic arrangements. In the later age competition became the mechanism of fulfillment of the just price, the function from which it derives its supreme significance. But competition accepts the acquisition of wealth. The fact that a man has made a fortune, even a great fortune, is not under competition proof positive of social waywardness. It may be and presumably is proof of his competitive efficiency. To better oneself is the spirit of the age. It has been identified as the characteristic mentality of the middle class and of middle class society. In apparently complete contrast to all this, medieval doctrine made the acquisition of wealth prima facie evidence that more-than-cost prices had been charged. The intent of the principle of just price was to freeze the orders of society in the proportions they assumed in the middle ages. What was interdicted was neither commerce nor wealth but the increase of commerce at the expense of feudal functions and the acquisition of wealth at the expense of feudal powers.

This effort was of course futile, as futile as giving a child a gun and telling him not to shoot. But what is most important is the fact that it established price as an authentic social mechanism. All that was required, once the principle of just price had been laid down, was a slight modification of the machinery of its enforcement, a mere redefinition of what constitutes just price, an elaboration of the theory of competition, to make commerce paramount over feudalism. This elaboration was implicit in the doctrine of price itself. In a very real and literal sense we have medieval theology to thank for the belief in price as an efficacious social mechanism which has long since become one of the deepest moral convictions of Western society.

Important as it is, however, this sense of moral concern for price as an instrument of justice is an insufficient basis for a science of price. The principle of parental authority is not less significant, surely, than that of just price; nevertheless no familial science has developed at all comparable to political economy, and the difference is due in considerable part if not altogether to the failure of family relations to yield a body of laws or system of relationships of an apparently quantitative character resembling at least superficially the quantitative relationships which in early modern times were already giving rise to physical science, as the price system did. To those who still follow the classical way of thinking the recognition of the price system seems to be quite a matter of course, like the recognition of the solar system; but here also there is a great difference. The price system has a meaning for human life and destiny which none but astrologers any longer impute to the solar system. In this respect for all its quantitative character it still resembles the system of family relationships. In truth our traditional economic thinking has occupied a unique place in the hierarchy of the sciences. Considered as a quantitative science, it is the only one which is also a philosophy of life; while considered as a branch of moral philosophy, it is the only one which has been able to establish any claim to consideration as a quantitative science. But this unique character was only gradually assumed. The question is, How? No one would aver that the meaning of price is a physical actuality like the moons of Jupiter at which Galileo peered. In later economic thinking empirical data and theoretical interpretation are so completely fused as to make it difficult for us to distinguish them; but historically the discovery of quantitative relationships and the imputation of meaning to those relationships were quite distinct. Not only was the price system—the quantitative system of pecuniary relationships—discovered first and "interpreted" afterward; the intellectual fascination which the newly discovered system exercised over the minds of social philosophers played an indispensable contributory part in the development of the way of thinking by which Western society later came to be obsessed.

As every student knows, certain "fields" of economics are much older than political economy itself, notably money and banking, public finance, and foreign trade. In each of these fields important discoveries were made and significant monographs were written centuries before political economy emerged as a full-fledged science. Taken by itself each of these developments seems to be more or less accidental, but taken together they have a common character which is immediately apparent. In each case what was discovered was the price nexus, and in each case the discovery resulted pragmatically from the attempt to deal with an immediate and pressing problem of a peculiarly enigmatic character—or so it seemed at the time.

A prince finds himself in financial difficulties. He exercises the power which we still call seigniorage, the power to issue disks of precious metal stamped with his superscription and authorized for use as a medium of exchange in specified amounts. As a matter of course he thinks of all this as his personal affair in a sense difficult for the citizens of modern states to comprehend. What more obvious economy can he effect than to reduce the weight of precious metal in his coinage? He proceeds to do so without let or hindrance. But then, what happens? To his dismay and annoyance he finds himself confronted with what we now recognize as the inevitable consequences of inflation: a general rise in prices extending over his whole currency-area the effect of which is to oblige his ministers of state to lay out in the "expenses of the sovereign" the same weight in precious metal as they did before, though now in increased denominations.

All this is very disconcerting to a sovereign. No overt resistance has been offered. What has transpired is the result of no organized opposition. It has just happened, naturally as it were, and universally; and so the local wise man is summoned and ordered to explain the mystery, in very much the same spirit in which Joseph was called upon to interpret Pharaoh's dream.

What he discovers is a strange and subtle reciprocity by weight and number between gold and goods. The purchasing power of money is indeed a natural phenomenon quite distinct in character from the powers of the sovereign and is determined by the weight of precious metal in relation to the quantities of goods. When the metallic content of a coin is reduced, its purchasing power falls in direct proportion; or, to put the same phenomenon in terms of price, the quantities of goods purchasable by the debased coinage falls, prices computed in terms of the debased coinage subtly rise, so that a constant ratio is maintained between weight of metal and quantities of goods irrespective of the superscription of the sovereign.

All this is quite obvious. Indeed, it is impossible to say when the relation between money and prices first became known. The ancients had an inkling of it, perhaps as early as metallic coinage was first used; and it cannot be said to be fully understood today. Even today economists repeat the aphorism of Queen Elizabeth's minister to the effect that bad money drives out good, although this proposition is plainly false. What "drives out" good money is not bad money but worsening money. There is no more reason why two coinages of different weight should not circulate freely together than guineas and sovereigns or quarters and dimes. It is only a falling currency which breeds inflation. None of the celebrated monographs on money problems which enrich the early literature of economics is wholly satisfactory though all show an extraordinary grasp of the central phenomenon, and this literature would have none but an antiquarian interest except for one circumstance.

What the early monetary studies revealed went beyond the difficulties of the sovereign, even beyond the money mechanism itself. More sharply than ever before they brought into focus the subtlety and pervasiveness of the price system. In every commercial community there exists a market mechanism, informal and unofficial, but so extraordinarily delicate and extensive that its adjustments are transmitted to every itinerant tinker and pedlar, every housewife and peasant, in a fashion calculated to inspire ministers of state with awe and envy. It was this extraordinary system which the authors of the early monetary studies were moved to dramatize. On virtually every page of this pre-economic literature the reader finds clear evidence of the fascination with which these prescient authors contemplated the amazing subtlety of the price system.

The same is true of the literature of public finance. Tax collecting has always been a grievous business. In the ancient folklore of all peoples the tax collector has always been represented as a close relative of the devil, and with considerable justice. Before the age of commerce, wringing taxes from subject peoples was a task so difficult and graceless as to require a special sort of character in which the talents of the secret police were combined with those of the racketeer. Too unsavory for the ordinary public official, the business was commonly farmed out, with the result of adding the exactions and cruelties of gangsterism to the necessities of state. The story of taxes through the ages is virtually one long uninterrupted tale of woe.

The emergence of the modern state marked the beginning of that process of expansion of the functions of government which is still going on, and so greatly enlarged the financial needs of public exchequer. But it also brought a new system of tax gathering. What was new was not any one specific tax. Excise taxes, franchise taxes, tariffs, and the rest have been employed in one form or another since time immemorial; but the growth of commerce vastly increased the yield of every sort of indirect taxation. Much has been written concerning the political importance of the alliance between crown and merchant for the formation of the modern state. At no point was the alliance more potent than in its bearing upon public revenue. In effect the whole merchant class became unofficial and unpaid tax gatherers, as they still are.

The merchants were able to perform this extraordinary function for two reasons. The practice of bookkeeping, which was itself a potent factor in the growth of the new society, made it possible for revenue officers to keep tabs on the merchants; and the price system made it possible for the merchants to pass the taxes on to their customers without informing them that they were being taxed. Thus the incidence of taxation came to be one of the major instruments of government.

Tax shifting of course gives rise to special problems. A tax on fuel or window glass may have widespread effects on health; a tax on fertilizer or agricultural implements may damage the whole economy. Taxes on imports or exports affect the whole community's schedule of consumption and even the level of consumption, and so on. Furthermore, as every modern student knows, these effects are often registered in curious and unexpected ways. The whole subject is so complicated as to have given rise in recent years to a special form of *expertise,* virtually a profession—that of tax expert.

As these difficulties began to be realized the same thing happened which was also occurring in the field of monetary problems. Sovereigns and ministers who were puzzled by the unexpected consequences of indirect taxation called for enlightenment, and special studies were undertaken in some cases by ministers of state or their subordinates and in others by scholars of demonstrated acumen. The result was the early literature of public finance which constitutes another chapter in the history of economic thought parallel and analogous to that on money; and at no point is the analogy more striking than in the preoccupation of the tax experts with the mysteries of the price system. For it was of course the mechanism of the market which had given rise not only to the anomalies of incidence but to the whole machinery of indirect taxation, so that at this point also the attention of serious students of public affairs was centered upon price.

Meantime the most difficult and insistent problem of all was that of foreign trade. Since nations are rivals virtually by definition it has always seemed axiomatic that one must profit at the expense of another, and in early modern times this "great illusion" was further accentuated by the bullion problem. It will not be necessary to review the pros and cons of mercantilist doctrine on the subject of bullion, favorable balance of trade, and national advantage. Students are now generally agreed that the ideas of the mercantilist writers were not as foolish as they seemed to the followers of Adam Smith; that bullion played a larger part in the statecraft of the sixteenth and seventeenth centuries than it has since, and that for nations unblessed with mines or treasure-laden colonies the sole access to bullion was piracy and its descendant, foreign trade. Under these circumstances the idea of a favorable balance of trade was at least intelligible, however stultifying it may be today.

Doubtless these circumstances were largely responsible for the fact that the demonstration of the reciprocal flow of goods and gold in foreign trade was deferred past the middle of the eighteenth century. Exponents of free trade are accustomed to assume a "normal" situation to begin with. The present situation in which the bulk of the world's monetary gold is sequestered in the United States is so extreme that many students doubt if an even distribution could now be effected by ordinary international trade in the absence of all trade barriers whatsoever, and the same question may well be raised with regard to the Spanish monopoly of gold in the sixteenth and seventeenth centuries. But these circumstances do not bear the whole responsibility for the slow development of the theory of foreign trade. The subject is itself extraordinarily complex. Only when the conception of the price system as an automatically self-adjusting mechanism had already been thoroughly assimilated was it possible for Hume to see not only that money and prices are reciprocal but that gold flows toward a low-price area and is repelled from a high-price area by a process which is reciprocal to the flow of goods toward high-price markets and away from low-price markets.

The effect of this demonstration was greatly to heighten

the charm which the price system had already begun to exercise over the minds of social philosophers as a result of the observations of revenue and monetary specialists. In trying to understand the significance of this development we must bear constantly in mind the prior commitment to a philosophy of price which was the heritage of medieval doctrine. There is nothing in the theory of foreign trade, nor in the subtle incidence of taxation and currency depreciation, which establishes any particular price pattern as just. This distinction is an awkward and uncomfortable one for modern minds. Five generations of classical price theory have so completely assimilated the idea of pattern to the idea of justice as to establish in the minds of modern students an all-or-none disjunction: either price has the social significance which classical theory has imputed to it, or it has no significance whatever. In this state of mind we read the early literature of economics and wonder how men who felt the subtle intellectual charm of the price system could still have failed to appreciate its larger significance.

But to deny its significance is not to deny the intricacy of the price system. As these early monographists saw, prices do form an extraordinarily complicated pattern. The adjustments of prices to each other are amazingly delicate and pervasive. A causal nexus does indeed run through the whole universe of discourse of price linking all price phenomena together into an integrated causal system. We talk of the laws of supply and demand, but in truth there is only one law: the law of the interrelatedness of all purchases and sales. In economics as in mechanics every action has its equal and opposite reaction. Is this just? Is the solar system just? In economics as in mechanics certain events are more closely related than others. It is possible to some degree to trace certain relationships—between crop prices and sales of fertilizer and agricultural machinery, and that sort of thing. These are the relations with which business men and statesmen are perennially concerned. Particular business men sometimes manage to learn a great deal about the situations to which their businesses are more intimately related and by which they are more immediately affected; and in recent years research organizations both private and governmental, employing trained analysts—economists, if you will—have learned a great deal about the planetary system of the market. They have learned such things as the relation between transportation costs and the distribution of industry, between volume of imports and the export of particular commodities such as cotton.

All this assumes causality. It assumes that nothing ever happens in the market without a cause or without effects. But it makes virtually no use whatever of the classical way of thinking about price and its significance, or of the theoretical formulas of which that way of thinking has been so prolific. Business men and bureaus of industrial research have formulas. They "watch steel," or car loadings. They devise indices of physical production or of wholesale prices. But they make no use of "indifference curves." They trace relationships between wage movements and wholesale and retail price movements, but not between wages and "productivity."

The distinction is the one which all elementary students are invited to make between "principles" and "problems." As a profession economics has come to consist of two distinct undertakings: one, a large and continually growing series of empirical studies of actual industrial relationships; the other, the theory, or social philosophy, of the meaning of economy. The former makes no use of the latter, nor the latter of the former, and the two would have no professional bearing on each other but for one circumstance: it is the "principles" which tell us what to think about the "problems." It is unnecessary for business men to think in this sense, and consequently business men can (and sometimes do) know a great deal about industrial relationships without being economists at all. But economists must think about the bearing of particular industrial situations upon the economy as a whole. To do so they must have some sense of the meaning of the economy as a whole. That is, they must have some way of thinking. No way of economic thinking emerges directly from empirical studies such as those of modern research institutions or those of the early students of money, taxation, and foreign trade. The classical way of thinking in terms of which most economists still interpret the results of their own empirical studies and those of others (who in some cases are not economists, that is interpreters, at all) makes extensive use of the phenomenon of price; but it is not implicit in price.

Price was not "discovered" to have social significance. That is not the lesson of the early monographs on money, taxation, and foreign trade. The significance which eventually came to be imputed to price was implicit in a certain conception of capital and a certain theory of value the origin of which was quite distinct from the discovery of the causal interrelatedness of prices. Nevertheless this discovery was an indispensable condition of the formation of the whole classical pattern of ideas, for it provided the vehicle of the whole system. Price was the catalyst by the action of which the ideas of capital and value were combined.

Two circumstances enabled price to play this role: the moral concern which found expression in the medieval doctrine of just price which strongly disposed the inheritors of this tradition to look to price for a solution of all social problems, and the intellectual fascination which resulted from the discovery that all prices are linked together in an amazingly extensive system of subtle and delicate relationships. The temptation to assume that such a system must have human, social, or moral significance is almost irresistible. To the seventeenth- and eighteenth-century mind it proved quite irresistible in astronomy and physics no less than economics. The natural sciences have been able to outgrow their former obsession with "the harmonies of nature." If economics has not yet altogether done so, that is due not so much to continued fascination by the intricacies of the price nexus as to the traditional ideas of capital and value for which the harmony of price is indispensable.

Chapter III

THE CONCEPT OF CAPITAL

EVERY SOCIAL ORDER rests upon a foundation of ideas or beliefs. These are of indefinite number and extent. Some are so deeply imbedded in the history of the race as to be shared by virtually all societies; while others, nearer the surface, are common only to the more recent and closely related cultures. Still others are peculiar to one particular society which is thereby distinguished from all others. Students of the social sciences would agree that modern civilization is no exception to this rule. Some of the ideas upon which it rests, like that of property, for example, are very ancient and are shared in some form or other by all human societies. Others, like that of free enterprise, are more limited in scope. Still others, it is to be presumed, are peculiar to the form and structure which commercial society has taken in the Western world during the last five or ten generations. Among these probably the most important is that of capital.

This is true for two reasons. No other idea epitomizes commercialism more completely, and no other idea carries greater weight in the exercise of rationalization by which commercial society has justified itself to itself. To use the language of Emile Durkheim, capital is the "collective representation" par excellence of capitalism. These two words identify and define each other, as indeed they should. For many years after it had come into general use among the socialists the word "capitalism" was refused admission to polite society because of the contemptuous tone in which it was always uttered by the followers of Marx. But no other term so neatly designates the economic structure of modern society, and so the word of the socialists has gradually found its way into general use; and since whatever is done by the right people straightway becomes right, "capitalism" has ceased to be a term of opprobrium and is now uttered with pride and even veneration by the adherents and defenders of the status quo. Many economists, more timid than their betters, bestow a scholar's frown upon this barbarism and profess not to understand what such a word might mean. But its meaning is perfectly clear to the world at large. "Capitalism" is that economy of which the dominant institution and idea is that of capital.

It is equally extraordinary as an institution and as an idea, and a perfect illustration of the extent to which the human mind can go in accepting and believing the folklore upon which it has been nurtured. The acceptance is so complete that few people are ever moved to reflect upon the enormities to which they have become accustomed. Under capitalism outstanding achievement, presumably of any sort, is rewarded by the elevation of its author to an aristocracy of wealth and power, and the guarantee of this position not only to the author himself for the duration of his life but to his heirs and assigns in perpetuity. So far there is nothing unique about it. The transmission of nobility to one's heirs is a feature of nearly every aristocracy. But in contrast to other forms of feudalism in which people are counseled to walk uprightly in whatever station in life it has pleased Almighty God to place them, capitalism fosters the belief that the acquisition of wealth is something that may happen to anybody—may and very probably will. From infancy the virtues of industry and thrift are sedulously cultivated in the young to the continually reiterated refrain that if they go to bed without protest and get up early without grumbling they will infallibly become rich. Not everybody, of course, will become very rich; but everybody may aspire to save his children from having to start life where he did, and even to provide them with "an independent income." So wise a man as William James, writing half-facetiously of his financial innocence, remarked in his letters that he knew just enough to know that he must never draw on capital. Having inherited a modest competence from his own father, he took it for granted that the next generation of Jameses must have independent means.

It goes without saying that a whole community cannot belong to the leisure class. Yet the institutions of capitalism provide no regular machinery for the termination of such claims. Wealth is extinguished in bankruptcy, and some economists have seen that such extinction is an indispensable condition to carrying on the system. But the community at large persists in treating such occurrences as calamities, not at all a part of the natural order of things, and no one enjoys more universal sympathy than people who having lived all their lives in idleness suddenly find themselves penniless, especially if their fathers and grandfathers before them also lived in idleness. In theory all capital is perpetual.[1] To set aside funds for the repayment of debt and the replacement of worn-out machinery is the most elementary and universal accounting practice. Indeed the idea is that industry does this on its own account and can do it by virtue of the potency it acquires from capital. The whole system is conceived to

[1] "... all capital is inherently perpetual ... in a society which is not planning for the end of all things, all property income is perpetual."—F. H. Knight, "Capital, Time, and the Interest Rate," *Economica* (August, 1934), pp. 10, 14.

derive from the peculiar character of capital as a "factor of production" and is not ordinarily regarded as an order of nobility at all, so that its beneficiaries are conceived not in terms of a social system of which they are the ruling class but in terms of a method of production in which they perform an essential function, that of "providing capital."

The concept of capital by use of which a social system is thus identified with a system of production combines two sets of meanings which are not only distinct but incompatible. These two meanings are frequently distinguished by the phrases "capital funds" and "capital equipment." The former represents a sum of "claims to income" measured in pecuniary units; the latter an aggregate of the physical materials and instruments of trade and manufacture subject to enumeration by inventory. To the modern student coming upon the problem for the first time in this form, there would seem to be no good reason for the mutual identification of these two distinct sets of phenomena, and every reason for clear differentiation. As Professor Frank A. Fetter has remarked,[2] "These two types of capital concepts are so distinctive in essential thought and practical application that confusion inevitably resulted from the use of one word to designate both." It is the practice of scholars to treat matters of this kind as if they were simple mistakes, to which earlier scholars were unfortunately prone, and to caution their readers against continuing to commit such errors as though nothing were involved but the discovery and elimination of simple mistakes of reasoning. This is the spirit in which virtually all the textbooks of the present day point out the two senses in which the word "capital" has often been employed, recommend that hereafter it be used in one sense only, usually that of physical equipment, and caution their readers against confusing this meaning with that of pecuni-

[2] In his article on "Capital," *Encyclopaedia of the Social Sciences*, III, 187.

ary funds. It is in this spirit that Professor Fetter proceeds directly from the sentence just quoted to remark that "this confusion occurred not later than the early years of the seventeenth century," and to trace its long inglorious career without any suggestion that anything more is involved than the obtuseness of earlier economists.

Scholarly as it seems, such procedure may be in the highest degree misleading. Undoubtedly it is so in this instance. To be sure, the identification of the social interests and attitudes which such "mistakes" express is no substitute for logical analysis. An idea is not proved false by identifying it with a social movement. But insofar as an idea derives its real substance from the social movement from which it did in fact result, analysis can scarcely presume to deal adequately with it which ignores the whole of that substance and undertakes to treat it as a pure intellectual abstraction. Such procedure may be itself merely a mistake if the social content of the idea under consideration is unknown. But that is not the case with the concept of capital. The confusion which is here under consideration did not begin with two sets of entities, funds and things, which were insufficiently distinguished from each other. It did not begin with entities at all. It began with capitalism.

The power of money—that is to say, of moneyed men—was growing throughout the middle ages and early modern times in spite of almost universal opposition and condemnation. By the middle of the sixteenth century, in England at least, it was paramount. "By the middle of the sixteenth century," says Max Beer,[3] "the career of canon law was at an end"; and to show that "mercantile capital was a powerful factor two decades prior to the Reformation," he cites a document dated 1559 to the effect that "since 1 Henry VIII there could never been won any good law or order which touched their liberty or estate, but they stayed it." Scholars

[3] In *Early British Economics* (London, 1938), p. 72.

have ascertained that the first use of the word "capital" in economic literature occurred just before the middle of this century. It was of this century that R. H. Tawney wrote in a passage which has often been quoted.[4] "A century before," he says, business men "had practised extortion and been told that it was wrong; for it was contrary to the law of God. A century later [they were] to practise it and be told that it was right; for it was in accordance with the law of nature."

The resolution which was thus effected by the concept of capital brought to an end a great historic controversy: that of "usury." As every student knows, the controversy over usury began in medieval theology and ended in modern economics, and reflected the process by which feudalism was supplanted by capitalism. What was at issue was no mere quibble over the morals of money-making. So much has been said in recent years about "the profit motive" as almost to obscure the larger social motive of which making money is only an elliptical expression. Making money, by whatever means, is obviously only a prelude to having money. To have money is to have moved permanently from one social class to another superior social class. It was this aspect of the case which constituted a direct threat to the feudal hierarchy, and it was this threat which the church, speaking again for the feudal order as it was already doing in the matter of just price, therefore undertook to meet.

As in the case of just price, the condemnation of usury by the doctors of the church was a fatal compromise. The medieval theologians condemned usury on the ground already occupied by the ancient philosophers that money is sterile, that it cannot and does not breed. Saturated with the doctrine of capital, modern writers have quite generally treated this idea as one of Aristotle's lapses. But was Aristotle wrong, after all? Does money breed? Corporations pay interest on

[4] *Religion and the Rise of Capitalism* (New York and London, 1926), p. 163.

bonds, and from the point of view of the bond-holder that is very nice of them; but what does it prove? Does it indicate that corporations know how to breed dollars, or that bonds are a feature of capitalism? To make money is to seize power, nowadays with the sanction of a society in which this is the accredited way of gaining power. What does this signify with regard to the birth rate of the dollar? Aristotle was not alone in his conviction. All the wisdom of all other cultures but our own has imputed sterility to money. It is our view of the matter which is ridiculous, as we should see at once if we were to substitute some other title to power for money in our neat formula. Does kingship breed kingship? Do feudal perquisites breed other feudal perquisites? Obviously Aristotle was right about money, and if the church had stood fast on this point and condemned money-power as such in all cases and in every degree, feudalism might have continued to prevail.

But the church compromised on usury as it did on just price, and for the same reason and in the same way. Economists make much of the ecclesiastical distinction between "consumptive" and "productive" loans. The distinction is of course one of class. The people who borrowed for "consumptive" purposes were princes, lay and ecclesiastical; consequently the doctors of the church were at pains to deny the power of the lender over them. The people who borrowed for "productive" purposes were other merchants; and with regard to them the church was content to maintain an attitude of dog-eat-dog. Furthermore commerce and finance had already become too important a part of the medieval world to be completely extirpated. Business must go on somehow. It was the medieval church which promulgated the doctrine of "Business is business." It did so in that amazing series of exceptions to the condemnation of usury of which later economists have made so much. The owner of money, it was thought, might be entitled to compensation for the loss he would sustain if his money were not employed in a given undertaking and therefore lay idle. One might ask, Just why? And what does the word "idle" mean with reference to money and in the light of Aristotle's doctrine? A man whose money was employed so as to make him in effect a partner in an enterprise might properly share in the proceeds of that enterprise. Again, why? Why does the loan of money make the lender a partner in the enterprise? A merchant lends money to a shipmaster. The ship goes down with all hands. The merchant loses his money and the captain and all his shipmates lose their lives. The case is even, then? The partners have shared the risks, have they, and so are entitled to share the proceeds of a less disastrous voyage? A great deal of casuistry has gone into the formulation of the doctrine of capital, and we owe much of it to the master hand of the medieval church.

For the doctrine of capital was already present in spirit in the medieval compromise. Indeed, as a theory of authorship it was only a new variety of an ancient species. In every civilization there exists some supreme power to which the fate of the people is attributed. In theocracies it is priests; in kingdoms it is kings. Modern readers often become very impatient with ancient chronicles in which every event of consequence is attributed to the personal agency of some king or other. This sort of thing is usually characterized as "over-emphasis," in such a case upon "the political factor." But the king is more than a political factor; he is the symbol of essential causality. Not only does such an interpretation of the life of a people impute supreme importance to political events; it imputes final responsibility for every event to the supreme authority. Since the king does exercise supreme authority—since his decisions are in some sense final—the destiny of the whole people is thus identified with his being, not without some show of plausibility. Capitalism is a theory of authorship in this sense.

It is the modern belief, perhaps the basic faith of capitalism, that the supreme author of modern civilization is business enterprise. This belief, like that of theocracies and kingdoms, derives from the power which is in fact exercised by capitalists. Everyone knows the part which science has played in Western civilization. But science is an impersonal force, a sort of vegetable growth, a highly cultivated hothouse plant which requires sedulous attention if it is to live and grow. The spokesmen of science—university presidents and the heads of research institutes—continually reiterate the common belief that the progress of science itself depends upon the will of business men in whose power it is to dispose or to withhold.

The same is true in the larger sense. Ours is an industrial society. As everyone knows, the whole community depends today upon what we call mass production, that is, upon the use of machinery on an enormous scale. But it is business men who exercise discretionary power over the use of this machinery. There is therefore a very literal sense in which the whole community depends upon the decisions of business men—hence the general belief in their essential authorship.

It was this belief which found expression in the medieval distinction between usury and legitimate commercial transactions. The money lender was in literal fact a partner since his decisions were paramount over the whole enterprise. If the decision was negative, the shipmaster could not sail. In medieval times the essential authorship of finance was confined to the relatively narrow limits of commerce in the strictest and meanest sense, and the stern prohibition of the exercise of financial power over princes was conceived to implement this limitation. If the doctors of the church could have looked forward to a time when financial power would be paramount over a whole society, they would certainly have been appalled and would probably have taken steps to obliterate the power of money. As their casuistry shows, they recognized the fact of discretionary power. That was something they understood, and their subtle distinction between usury and *lucrum cessans* and the rest is intelligible in no other terms. What they failed to reckon with was the industrial revolution.

The period which separates medieval from modern times has usually been described as one of spiritual awakening, but it was also and perhaps primarily one of very great material change; and it was as a consequence of this change that finance came to bestride the world like a colossus until by the middle of the sixteenth century it seemed to some contemporary observers that business men were already in a position to dictate to parliaments and kings. The stage was then set for the appearance of the pure theory of capitalism.

The pure theory of essential authorship always postulates identity, the identity of discretionary authority with social process. "*L'état, c'est moi!*" is the pure theory of kingship. The state and all its functions are sublimated in the person of the king. This is the identity which was established by the concept of capital. Modern critics describe it as a confusion of meanings, but it was not a confusion in origin and function. It was the intentional identification of discretionary power with all that over which the power was exercised. Already science and industry had transformed the world. Europeans had crossed all the oceans. No other people in the world was a match for their new weapons. The curtain was rising on the age of machinery. All this was the work of the community, as anyone could see. There has never been a time when prevailing beliefs have completely blinded men's eyes to the physical facts of life. Throughout the literature of this period passages may be found which show that ships and instruments of navigation, farm implements and methods of cultivation, iron, wood, and other "natural resources," did not pass altogether unnoticed. Obviously the life of the Western peoples depended utterly on the existence and use of an already considerable accumulation of tools, materials, and "know-how." But in a community in which everything is for sale not only can nothing be done except with the consent of those who control the power to purchase; where everything is for sale even the instruments of production are identical with a sum of money values. In effect they are money values.

It was the historic function of the term "capital" to establish this identity. Etymologically the word derives from the Latin for "head," and means "chief" or "principal": that which is indispensable to whatever is under consideration. For economic activity tools and materials are indispensable; but especially money is indispensable. The term capital, which combines these meanings, thus expresses the joint meaning. Furthermore it does so in terms of money. For it is in terms of money that industrial tools and materials are symbolized, not vice versa. It is money which is "invested" in tools and materials. The process of investiture never works the other way since, like every investiture, it is a ceremonial transfer of authority of which in this instance money is the source. And since money is the source of the industrial power which is thus vested in moneyed men, the source and origin of capital is the accumulation of money. That is why no economist, however much he may take to heart Professor Fetter's lesson, can avoid using "capital" in both senses. If he follows common practice and defines capital as the physical equipment of industry, he must proceed to attribute the origin of capital to saving, since that is the universal dogma. No orthodox economist has ever attributed the growth of capital to science and technology. Civilization may, in a sense, depend upon science and technology, but capital comes into existence through saving; and it is money which is saved, not the physical equipment of industry. No one secretes steel rails by going without lunch. But if, on the other hand, the economist follows Professor Fetter's own practice and taking his cue from the process of accumulation defines capital as a sum of money claims brought into existence through saving, he is then obliged to identify these capital funds with the physical equipment of industry, as Professor Fetter does, since otherwise they are functionless and meaningless.

The whole formula may be put quite simply. The very existence of the community together with all the material progress which recent centuries have witnessed depends upon the existence and use of capital (meaning the physical tools and materials of industry, the knowledge and skills of the community); but it is only by "saving" that we are able to accumulate capital (meaning funds of money values capable of being "invested" in capital equipment); consequently it is upon the accumulation of capital (funds) that the whole life of the community depends.

The expression "saving" used with reference to the accumulation of capital (funds) is such a travesty of the ordinary meaning of this word that it has become a cynosure of dissident opinion. It has always been quite obvious and is now a matter of statistically established fact that a very considerable part of all "saving" is accomplished by the rich, nowadays in large part on the books of corporations which do not even trouble with the formality of assigning their "savings" to their putative owners; and since it is not the habit of the rich to stint themselves in the matter of their personal expenditures, it is quite evident that their accumulations, whether personal or corporate, do not constitute "saving" in the Christmas-club sense as the community at large conceives it. Various attempts have therefore been made to reinforce the theory of capital at this point.

The most notable of these is perhaps the theory of "abstinence" promulgated by Nassau Senior, one of the most devoutly uncritical adherents of classical doctrine. The idea is that funds may be consumed in more spacious living or they may be accumulated for the endowment of future legatees. Since the latter necessarily involves a sacrifice of present consumptive spaciousness, the advantages which accrue to future owners of the capital so accumulated is a proportionate payment for this abstinence, quite without reference to the quality of spaciousness from which present income-receivers thus abstain. The idea that anybody should be rewarded because somebody has refrained from still wilder flights of ostentation than those to which the community is already inured is so ridiculous, however, that later economists have expunged the word "abstinence" from their vocabularies. The modern formula is "time preference." This phrase has two advantages over abstinence: in appearance it is morally neutral, since it ostensibly makes no reference to any quality of expenditure except date; and it purports to derive the whole theory of saving from the fact that rates of interest do actually vary inversely with the term of the loan. Higher rates are in fact asked and bid for short-term loans than for long-term loans. Does this mean that time is what is thus bought and sold? And does this mean that saving and investment can be conceived wholly with reference to the time span, without raising any question of the quality of abstinence? A vast amount of scholarship has been lavished upon the analysis of time spans and interest rates in recent years, apparently under the apprehension that these considerations are all that matters. Yet it requires only a little reflection to establish that such is not the case.

In the first place, the fact that interest rates vary inversely with time spans does not mean that the original motive for the accumulation of the funds for which investment is thus being sought was a "preference" for time. Food prices vary, too, but no one would say that the price of food is the incentive to eating. One might assume that fund-accumulation is an inescapable consequence of large incomes, that funds exist willy-nilly for which investment must be found; different types of investment might still appear in a competitive economy at different rates of interest. Since short-term loans threaten a speedy renewal of the bother and risk of reinvestment, they might well find it necessary to offer higher rates than long-term loans, quite without reference to the circumstances which have brought into existence an accumulation of funds available for investment. In short, even within the universe of discourse of the investment process, it is never pure duration that is at issue.

But, secondly, whatever happens to funds after they are accumulated is quite a different matter from the circumstances by virtue of which accumulation has occurred. To say that the willingness of investors to loan money for long terms at low rates of interest proves that people prefer having money in the sweet by-and-by is as ridiculous as anything Nassau Senior ever said. What does "having money" mean in such a formula? Whatever it means, that is the substance of the matter, of which time is only a concomitant variation. One cannot speak of a time span without it being a span of something or other. If the issue is between present and future money-having, enjoyment, consumption, or what have you, the substantive issue is still Senior's abstinence, for which "time preference" is only a substitution mechanism.

The truth is that economists have used time preference, with its empirical reference to the facts of interest rates, as a means of averting their eyes from a very embarrassing spectacle: the great inequality of income which is one of the most conspicuous features of capitalism. There is no boggling the fact of inequality by any amount of talk of abstinence, or even of time preference. Funds are accumulated not because some people are more abstemious than others, or more far-sightedly prone to idealize the sweet by-and-by, but because some people are richer than others, and for no other reason. All attempts to idealize the accumulation of money are beside the point, and so are all attempts to discredit capitalism on the ground of the cruel inequalities on which it rests. Capitalism is neither sustained nor discredited by the facts of inequality; it is inequality which in the last analysis is to be justified by capitalism. If the existence and progress of industrial society are contingent upon the accumulation of capital (funds) as the condition of the existence and growth of capital (equipment), then inequality, however cruel, is the price civilization pays for its existence and development. To the credit of the classical tradition it must be admitted that this is the issue to which in the main it has been addressed, an issue with reference to which the pros of abstinence and time preference and the cons of injustice and cruelty are mere byplay.

Is fund-accumulation indispensable to industrial process? Economics has never rested content with mere legerdemain. The identity of the two meanings of capital has supposedly been proved. The most specific proof is one which was devised by the Austrian, Boehm-Bawerk, in the latter part of the nineteenth century as an answer to the strictures of Karl Marx. Since it turns upon the so-called "roundabout" character of industrial production and is reproduced in most current textbooks, it is familiar at least in substance to virtually every elementary student. Briefly it runs as follows. Dependence upon the machine process, for example for the baking of bread, means that before the first loaf can be baked a lot of machinery must be installed. This takes a considerable interval of time during which the mechanics, the future bakers, and their potential customers must eat. Their sustenance must therefore be provided in advance of the operation of the projected bakery. In short there must be, in advance of every industrial operation and as a condition of the "roundabout" method of production by machinery, an accumulation of the means of subsistence proportionate to the length of the interval. This accumulation is capital. It is the accumulation of capital funds which makes it possible for the capitalist to "advance" the means of subsistence without which the community cannot wait for the delayed product of the machine process.

So convinced was Boehm-Bawerk of the physical actuality of this situation that he undertook to show that it would obtain even on Robinson Crusoe's island, and he is therefore largely responsible for the reproach of "Crusoe mentality" under which economics has labored ever since. On the supposition that Robinson Crusoe was living on berries, literally from hand to mouth, but could achieve greater security if he could build a boat, Boehm-Bawerk argued that he could build the boat only if he could accumulate enough berries in advance to sustain him during the building operations. Thus capital accumulation and investment were demonstrated to be a condition of expanded production in a one-man economy in which no exchange took place and no money was employed.

The fatuity of this argument is so extreme that it would be apparent to the most elementary student if he could escape the atmosphere of intimidation in which such instruction commonly proceeds. Society does of course make "advances" to every new industrial operation. The whole existing apparatus of industry is available as the foundation of further industrial operations. This includes, in the case of the baking industry, a highly organized industry for the production of baking machinery and behind that the smelting and mining industries which supply the raw materials for baking machinery, the machine tool industry, the whole constellation of the milling industry from which comes flour for the large-scale production of bread, and so the industrial system generally.

At any given moment the development of any industrial operation assumes industrial society as a going concern. This is indeed a sort of accumulation: it is the cumulative process of industrial technology. To give plausibility to Boehm-Bawerk's argument it is necessary to ignore industrial technology altogether, as he did, and use the word "advances" in so vague a sense that the whole going concern of industrial society may be mistaken for the pecuniary advances of the capitalist. Even in the case of Robinson Crusoe it is evident that if the hermit could never pick more than enough berries to keep body and soul together for another day, no accumulation would be possible. The indispensable condition to boat-building must be an improvement of the technology of berry-picking. All industrial operations are so conditioned and would be even in a one-man, non-exchange economy; but this has nothing in common with the accumulation and investment of funds. What could be done with the funds of the investor in a bakery if no source of baking machinery existed?

Not only does the "roundabout" theory confuse industrial integration with financial power; it completely misrepresents the industrial facts. Generation after generation of students have been learning from the study of economics that industrial production is a particularly slow and cumbersome affair in which speed is sacrificed for eventual quantity. This is utterly untrue. In the automobile industry, for example, it is only a matter of days for a scoopful of earth from the Mesabi range to be rolling down the highway as a motor vehicle. In actual operation machine production is the reverse of roundabout. It is prodigiously direct. Any given operation is conditioned by the whole industrial system of which it is a part and without which it would be unthinkable in spite of all the gold of Midas. It is also conditioned by financial control. The "advancing" capitalist decrees that the product of the baking-machine industry shall be set up in his town, and this is important. But it is quite another matter.[5]

[5] This distinction is further analyzed in Chapter IX.

The identity of these two processes—of capital equipment with capital funds—has never been established by any specific demonstration. It is rather implicit in the whole way of thinking which has been traditional in economics, and in this tradition it has been assumed rather than discovered or demonstrated. As Professor Fetter pointed out, it was assumed before the classical system of ideas was formulated and is one of the basic assumptions of that intellectual system. This is the assumption of the creative potency of funds. It finds expression in two forms: in what Veblen used to call "conjectural history," and in the analysis of production. Nearly all economic writers have indulged at some time or other in chapters on "the progress of opulence" in which they have in imagination represented the accumulation of "wealth" as preceding and conditioning industrial development, and professional historians have taken their cue and done their best to discover the sources of the (conjectural) funds which, supposedly, made later industrial development possible. These efforts have been notably unsuccessful, so that economic orthodoxy has never been able to cite history to its purpose at all extensively or with any great force of conviction. Nevertheless the historical assumption remains as a challenge to any other way of thinking to show how on any other basis Western society could be conceived to have developed as it has. Fortunately there is a profusion of evidence with which to meet this challenge.

But the chief preoccupation of economists has been with the analysis of production, as they have called it. In this analysis—the major task of classical political economy—there has been no thought of apology for or justification of the established order or its symbol, capital. It did not even have the conscious purpose of furnishing "laws conducive to abundant and reliable supplies of capital and labor at reasonable prices." [6] Nevertheless it is in this main body of

[6] J. A. Hobson, *op. cit.*, p. 80.

economic theory, if at all, that the duality of the concept of capital is explained and justified.

Economic theory has never been concerned with physical production in the sense of what goes on in factories and machine shops. Learned opinion has usually credited William Petty with a more realistically physical conception of the productive process than was true of later and maturer economic thinking because Petty analyzed production in terms of man-hours and man-hours in terms of the corn necessary to the physical sustenance of the laborer. But this is plainly not job-analysis in the engineering sense. No less than later economists, Petty was fascinated by the subtleties of the pricing mechanism into which like his successors he tried to read a social meaning. Already, in the seventeenth century, the problem of economic theory was not to analyze what was actually going on in mine and factory but to establish a relationship between price and value. The problem is to establish a price equivalence between the value which is extractable from commodities in consumption and the value which has been put into them in production. Since value is by immemorial tradition a subjective phenomenon,[7] its cost-equivalent must also be subjective; and since for social reasons capital is the factor which is chiefly at issue, the analysis must from the outset do two things. It must identify capital with labor, and it must subjectify labor. Both of these projects were well under way by the time of William Petty. Petty's corn has a more physical appearance than the plainly subjective "toil and trouble" in terms of which Adam Smith reckoned labor cost. But why corn? Why not skill? At no time in history could any genuine attempt to understand the physical operations of production have failed to take cognizance of labor's "know-how" as having at least no less significance for the production of goods than spiritual anguish. Not only did Petty ignore the realities of production; the

[7] This conception is further analyzed in the following chapter.

truth is that whereas later economists thought of general discomfort, Petty thought specifically of hunger as the particular form of anguish which labor incurred in the exercise of production.

From this point on, the classical analysis of the factors of production has been in terms of spiritual wear and tear. The terminology which has been generated by this effort has been encyclopedic, ranging all the way from Petty's corn to disutility and, nowadays, opportunity. But always the effect has been the same. Many critics have noted that the so-called factors of production are really distributive, and that their relation to value is one of imputation. That is, land, labor, capital, and management are identified not by virtue of what they do in the shop but by virtue of what they receive in the division of social income under the rubrics of rent, wages, interest, and profits, payment of which imputes to their recipients some sort and degree of social value. Furthermore it is generally agreed that the problem of imputation is most acute with respect to labor and capital. By common consent the profits of management are not a fixed charge on society since they vary directly with economic frictions and might be expected to approach zero as a limit in a state of perfect competitive equilibrium. Orthodox theory has also long since ceased to concern itself with the claims of landlords. More than a century ago Ricardo proved that rent plays no part in the determination of prices but is only a differential corresponding to physical differences between different parcels of land. Unfortunately this demonstration proves too much. As a number of students have lately seen, both capital and labor can be treated in the same way. Their receipts also can be shown to vary with physical circumstances; and any one may be proved not to determine price if the theory of imputation be observed with respect to the others, as it was in the case of Ricardo's theory of rent. But this anomaly has not been recognized by orthodox opinion generally, in which therefore capital and labor continue to stand by themselves as the major factors for consideration in the imputation of value.

The authenticity of capital was thus established by its identification with labor. For nobody challenges the moral claim of labor. In contrast to feudal attitudes, modern society has all along made a fetich of the dignity of work. Contemporaneously with William Petty, Locke based his whole theory of property on the indefeasible claim which is established when man mixes his labor with the soil. The right of the laborer to the product of his toil was one of those rights which seemed to the philosophers of the eighteenth century to be inalienable. So strong is this sentiment that it dominated even the mind of the revolutionary Marx, who made it the basis of the claim of the proletariat to the "surplus value" of which they had been immemorially robbed. The laborer is worthy of his hire. If the same is true of capital, it is enough.

But the complementary nature of capital and labor does not derive from the working partnership of capitalists and laborers, very fortunately perhaps. Indeed the founders of the classical tradition were singularly candid in their treatment of the actual working relations of owners and employees. "From the writings of many, if not most, of them can be culled passages expressing a benevolent attitude to the claims of labor," as Mr. Hobson says.[8] The truth is that whatever the spotted actuality, owners and employees must be partners, since capital and labor are complements; and they are complements not because of any actuality but by virtue of their conceptual character as intellectual abstractions. This is true of labor no less than capital. From what human quality, for example, do the supposed rights of labor devolve? Clearly they have nothing in common with technical skill, which appears in quite another universe of dis-

[8] *Op. cit.*, p. 85. See also Chapter I, above.

course.[9] Locke said nothing about property rights being established by the degree of skill with which men till the soil. The quality in terms of which labor is identified with capital is wholly subjective, a spiritual quality, a creative potency, a matter of dignity and anguish, hunger, toil, and trouble, disutilities endured, opportunities foregone.

In the last analysis classical political economy is a theory of final causes in the theological sense. Production having been conceived as the creation of value, the question is: By virtue of what creative potency do labor and capital contribute jointly to this process? The answer to this question is implicit in the word "virtue." Modern usage retains this expression as a cliché, but in the past it was taken literally. To all the simpler peoples, creation is indeed a matter of virtue—of *mana,* as the Polynesians say.[10] Even today this is the popular conception of genius. In "creative" activity man mixes his personality with the inert materials of nature and so endows inanimate objects with something of his virtue. "Claims" and "rights" can be conceived in no other terms. It has often been remarked that Locke established the right of property on grounds identical with those of the rights of kings, which he denied. In this respect the virtue of labor is not only identical with that of capital; it is one with all the mystic potencies which have prevailed since the dawn of history.

Thus classical theory justified the duality of capital by extending its schizophrenia to the whole economic process. Capital means two things: the physical equipment of industry, and the funds by which control is exercised. It is the physical equipment which conditions actual industrial operations; but it is the funds which impart "value" and establish claims. In like fashion labor also means two things. It means the exercise of skill, which is the actuality of industrial pro-

[9] See Chapter VI, below.
[10] See Chapter VIII, below.

duction; but it also means the infusion of creative potency, which likewise imputes value and establishes all rights and claims. All the terms which are used in the formulas of value theory are similarly schizophrenic. Thus for example we speak of the "productivity" of either labor or capital, meaning in some cases the ratio of physical product to number of machines or man-hours of operation, and in others the ratio of creative potency to pecuniary remuneration.[11] It is for this reason that the anomaly of capital passed unnoticed for so many generations and continues to persist even after it has been explicitly recognized. The confusion of the concept of capital is concealed in a general confusion, and it can be resolved only by a resolution which is likewise general.

Certainly the concept of capital is not altogether responsible for this general confusion. Something of the sort was bound to result from the effort to find a meaning in the price system which it does not have, and the condition was further aggravated by the "discovery" of a conjunction between price and the metaphysics of value. But economic theory has never been a merely intellectual exercise. The effort to establish a relation between price and value has been made in the interest of understanding what is happening in the economy of modern Western civilization. Two sorts of things are happening, each of which can be indicated by a single word: industrialism and capitalism. These two aspects of the modern economy are in fact quite distinct. Nevertheless in the apprehension of modern society during the past four hundred years they have been identified; and this identification, symbolized by the word "capital," has imparted its own peculiar quality of confusion to the economic thinking of this entire period.

[11] The concept of productivity is further discussed in Chapter IV, below.

Chapter IV

THE THEORY OF VALUE

THE CLASSICAL tradition of economic thinking was formed in the eighteenth century in a climate of opinion one of the principal features of which was the idea of natural order. It also embodied an eighteenth-century conception of human nature which antedates the modern science of psychology. Much has been made of both these points by later criticism, but without notable effect. No one doubts the influence of the philosophy of natural order upon eighteenth-century economists; but contemporary economists protest vehemently that their use of such terms as "normal" and "equilibrium" has nothing in common with eighteenth-century ways of thinking. Similarly no one doubts the psychological naïveté of the eighteenth-century writers, but our contemporaries insist that no traces of it are to be found in their work. So long as such charges are preferred and answered one at a time, the defense may be disconcertingly effective. How is the critic to prove, in the face of vigorous denial, that the phrase "normal price" is an evocation of the "laws of nature" of another age? The answer lies in the cumulative character of intellectual guilt. Modern representatives of the classical tradition may or may not talk the language of bygone ages at any particular point; nevertheless the whole theory of value which lies at the heart of all their reasoning is the embodiment and summation of all they disavow.

The issue of natural order is, of course, teleology. This way of thinking has been aptly characterized as that of people who think it very wonderful that fishes which after all can live in nothing else should be provided with so much water. The word "natural" is harmless enough. Indeed its implication is that of an order of things which exists outside ourselves and quite independent of our wishes and intentions or even, perhaps, of any wish or intention. The idea of order is likewise unexceptionable. Both words are widely used today in unimpeachably scientific senses. But trouble develops when they are used together. Although we do use the word "order" to designate patterns in the formation of which guiding intelligence has had no hand, as in zoological classification, we also use it quite generally to characterize human activities, so generally that we can scarcely think of "the order of nature" without implying that nature reveals the kind of order to which housekeepers aspire.

This was the intention of the eighteenth-century philosophers, and it was an idea which they had "come by naturally." Their way of thinking was inherited from medieval theology. As the saying goes, "Some people call it Nature, but others call it God." In a very remarkable little book, *The Heavenly City of the Eighteenth Century Philosophers,* Professor Carl Becker has pointed out the essential continuity of the "age of reason" with the age of faith. The schoolboy who wrote that Newton discovered three laws of motion which it would be well for all of us to follow was closer to the mark than he realized. To the mind of the seventeenth and eighteenth centuries the laws of nature seemed to have been enacted for the guidance of rational beings. Early modern science, as Professor E. A. Burtt has pointed out and students now generally realize, rested on metaphysical foundations, especially on the conception of the universe as rational in the sense that man is rational.

This was of course the medieval idea. According to the doctors of the church both statutory and natural law embody those faint glimmerings of Infinite Wisdom which the imperfect mind of man has been able to apprehend. Indeed the distinction between statutory law and natural law was much less sharp than it seems today. "Natural law" had a legal as well as a scientific content and was one of the foundations of modern jurisprudence as it was also one of the sources of the medieval way of thinking.

For what is most significant is the wide dispersion and great antiquity of this state of mind. It is by no means limited to Christian theology. On the contrary, a theory of the orderliness of nature and its application to human affairs is to be found in the literatures of all peoples who had literatures, and in Western culture it goes back as far as the records go. Scholars have pointed out at least three clear sources of the medieval complex: ancient philosophy with which the medieval mind re-established direct contact; the early Christian tradition (*e.g.*, St. Augustine) upon which Greek philosophy had impacted in the formative period; and the Justinian codification of Roman law with its Stoic tradition of *jus naturale*. And behind all this lay the rubrics of primitive culture. Some years ago Professor F. M. Cornford demonstrated in a book which ought to be much more widely studied than it is, *From Religion to Philosophy*, that a sense of fate (*moira*) anticipated all the gods, and that when advancing sophistication exorcised the gods, what remained to dominate the grand tradition of Greek philosophy was that aboriginal sense of fate.

This sense of a fateful order by which the universe and even the human economy are shaped is more than a historical survival. The wide dispersion of the concept of a natural order in the universe is probably a case of convergence of cultures upon this point rather than of universal diffusion, and the convergence is probably due to circumstances which affect all "abstract" thinking and of which the general disposition to impute human qualities to the non-human universe is the result. In his pioneer studies of the social character of the conceptualizing process, the French sociologist, Emile Durkheim, used the phrase "collective representation" to describe the way of thinking by which all societies impute their special arrangements to the universe.[1] Durkheim and his followers made the mistake of contrasting this "prelogical" conceptuology of "primitive mentality" with the supposedly logical thought processes of modern Frenchmen; but the usefulness of his analysis of "collective representation" is only heightened by the realization that modern thinking is full of collective representations.

The conception of "the order of nature" is a collective representation. Just as contemporary theologians and moralists read a social meaning into the physical theories of the "relativity" of space and time and the "indeterminacy" of the atom, so the eighteenth-century philosophers read social meaning into the terminology of Galileo, Newton, and Harvey. Professor Becker remarks that although not everybody read Newton's *Principia* even in the eighteenth century, everybody talked about it, just as virtually the whole of the last generation has talked about Freud. In his *Growth of Philosophical Radicalism* Elie Halévy called attention to the use Adam Smith made of gravitational figures of speech, metaphors which are still repeated in current economic textbooks apparently without any realization on the part of contemporary writers that they are perpetuating eighteenth-century obsessions. The same significance attaches to the fact that when the physician, François Quesnay, came to discuss economic process he did so in the language of Harvey's great discovery. For Adam Smith, current prices "grav-

[1] This way of thinking is further discussed in Chapter VIII, below.

itate about" normal price; for Quesnay, riches "circulate." Galileo's pendulum has swung its way through the whole of modern thought.

In economics the chief repository of this way of thinking is the concept of equilibrium. Since this term is more widely used by economists today than ever before, contemporary theorists are faced with two alternatives. Either the collective representation of the eighteenth century still dominates economic thinking, or the term "equilibrium" is used today in a quite different sense from that which dictated its first employment. The latter is of course what economists now say, and in making this claim they derive aid and comfort from modern physics. The term "equilibrium" is, to be sure, still employed in physics where it no longer has any connotation of a far-off, divine event but means only whatever sort of balance of forces may conceivably obtain in any given situation. This, modern economists protest, is just what they mean by equilibrium. The relation of supply and demand with respect to price is that of two springs attached to a moving peg. Any increase in the tension of one spring will cause the peg to move that way until the tensions are equalized and the peg comes to rest. That, they say, is just what happens in the case of price: a change of tensions, a price adjustment, and a return to equilibrium.

But there is an important difference between physics and economics of which this interpretation takes no account. Physicists set no store by equilibrium but economists do. They must. The whole significance of equilibrium in economics is that it is beneficent. Equilibrium is good. Disequilibrium is bad. That of course is the older significance of "natural order." The order of nature was conceived to be beneficent. It was the glory which the heavens revealed. This is the content of the idea of equilibrium with which modern physics has dispensed. Physics no longer hymns the "natural harmonies" of the universe; but economics does. It does so today with a certain obliquity of language. No contemporary economist makes "the natural harmonies" of supply and demand a matter of "Christian evidences," as Archbishop Whateley did a century ago. Nevertheless price equilibrium is a consummatory state even in contemporary economics, not merely an analytical device as it is in modern physics.

In recent years certain economists have showed a disposition to deny this. A remark to this effect by Professor Lionel Robbins, that "equilibrium is just equilibrium," has been very widely quoted. The motive of such a declaration is obvious. It betrays consciousness if not of guilt at least of general suspicion. Few physicists take the trouble any longer to clear their use of the concept "equilibrium" of taint of beneficence, since their context implies no such beneficence. That of economics does—hence the denial. It goes without saying that this denial is sincere, but it is nevertheless highly paradoxical. For the question at once presents itself: if equilibrium is just equilibrium, why are economists so much concerned about it? Why is it so necessary for economists to prove that all prices "gravitate about" a point of equilibrium if equilibrium has no more significance than that of a pair of springs?

As a matter of fact one of the most recent and startling developments of price theory, that of "monopolistic competition," seems to be well on the way to establishing the insignificance of equilibrium, with effects which are not yet fully appreciated. The whole upshot of classical price theory was that prices are "naturally harmonious," as the universe was once conceived to be, and that in the absence of "unnatural restraints" the whole system would come to rest at a point at which the factors of production would be used with maximum efficiency and utilities would be distributed in such a way that the total satisfaction of the whole community could not be increased by any change. It now appears that whatever the situation with regard to restraint of trade there is some point or other at which prices come to rest. The theory of monopolistic competition is the deductive determination of the various points at which equilibrium occurs under various conditions of restraint of trade. This is indeed the demoralization of the concept of equilibrium. But it is the reduction of the whole classical theory of price to an absurdity. The essence of that theory is that the price system forms patterns which are significant, whereas the essence of this new theory is that price patterns are without significance. This may be so. But if so, why are we concerned about them?

The present discussion, however, is not concerned with criticism of price theory, ancient or modern, but only with tracing the formation of the pattern. For this purpose the theory of human nature is more important than that of equilibrium. The conception of value in which price theory eventuates has its source in human nature; and this conception of human nature as the locus of value was the psychological counterpart of the harmonies of nature. The eighteenth century was greatly exercised about human nature, and for a definite reason. As Leslie Stephen pointed out in his classic *History of English Thought in the Eighteenth Century*, the development of the natural sciences posed a conundrum. It was no longer possible for educated men to account for such moral decency as human behavior does after all exhibit in terms of the direct intervention of a guiding Deity. The Hand, if it existed, had at least become invisible. Consequently the patterns of moral action must be somehow implicit in the "natural order" of things. The question was, How? Two types of answer can be made, along the lines of what philosophers call rationalism and empiricism. Rationalism has had its British representatives; but it has flourished chiefly in Germany and its influence upon economic thinking has been principally through the metaphysical background of Karl Marx. The climate of opinion in which classical political economy germinated, for the most part in England, was that of "British empiricism."

The influence of this tradition of moral empiricism upon the classical way of thinking in economics is notorious. Every undergraduate knows that Adam Smith occupied a famous chair of moral philosophy and made an outstanding contribution to the literature of ethics and psychology years before he wrote *The Wealth of Nations.* It is also notorious that classical economic theory makes certain important assumptions with regard to human nature by which that whole way of thinking has been conditioned. Nevertheless economists have showed very little disposition to investigate these assumptions and their sources.[2] The reason for this neglect is apparent in what such investigation reveals.

Adam Smith's theory of moral sentiments was the behaviorism of the eighteenth century. By intention it was a wholly objective account of human nature, at least so far as the mechanism goes. What Smith called "sentiment" his predecessors had called "sense," and they had done so with the intention of identifying the springs of conduct with the "five senses." It was a sort of eighteenth-century stimulus and response, or push-button, theory of behavior. The third Earl of Shaftesbury, who had been brought into the world by John Locke and was the inspiration of Smith's teacher and predecessor, Francis Hutcheson, regarded the sense of smell as the prototype of the moral sense. The reason a man avoids nastiness even in the absence of reproving associates, he

[2] Following the work of Leslie Stephen and the German, Wilhelm Hasbach (in which Veblen was the only economist to display much interest), the only published work which goes into these materials at all extensively is *The Individual and His Relation to Society as Reflected in British Ethics,* by James H. Tufts and Helen Thompson (Chicago, 1904), which has been out of print for many years. An exhaustive study by Professor Gladys Bryson, presented as a dissertation at the University of California in 1930, has never been published.

said, is because he has a nose. Similarly he avoids wrongdoing because he has the moral equivalent of the olfactory sense.

All this sounds very quaint today. Noses, we now realize, detect odors but do not select them. The selection is done by society, by social habit and tradition; that is, by the mores. There is no odor, however foul it may seem to certain people, which is not enjoyed by other people with different traditions; and the same thing is true of behavior generally. There is no act which is universally condemned. "Crime" is universally condemned. But "crime" is an abstraction, not an act. What is crime in one set of circumstances or to one set of people may be highly meritorious in other circumstances or to other people.[3] The eighteenth-century behaviorists did just what so many of us have done in one way or another: they tried to give a thoroughly scientific explanation of something which is not scientific at all. In our own time the device of instinct has been used in just this way. An instinct purports to be a bodily behavior mechanism; but what it purports to explain is a matter of social opinion, the opinions of the explainers. The British empiricists were disposed to be as empirical as possible with regard to their devices. Their moral sense was conceived to be virtually a bodily mechanism. Since their knowledge of the olfactory mechanism was very limited as compared with our own (which is still far from complete), it was possible for them to suppose that the moral sense functions just like the sense of smell. But what they sought to explain (in the case of both these senses) was wholly preconceived.

It was, in fact, the pre-established harmony of the theolo-

[3] To dispose of an enemy sentry, "jump on his back, reach both arms around his neck and shove a foot against the back of his knee. The impact is guaranteed to double him up like a jackknife and if you twist at the same time you'll sever his spinal cord." Quoted by *Time*, June 22, 1942, from an article entitled, "Learn to Fight Dirty," in the first issue of *Yank*.

gians. Science had eliminated the guiding hand of Providence but not the conception of a providentially well-ordered universe. Consequently there was only one possible explanation of this state of affairs: contrived at the outset with Infinite Cunning, wound up at the beginning of time like a transcendental clock, it would tick on through infinity according to the beneficent laws of nature, a perpetual manifestation of the rationality of things. Human nature was thus conceived to be a part of the universal clock. For generations students of economics have quoted the famous passages in which, for example, Adam Smith says that the prudent investor "is led as though by an invisible hand to promote an end which is no part of his intention," smiling tolerantly at this quaint conceit. No misinterpretation could be more complete. Economists should read Hume's account of the sexual instinct whereby, as he virtually says (and his conception of human nature was closer to Smith's than any other), man is led as though by an invisible hand to promote an end which is no part of his intention, to wit, the perpetuation of the species.

This way of thinking is no mere byplay. To regard it as having none but a literary connection with classical economic theory is to misconceive that whole system of ideas. Central to that way of thinking is the conception of a "community of interests" in economic life. Price is the mechanism and competition is the spirit of this supposed community of economic interests to the analysis of which the whole of classical theory is devoted. But its substance—that of which an explanation is being sought—is the conception of human nature and social order in terms of pre-established harmony, the harmony of a world which acts as though guided by an invisible hand because it was indeed devised by an All-wise Artificer and wound up to run precisely along these lines.

Of all the rubrics of classical theory competition is perhaps the most extraordinary. What this word has reference to is presumably the struggle for existence on the economic level. As such it is red in tooth and claw. The life of the competitive business man is one of unremitting asperity and subterfuge, and this is not only true of the great barons of the business world. For sheer meanness, deceit, trickery, subterfuge, and intrigue the corner grocer has no equal. Furthermore to suppose that monopoly and competition are "natural" opposites or contraries is the height of absurdity. The ambition of every competitive business man is to put his rival out of business and absorb his trade. Conspiracy to this end is not confined to the skyscrapers of the New York financial district. Every butcher and plasterer has his "friends." And all this is a matter of common knowledge. To be sure, every particular act of petty knavery is more or less concealed from public view. But ten days' apprenticeship in any competitive establishment would be sufficient to open the eyes of the inquiring student to the character of competition. Why, then, does competition play the role of savior in the traditional economic drama?

Leslie Stephen remarks that Adam Smith was not the keen observer of the humble actualities of economic life that he is reputed to have been. Indeed, he was not an observer at all; he was a philosopher. His interest was focused on ideas, and his system was "simple and obvious" because it was compounded of familiar and generally accepted ideas, at this point the idea of sympathy. Both Smith and Hume, in whose *Theory of Moral Sentiments* and *Inquiry Concerning the Principles of Morals* the idea of moral sense reached its apogee, summed up the moral nature of man in "sympathy." The idea was that human beings are so attuned to each other that each one responds to his fellows, automatically so to speak, in such a way that the total pattern of behavior forms a natural concord. This concord is not an adventitious thing; it is implicit in human nature. It is Nature's master device for effecting harmony in the human sphere. This is what competition assumes. It has been a favorite maneuver of economists throughout the classical period to "simplify" specific economic situations "for analytical purposes" by postulating certain specific economic changes while "all other things remain equal." In a recent and searching study of assumptions of this kind T. W. Hutchison has given especial attention to this "ceteris paribus" assumption and has concluded that it is meaningless.[4] It is indeed devoid of economic actuality, but not wholly without content. Its content is the idea of sympathy. What economists assume when they undertake to infer the "natural" reactions of business men to a given shift of demand or supply "all other things being equal," is that business men do not naturally kick and gauge but do behave with "sympathy."

This, it goes without saying, is a tremendous assumption, for it locates the well-spring of all economic behavior in the human soul. From the modern scientific point of view, what is wrong with eighteenth-century psychology is not so much its fatuousness as its subjectivity. Empirical as they were, the moral-sense philosophers assumed as a matter of course that the senses—all the senses—are organs of the soul. When Shaftesbury discussed the nose, it was as a projection of the mind. Sensations were of course "mental" phenomena, and so was "moral sense." That is why the analogy was not crippled at the outset by the absence of a moral sense organ. The organ is only the window. Since the sensation, even of smell or taste, is a figment of the mind, and since morality is otherwise inconceivable, the two may be identified with perfect ease—on the mental level. Eighteenth-century empiricism was the purportedly objective analysis of avowedly mental phenomena.

This is what it means to speak of classical economic theory as "deductive" reasoning. Obviously there is nothing amiss

[4] *The Significance and Basic Postulates of Economic Theory* (London, 1938).

with deduction, which is only a name for the process by which its meaning is elicited from any given proposition; and if this were all that is wrong with the traditional way of thinking in economics, it would be virtually blameless. That is why its proponents are so ready to admit its deductive character. But the validity of any given deduction is proportionate to the validity of the propositions from which meaning is deductively elicited. The trouble with the classical way of thinking is its basic propositions, the theory of human "nature" of which all economic activity is conceived to be the "natural" expression.

This conception of human nature in subjective, mentalistic, terms not only inspires the idea of a competitive "community of interests" which was political economy's answer to the medieval doctrine of just price; it also inspires the conception of interest in terms of which the whole theory of value is conceived. For the moral sense of the eighteenth-century philosophers was a principle of morals no less than of psychology. As such it was a variant of a very ancient moral philosophy, namely hedonism. As every student knows, hedonism is the theory that in his moral life man is guided by the "senses" of pleasure and pain, happiness and unhappiness, utility and disutility. Since these "senses" or "sentiments" are conceived to be "natural" responses to stimuli of the same sort as the senses of hearing, sight, smell, and the rest, for which they are named, the theory of moral sentiments has always been regarded as a "naturalistic" and therefore quasi-scientific way of thinking to which accordingly men have repeatedly turned in those ages (such as that of the ascendancy of Greek philosophy in the ancient world) when the grip of revealed religion has relaxed. Such was the situation in the eighteenth century and such was also the response.

When the gods resign, the sense of destiny remains, in the moral sphere no less than the natural universe. To suppose that men are impelled "by nature" to seek happiness and avoid pain and effort was altogether consonant with the natural philosophy of the age of Newton and Harvey. But the application of this supposed axiom has always been obscure. To just what way of life does the pursuit of happiness (or satisfaction) lead? That is the question which the philosophers have always found it difficult to answer.

Whereas the general public pictures a life of "happiness" in Sybaritic terms and defines an "epicure" as a devotee of physical indulgence, Epicurus himself and all thoughtful students of the problem have tried to represent the pursuit of happiness as the road to spiritual ideals. The difficulty is that it is not a road but only a synonym. The body winces with pain, but happiness is defined by society. No less than modern psychology, modern social studies have now enabled us to see that such ideals as those of the American Declaration of Independence are never deduced by philosophers from such "axioms" as "the pursuit of happiness." On the contrary, they are projections of the actual life of the community—the "mores," in this case of actual democracy. What seems morally "pleasant" and "unpleasant" to any community of men is determined by their mores, and not vice versa. Hedonism in all its forms is a vicious circle for this reason. "Pleasure" (or "satisfaction," or "utility") is not a natural phenomenon like the "five senses" of the physical organism. For every man it is determined by the social medium in which he lives; and consequently when it is adopted as a tool of analysis or a term of explanation of that social order, its adoption means the assumption in advance of all that social fabric of which an explanation is being sought. We hold this truth to be self-evident, that men who live by democracy, or by capital, will find in it their happiness, and that is all that is self-evident.

The philosophers of the eighteenth century must not be held responsible for the social studies of the twentieth, but they were quite aware of the difficulty of their situation, and it was in this difficulty that the price system appeared as a god from the machine. Whereas in other ages hedonism has foundered upon the inescapable vagueness of its categories, Adam Smith and the other creators of political economy were inspired to seize upon the pricing mechanism as the vehicle of the pursuit of happiness. It is to this "discovery" or synthesis, more than to any other inspiration, that we owe the whole system of ideas by which the economic thinking of the past five generations has been dominated. Obviously Adam Smith was not its sole author. Indeed it is impossible to say when and where and how the idea of a correlation between price and value first occurred. The physiocrats had a glimmering of it, and Adam Smith doubtless owed his first perceptions directly to them; but fainter glimmerings may be detected far back in economic literature. From the time when the price system first began to exercise its fatal fascination, its students have caught glimpses, beneath the surface, of the promise of a larger meaning, one in which the meaning of commercial society itself seemed about to emerge.

For price seems to solve the immemorial enigma. To the question, "What is happiness? Who shall say?" the classical economists seemed to have found a final answer. No one can say; but no one need say, since the price system provides an instrument through the subtle operation of which every man can have his say. Since consumption seems by axiom to be the consummation of all economic effort, and since consumption is actualized in demand, and since demand impacts upon the scarcity of nature to determine the form and direction of every economic undertaking, it seems to follow that commerce itself expresses in this subtle fashion the aspirations of the race.

According to classical theory consumption is the "end" of all economic activity. It would be interesting to know who first laid down this "axiom." Adam Smith states it in the clearest and most categorical language, and it is still repeated in virtually identical wording in current treatises and textbooks. To most people, apparently, this proposition still has the sound of an axiomatic truth. But why? What, exactly, does it mean? Clearly the word "end" is not used here in any chronological sense. That is, no one supposes that economic activity "comes to an end" with consumption. Obviously it never comes to an end at all but goes on continuously. Each act of consumption is followed by other acts of a productive character and so by an indefinite series of successive consumptions and productions. If the "axiom" means anything, it can only mean that acts of consumption are somehow "consummatory," that they are what philosophers have called "final causes." That is, they have the same relation to production which "salvation" has to "repentance." There is presumed to be a certain state or spiritual condition (consumption, or "salvation") which is conceived to be valuable "in itself," to which the other state conduces; so that the other state (production, or "repentance") is conceived to be valuable not "in itself" but only as a "means" to the transcendent "end."

It is this transcendentalism which has kept economic thinking in bond to price theory. It was implicit in the whole conception of human nature in terms of natural harmony from which the classical tradition was derived. One might suppose that a theory which treats consuming as in effect the salvation of the race would proceed at once to identify economic welfare with more abundant consumption. But this, it seems, would be naïve. In classical theory consumption is no vulgarly physical activity such as eating, or sleeping under shelter; it is a matter not of the use of things but of the consumption of "value." What matters is not the calories and vitamins the food contains but its "utility," that is to say, its "want-satisfying" quality, that is to say, the "feelings" it excites in the breast of the consumer. Experiences such as these are uniquely individual in the metaphysical sense, locked within the spiritual being of each individual. Consequently the economist can know economic value only as it is revealed in the "wants" with which each individual reports his own unique spiritual experiences; and since these are made known by purchases which in turn are gathered up and synthesized in the price system, it follows that the price system is the only locus of value and guide to economic welfare.

Such being the case, the task of economic science is to analyze the subtle and complicated process by which value is created and consumed; and it has proceeded to do so by the elaboration of a series of formulas the bewildering complexity of which has steadily increased from generation to generation. But throughout all this complexity of detail the gist of the matter remains quite simple. It is a misrepresentation to say as Mr. J. A. Hobson has done [5] that "the main concern" of economic theory is "to furnish 'laws' conducive to abundant and reliable supplies of capital and labor at 'reasonable' prices." The laws and institutions of commercial society do this quite effectively. The task of political economy is to "interpret" the situation which the institutions of capitalism have brought about, in particular the role of capital. To accomplish this it is necessary to show that capital and labor are "worthy of their hire," that prices are just, and that the over-all situation which is induced by the free play of the price system is one of maximum efficiency in the use of the factors of production and maximum satisfaction in the distribution of the product of industry to the community.

For this purpose two sorts of variables must be employed, those now generally identified by the terms "utility" and "productivity." These are the entities which Alfred Mar-

[5] See Chapter I.

shall's famous simile likened to the opposing blades of a pair of shears; in trimming the cloth of capitalism they cut against each other. They are the "quantities" which require to be equated in the formulas of value theory. Although both these terms are commonly identified with the "neo-classical" period, both are in fact very ancient. In one form or another "utility" may be found as far back as economic literature goes.[6] Perhaps the first articulate form in which the problem of value theory appeared was that of the relation between "value in use" and "value in exchange," which is as much as to say "utility" and price. If price may be regarded as "setting a value" on things, then what is the relation between the value which price sets and the value things "really have" in the estimation of those who use them? This was the issue between "value in use" and "value in exchange," and it is still the issue of utility conceived as the "want-satisfying" quality of things. All that was added in the last third of the nineteenth century was the resolution of the want-satisfying quality into infinitesimal increments for purposes of mathematical treatment.

The term "productivity" also is of indefinite age. It was one of the leading categories of the physiocrats nearly a century and a half before its exploitation by Professor John Bates Clark, and the significance which the physiocrats attached to it is still the essence of the case. They wished to discriminate in favor of agriculture and against commerce and industry,[7] and they employed the term "productivity" for this purpose. What it imputes is a very special kind of creative potency, an "effective causation" in the metaphysical sense, by virtue of which its agents may be judged to be socially deserving. Because Adam Smith and all his succes-

[6] *E.g.*, Gabriel Biel (d. 1495), *Treatise on the Power and Utility of Moneys* (Trans. by R. B. Burke, Philadelphia and London, 1930).

[7] For reasons most clearly stated by Norman Ware in his article, "The Physiocrats: A Study in Economic Rationalization," *American Economic Review*, XXI, 607.

sors rejected this particular discrimination, later students have failed to notice that the term "productivity" has retained all its discriminatory significance and still continues to pose the physiocratic question of social deserts. For John Bates Clark and his successors, the question is still one of the relation between the pecuniary payments to labor and capital and the value they create.

It would be very nice indeed if it could be shown that the social deserts of the increments of capital and labor which are employed in making any given article are exactly equal to the real satisfaction which the article actually gives in use, and that both are correctly measured by the price at which the article is sold and bought. But there is a difficulty. Both of these quantities are unknowns. This situation is so fantastic that the mind almost refuses to entertain it. Nevertheless it is clear and unmistakable. Economic science has no technique of independent measurement of any of these entities, utility, productivity, or value. How do we know that price measures any one of them, let alone equating them? We do not know; we only assume it to be so. The utilities for which a customer pays and the productivities for which labor and capital are paid are equal by assumption, and that is all there is to it. We have no more evidence of their actual caliber than we have of the quantities of sin, repentance, and divine grace which are equated in salvation.

As scientific methodology this sort of thing is so outrageous as to pass belief. How could intelligent students have engaged seriously in exercises of this kind? The answer is that each of these terms is capable of precise definition, from "value" on down. Thus economists usually define "value" as the relation between the price of a given commodity and the prices of other commodities. The distinction between absolute price and such a ratio is of course a genuine and useful one. Indeed it is the same distinction as the one we make between "money wages" and "real wages." The price of wheat may go up while its "value" (price ratio to other commodities) goes down, just as money wages may go up while real wages go down. In similar fashion "demand," for example, may be defined in terms of actual purchases with the proviso that we know nothing of it except in terms of actual purchase. Without doubt it is this apparent precision which has sustained these amazing theoretical exercises down to the present day. But it raises two questions.

If "value" means "price ratio," why is it called "value"? If "demand" means "purchase," why is it called "demand"? Each of these words is derived from common speech in which both have very extensive connotations of a highly ethical character. Many students of economics have labored mightily to purge their lucubrations of "ethical implications" of this character. With regard to "demand," for example, it is now standard practice for textbooks to warn their readers that in speaking of the "demand" for unhealthy, vicious, and even "anti-social" goods and services economists have no thought of endorsing the human attitudes at issue; what they have reference to is only the actuality of purchase of these things and services. But in that case why have they used such words as "demand" with their indissociable reference to appetites and attitudes? If demand means only purchase, the obvious way to purge economics of untoward ethical implications would be by simply saying "purchase." If that is what economists want and mean, why do they do otherwise?

If they did this, there would be no theory of value. Many members of the profession insist that they are prepared to face that outcome with equanimity. Their task, they declare, is the investigation of the actualities of price behavior. In the performance of this task they are not concerned with any theory of value in the philosophic sense and would be quite able to use the phrase "price ratio" as a substitute for "value" if such a practice were to be generally adopted. This is all very well as far as it goes. To the credit of the profession, very extensive empirical investigations of a highly exact and untheoretical character have indeed been prosecuted. But the proposal to confine economic discussion to this empirical universe of discourse raises another question. Very few of the empiricists refrain altogether from harboring social convictions or, as Professor Eric Roll has pointed out,[8] from expressing them in public in such a manner as to suggest that the convictions somehow emerge from the empirical studies. According to their own avowals, this cannot be the case. Then where do they come from? Only one answer is possible: they come from the theory of value in the philosophic sense which these scientists as scientists have clearly and definitely disavowed.

The truth is, it is impossible for economics to disavow the ethical implications of value theory or to dispense with the terminology in which those implications are imbedded, since economics is, and always has been, concerned primarily with the meaning of price patterns. The demonstration that fertilizer sales vary with the price of wheat does not reveal the meaning of the economy. Only a theory of value can do that, for it is after all a matter of value in the largest sense.

That is why economists persist indefatigably in the effort to elicit meaning from the price system. The absurdities of traditional theory are only too apparent. Critical study after critical study reveals the tautological character of economic reasoning with respect to this category and that. When criticism becomes too intense, economists abandon the offending term, not without a struggle, and triumphantly adopt another to the same effect. The history of these maneuvers is long and involved, and no important purpose would be served by reviewing it again. It is only the outcome that is

[8] *A History of Economic Thought* (New York, 1942), pp. 550, 551.

significant. Professor Pigou declares that value is "indefinable,"[9] though we know that it is a spiritual quality and that it is measured by price. Professor Cassel rejects this conception of value "as an intensity of feeling in the individual soul" on the ground that "we have no measure of such an intensity," and therefore proposes that we abandon the category "value" in favor of price, since "'values' are then represented by arithmetical figures which we call 'Prices.' Thus we gain the great advantage that our valuations become measurable quantities."[10] Professor Cassel likewise insists that "it is impossible to speak of the marginal productivity of any factor in the great social process of production except when the prices of the different factors are assumed to be known. But in this case the marginal productivity of each factor is simply its own price."[11] Similarly the concept of "utility" with its unconcealable subjectivity has been abandoned in favor of Pareto's subterfuge of "indifference," the present popularity of which[12] is based on the assumption that "indifference" is not subjective, though dictionaries persist in defining it as "the state of being unconcerned; lack of interest or feeling; apathy."

The net result of this extraordinary situation has been an increasingly general disposition on the part of economists to refer all their troubles to the philosophers. Economics, it seems, is limited to "the impact of human wants upon the limited resources of nature." For the economist both the resources and the wants are "given." They are "primary data."[13] This statement of the case represents a sincere

[9] Following G. E. Moore who had made indefinability the basic principle of ethics in his *Principia Ethica.* See *Wealth and Welfare* (London, 1912), p. 3.

[10] *On Quantitative Thinking in Economics* (Oxford, 1935), p. 31.

[11] *Ibid.,* p. 125.

[12] For example, J. R. Hicks, *Value and Capital* (Oxford, 1939).

[13] F. H. Knight, *The Ethics of Competition* (London, 1935); Lionel Robbins, *The Nature and Significance of Economic Science* (London, 1935).

attempt to approach the problems of economics in the spirit of scientific objectivity and caution, and is all the more remarkable on that account. For neither wants nor resources are "primary data" in the sense that no one can say any more about them than that they are what they are; and even if this were so, as Wesley Mitchell pointed out thirty years ago, it would then be the duty of the economists to proceed to repair this defect.[14] If anything is known anywhere in the field of the social sciences today, it is that "wants" are not primary. They are not inborn physical mechanisms and they are certainly not spiritual attributes. They are social habits. For every individual their point of origin is in the mores of his community; and even these traditions have a natural history and are subject to modification in the general process of social change. No business man assumes that "wants" are "given." One of the axioms of business is that markets must be created. Resources also are not fixed by the "niggardliness of nature." They are defined by the state of the industrial arts. Every thoughtful and informed student can enumerate resources which have come into being within his lifetime as the result of new scientific discoveries and technological processes.

The truth is that these simple phrases in which economics is defined in terms of "human wants" and "limited resources" conjure up the whole climate of opinion of the eighteenth century. The resources represent "the order of nature," and the wants evoke the transcendental metaphysics of the human "spirit." And they do so not because of any deliberate recalcitrancy on the part of modern economists but because these are the only terms by use of which price can be conceived to be the locus of value, and because no other conception of economic value as yet exists.

For whether or not it continues to be a science of price,

[14] "Human Behavior and Economics," *Quarterly Journal of Economics*, XXIX, 2.

economics must be a science of value. If the economy is meaningless, no science of economics is possible. If it has meaning, the problem of economics is to elicit that meaning. The way of thinking which has prevailed hitherto has sought the meaning of the economy in price. It has done so because the subtlety of price relationships seemed to give promise of hidden meaning, because the justification of the dominance of money power involved the identification of "money values" with industrial actualities, and because the prevailing conception of the well-springs of human conduct seemed capable of fulfillment in the calculus of price. These promises have not been realized and that way of thinking has therefore failed.

But other ways of thinking are still possible, and not only possible but actual. All that economic thinking has hitherto been obliged to exclude and reject—all that is excluded when it is assumed that "wants" are "primary" and that "scarcity" is defined by "nature"—all that we know today of social change, including the factors which actually shaped the industrial revolution: all this stands ready for assimilation into modern economics. It is only the barrier of price theory which prevents.

ECONOMIC BEHAVIOR

Chapter V

ELEMENTS OF HUMAN NATURE

SINCE ECONOMIC activity is a part of the whole of human behavior, the analysis of that activity must comport with the analysis of behavior generally. The classical economists were quite right in deriving their economic principles from the theory of human nature; the fault, as we have seen, lay in the conception of human nature which prevailed in the eighteenth century. A quarter-century ago, when "institutionalism" first began to attract general attention as the chief contestant with the classical way of thinking, at least on the stage of American academic economics, commentators remarked apparently with some surprise that this new way of thinking in economics seemed to derive from the psychological doctrine known as "behaviorism." [1] Doubtless the surprise was due not so much to the coincidence of economics with psychology as to the peculiarities of that particular school of psychologists. The original "behaviorists" have been singularly truculent and have embroiled themselves in argument with all other shades of psychological opinion insisting all the while that theirs is

[1] *E.g.*, Theo Surányi-Unger, *Economics in the Twentieth Century* (New York, 1931), p. 224 and elsewhere.

the only true behaviorism. But there is a larger sense in which virtually all psychologists, in America at least, are now behaviorists; and it was in this sense that the "institutional" economists, who after all stood outside the family disputes of the psychologists, were resolute behaviorists. As it was presented to them, the issue was between the modern point of view in psychology and the traditions of the past.

A valid way of thinking in economics must derive from a valid conception of human nature. But what is a valid conception of human nature? As it is presented to the student of economics, this problem is complicated not only by parochial disputes among contemporary psychologists but by issues which go beyond psychology proper and involve the whole roster of biological sciences on one hand and on the other the whole roster of social sciences, all of which are in some sense or other sciences of "man." Is psychology a physical science or a social science? Is human behavior to be explained in terms of minute currents of electricity conducted by nerve fibers, or is it to be explained in terms of the configuration of social situations? Or are these absolute alternatives?

To the economist it would seem that they are not. Indeed, to anyone who stands outside the special controversies by which modern scientists are divided, their agreements seem to be much more important than their differences. On two related points which are of supreme significance for economics all modern students of human nature are agreed. Throughout the past the phenomena of human nature were conceived to be of a different order of reality from those of physics and even anatomy. This distinction is perpetuated in the etymology of the word "psychology," which was originally the study of the "mind" or "soul" as distinguished from the body and the physical universe which it inhabits. These two realms of being were conceived to be related in some fashion, to parallel or even touch each other in some mysterious way, but nevertheless to be quite separate and distinct: a phenomenal realm of the physical universe including the physical organism, and a noumenal realm of mind. "Mind," it was thought, could be known only by "direct" inward contemplation, since "knowing" was assumed to be an act of the knower's "mind" which thereby "knew itself" in a metaphysical self-embrace. And this meant that each mind was in a very important sense unique, since the only mind which is metaphysically accessible to any knower is his own. All this is what is conjured up by the economic assumption that wants are "primary data."

With respect to this tradition there is general agreement among contemporary students all the way from anatomy to sociology. It is the issue which the "behaviorists" seemed originally to raise. When they first declared "introspection" out of bounds it was the metaphysics of self-contemplation which they were attacking. In their enthusiasm they extended the attack to include laboratory techniques which seemed to others scientifically useful, so that the issue of introspection soon lost its edge. But whatever they may call their laboratory techniques, there are today no psychologists, at least in America, who are engaged in exploring the recesses of the soul. The metaphysical dualism of body and mind has been completely abandoned throughout science, and with it the metaphysical uniqueness of the individual soul. Anatomists are no less insistent than sociologists on the continuity of the phenomena with which they are concerned, and could declare with no less emphasis that "a separate individual is a phenomenon unknown to experience." [2]

This principle of continuity is a basic postulate of modern science (for reasons which will be examined later), and extends even to the issue between the physical and the social patterns of behavior. No modern scientist on either side of

[2] C. H. Cooley, *Human Nature and the Social Order* (New York, 1902), p. 1.

the perennial controversy over "nature and nurture" would state this issue in terms of the metaphysical dualism of physical and spiritual realms of being. Geneticists do sometimes declare (outside the laboratory) that issues of tax policy over which they find economists contending "are just a matter of breeding"; but they know that even the super-race of which they dream could scarcely settle their tax problems in the maternity ward. These outbursts are only acts of self-assertion on the part of specialists who are always fearful lest the importance of their researches be forgotten, and they have perceptibly slackened as it becomes more and more certain that modern civilization is not going to favor sociology at the expense of genetics, or vice versa, since each is plainly indispensable to the sum of knowledge.

The issue, it is becoming more and more apparent, is between universes of discourse, or levels of generalization as the logicians and semanticists prefer to say, not realms of being. To insist that tax problems are a matter of public finance is not to deny the validity or importance of Mendel's laws, any more than to insist that heredity is a matter of genes is to deny the validity and importance of Einstein's general theory of relativity. Problems of taxation do not appear in the bottles in which geneticists breed *drosophila melanogaster*, any more than genes appear in the cyclotrons in which physicists decompose the atom. Different levels of generalization are of course not unrelated. The relationship between the physical and the social levels of generalization with regard to human behavior are especially intimate and subtle. Furthermore our knowledge is very far from complete. Future discoveries in physics or chemistry may bring unexpected developments in the physiology of the nervous system; these may substantially alter our conception of the learning process; and this may effect substantial changes in our analysis of the social patterns of behavior. Nevertheless our scientific maturity is already sufficient for general agreement not only on the principle of continuity and the distinction of levels of generalization but even with regard to the relation of different levels to each other in the analysis of behavior as a whole.

This relationship is one of complete alternation. It is the same for human behavior as for any other phenomenon. Any given substance such, for example, as table salt may be said to be composed entirely of electrons, protons, neutrons, etc.; or it may be said to be composed entirely of atoms; or it may be said to be composed entirely of molecules; or it may be said to be composed entirely of crystals. None of these propositions invalidates any other. None can be substituted for any other, and especially not in part. Thus it would be a complete misrepresentation of both the physics and the chemistry of sodium chloride to say that this substance consists in part of electrons and in part of molecules. Insofar as molecular structure is concerned at all, it is co-extensive with the salt. A given quantity of salt may be partly crystalline and partly in solution in water, but it may not be partly crystalline and partly atomic.

In exactly the same sense human behavior is wholly organic and wholly social. There is no movement, position, function, or condition of the human body which is not that of a physical organism and which therefore is not what it is because that organism is of the biological species *homo sapiens;* and similarly there is no organized activity of any human being which is not socially organized. All human behavior is organically conditioned in the same sense in which all other human behavior is organically conditioned; and all human behavior is socially organized in the same sense in which all other human behavior is socially organized. To say that part of the actions of human beings are to be accounted for in social terms, while part are to be accounted for in physical terms, would be as complete a misrepresentation of the case as to say that part of a handful of table salt is molecular while part of it is atomic. The articulation of the joints of the legs by virtue of which the legs can be folded so as to rest the weight of the trunk directly on the ground (or any small object) is a wholly physical phenomenon, determined by physical heredity, the biological characteristics of the species, and all the rest. The practices of sitting down to eat, to hold court, to listen to music, and the like, are social practices and as such are neither determined nor explained by the structure of the body. To say that we sit down to eat because politeness dictates this behavior, but that we sit down to listen to music because of the way the bones articulate, would be an outrageous confusion of the physical and the social aspects of behavior—both of which are of course present in both instances.

These two aspects of behavior are related, just as the physical and chemical aspects of all substances are related. We are told that the reason sodium chloride is a stable compound although both elemental sodium and elemental chlorine are violently unstable is because sodium and chlorine atoms swap electrons. Thus the electronic character of these elements defines the character of their combination. In similar fashion it is of course true that the articulation of the bones, muscles, and nerves of the human hand, the structures of the throat, the whole organization of the central nervous system, all constitute the physical equipment of a species which, because of this physical equipment, is capable of the organized activities of tool-using, language-speaking, and so on. Yet no one may be said to "speak a language" because of the structure of his throat or the function of his brain. No one speaks a language except by virtue of having learned that language, and the same is true of all organized behavior.

All students of man, from anatomists to sociologists, agree on these principles without any reservation of principle. Nevertheless it is important, especially for students of economics, to review them, for two reasons. Science has arrived at this resolution of the different levels of generalization in the analysis of human behavior only within recent decades and many special cases still remain as holdovers from older ways of thinking in which these principles are violated. The disposition of economists to abstract "motives" from other patterns of behavior is one of these. Whereas the organization of an industrial assembly line is patently a social pattern, there is still a common disposition among economists to think of "motives" as being somehow aboriginal, a sort of well-spring of economic conduct from which all the rest of economic activity flows, and so to think of the "psychological basis" of economic activity as being limited to "motives." This way of thinking is of course derived not from modern scientific studies but from old ways of thinking in economics. In the view of modern science there is nothing unique about "motives." Indeed that very term is itself a holdover. If the scientific analysis of behavior is trustworthy at all, we must accept the principle of alternate levels of generalization and its inevitable economic corollary. All economic behavior is equally social in character. No economic act or function is uniquely physical (let alone spiritual) or uniquely determinative of all the rest—not motives, or consumption, or anything else.

A second reason why it is important to hold general principles of analysis in clear view is that this means that the phenomena with which all the social sciences, including economics, are concerned are those of culture. This is what various modern economists have had in mind when they have urged their students and their colleagues to study anthropology. Culture, the organized corpus of behavior of which economic activity is but a part, is a phenomenon *sui generis*. It is not an epiphenomenon, a result of something else, explicable in other and non-cultural terms. It is the stuff of social behavior, the universe of discourse of the social sciences, the aspect which the data of observation assume at that level of generalization.

As such it is self-explaining and self-perpetuating. Some years ago Professor Robert Lowie adapted an axiom of biology to the social level of generalization. Following the final explosion of the ancient myth of spontaneous generation, the biologists laid down the principle, *omne vivum ex vivo,* meaning that living organisms come only from preexisting living organisms, and that the form, structure, functions, and all the rest, of living organisms are to be explained only in terms of the forms, structures, functions, and the rest, of other living organisms. In similar fashion Lowie laid down the principle, *omnis cultura ex cultura,* meaning that every cultural phenomenon is derived from some other cultural phenomenon and can be explained only in terms of other cultural phenomena.[3] This is not to deny that human beings have skeletons, or that the lining of the stomach secretes hydrochloric acid. But it is to deny that any social pattern whatsoever derives from the bones or the secretions of the stomach or can be explained in such terms. Cultural phenomena (including the economic) derive exclusively from other cultural phenomena and can be explained only in terms of other cultural phenomena.

Most particularly this is to deny that social patterns derive from or can be explained in terms of the behavior of "individuals." The dilemma of the individual and society has been a particularly troublesome one from which science has begun to extricate itself only within the past generation; and yet the difficulty is not intellectual. The relationship of the individual cell to the organism offers an exact analogy. Every function of the body is in fact performed by a multitude of individual cells without the action of which it could not occur. No one denies this. Nevertheless in the analysis

[3] *Culture and Ethnology* (New York, 1917), p. 66. See also John Dewey, *Human Nature and Conduct* (New York, 1922), pp. 59 ff.

of organic functions the individual cell is irrelevant. The functions of the organism constitute another level of generalization to the analysis of which the actions of the individual cell do not pertain. This does not mean, as some nineteenth-century sociologists were tempted to say, that society is an organism, any more than it means that men are cells. The analogy is between the distinction of two levels of generalization in each case. All human activities are the sum of the acts of individual men. This is the level of generalization on which ordinary human affairs are conducted and for which the question is all-important, "Who has acted how, and why? The functions, factors, and forces into which culture is resolved by analysis do not "act" as men act; but they do constitute a causal nexus the analysis of which is the problem of the social sciences, and in this analysis of social causes and effects the acts of individual men are not at issue. All this is obvious today and would have been obvious long ago but for the persistent belief in the metaphysical ultimacy of human individuality which has prevented our viewing men as we view cells and molecules. A compulsion neurosis, inspired by immemorial tradition, has perpetuated a fixation on the human individual to the confusion of cultural analysis.

For the student of economics, then, what is at issue on the level of generalization of cultural analysis? Anthropologists study kinship systems; taboos, ceremonials, and esoteric rites; the lore of myth and legend; collections of artifacts representing material culture traits. Sociologists study primary and secondary groups; family, neighborhood, region, and the like. Political scientists study governments. But what do economists study? The textbooks have an answer ready: the activities in which men engage in getting a living. But these glib phrases with their plausible citation of the common tongue commit the error for which economists have so often had occasion to reproach themselves, that of defining the problem on the individual level and then raising it to the cultural level by a sort of algebraic multiplication the way a variable is raised to the *nth* power. The question still remains, What social functions and activities are included in "getting a living?"

If this question could be raised *de novo,* and on the cultural level at the outset, it would be almost self-answering. A component part of every culture is a vast system of tools and tool-using activities. Economists are certainly interested in this sort of thing, and their interest is focused not on the engineering aspect of the tools as artifacts but on the pattern of the system of activities so constituted. Furthermore the interest of economists is not limited to these activities. A further component of every culture is another system of activities in which all these tools and all the products of their use are employed to very curious effect. They are employed ceremonially, and their manipulation in this fashion has the effect of establishing claims, exhibiting prestige, dividing the community in terms of "ceremonial adequacy" along lines more or less coincident with those which are objects of interest to anthropologists, sociologists, political scientists, and the rest. These activities also constitute a system which is part of the total system, which is the culture. Students of economics are not primarily interested in the coincidence between these and other ceremonial activities, but they are necessarily concerned with the relation between the use of tools to make things and the use of tools to establish social distinctions. For these two sets of activities inevitably condition each other. Professor Melville Herskovits has remarked that there is no community of which we have any knowledge which does not engage in some sort of organized, ceremonial waste, usually on a considerable scale.[4] What they waste—yams, for example—is the very thing they have been at greatest pains to produce and accumulate;

[4] *The Economic Life of Primitive Peoples* (New York, 1940), pp. 355 ff.

and what we, and they, mean by "waste" is a performance in complete contrast to the meticulous, grubbing care which has gone into production and accumulation. These two activities condition each other in both directions. Yams are ceremonially wasted because they are hard to produce; and they are hard to produce in sufficient quantity because they are ceremonially wasted.

The business of "getting a living" includes both these functions. That is, it includes activities of a technological character, and it also includes activities of a ceremonial character; and these two sets of activities not only coexist but condition each other at every point and between them define and constitute the total activity of "getting a living." It is the problem of economic analysis to distinguish and understand these factors, and their mutual relations, and the configurations of economic activity for which they are responsible. The great economic pioneer, Thorstein Veblen, was the first to see this clearly and to make this analytical distinction between technology and ceremony the point of departure of all further economic analysis. Probably his insight was due to the great impression which was made upon his mind in its formative period by the then infant science of anthropology, and perhaps also to the fact that he was socially and academically an "outsider," and an amateur both in anthropology and economics.[5] Critics of his work are generally agreed—indeed, it is almost their only point of agreement—that this distinction is fundamental to all Veblen's thinking and is his most significant contribution to modern thought. It is equally fundamental to the thinking of an even greater pioneer, John Dewey, who has himself acknowledged the influence of Veblen, perhaps with more generosity than justice.[6]

[5] The case of Veblen is thus an instance of the process of discovery analyzed in Chapter VI, below.

[6] Joseph Dorfman, *Thorstein Veblen and His America* (New York, 1934), p. 450.

As a profession, economists have not followed Veblen's lead, for reasons which have already been discussed. Consequently this approach to the study of economics is still outrageously unorthodox. Nevertheless Veblen's basic idea has become almost commonplace during the last generation or so, chiefly as the result of work in other fields. In modern studies of the social functions of language, for example, the contrast has become quite apparent between the technical, or instrumental, or denominative use of words and the ceremonial use. Indeed this distinction has become the chief preoccupation of the semanticists. Exploration of the ceremonial patterns of contemporary civilization has become the subject of a large literature. Indeed the general recognition of the ceremonial elements in present-day living is doubtless responsible for the fact that *The Theory of the Leisure Class* has been the most widely read and the most fully understood of Veblen's books.

Researches in the field of technology have also been contributed by a wide variety of participants. The establishment of industrial museums has stimulated the investigation of the nature and history of invention. Even the history of science has been more carefully and extensively explored in recent years than ever before, as a result, perhaps, of increasing awareness of the great responsibility of science in modern civilization. Even the fine arts have quite generally emerged from the leisure-class dilettantism which has always been their curse and become material for objective social analysis.

In spite of all this, however, there is still an apparent reluctance to dichotomize the technological and ceremonial aspects of civilization. Many writers who discuss tool-using and ceremonializing as though they were the obverse and reverse of social behavior still seem to refrain from saying so. Students of science and of industrial engineering frequently hazard the assertion that it is science and engineering which is responsible for the progress of civilization, but usually without raising the issue of the other aspect of culture. This hesitancy may express a common distrust of dualisms, distrust which is only too well justified. Metaphysical dualisms of body and mind, phenomena and noumena, the physical universe and the world of "spirit," have been persistent and pestilential in our thinking. Our worst confusions have had their origins in dualism.

This difficulty could be resolved if it could be clearly understood that the distinction of the technological and the ceremonial aspects of organized behavior is a dichotomy but not a dualism. That is, it undertakes to distinguish two aspects of what is still a single, continuous activity both aspects of which are present at all times. Indeed, they bound and define each other as do the obverse and reverse of a coin. Such a distinction need not and does not set up two separate realms of being such as have characterized the historic dualisms. On the contrary it is the essence of the case that these two behavior functions are not only functions of one continuous whole of human behavior but even that both employ and give expression to the same basic faculties of which all organized behavior is the expression.

These two behavior functions do have widely different results on which, inevitably, very different judgments must be made. Such judgments are well-nigh universal. It is a commonplace that man as a species has proved himself capable of the most prodigious achievements and the most abysmal follies, achievements and follies both of which have no parallel in the behavior of any other species. With a very few most rudimentary exceptions, no other species uses tools at all. We admire the labors of the ants, but they are still incomparable with the works of man. The follies of mankind are likewise incomparable. Both sets of achievements, however different in outcome, are peculiarly human. Both are works of intelligence and imagination. Both are social accretions made possible by memory and habit, the capacity for organized behavior, the background of culture by which the behavior of successive human generations is socially organized.

This does not mean that there are no differences of pattern between technological and ceremonial behavior, nor that there may not be important differences of an elementary character. But these differences certainly are not total. Both are aspects of the behavior of human beings in society. In particular it must be emphasized that both employ intelligence and both employ tradition. As they are commonly used, these words have feeling tones—"intelligence" one of approval, "tradition" one of disapproval. There may be a sense in which such discriminations are justified, but it is a very special sense.[7] If we mean by intelligence that which is measured by an "intelligence quotient," the behavior-organizing capacity, it is obvious that the creation of myths, the performance of sacerdotal functions, the exploitation of one's fellows, and the commission of crime, all call for intelligence no less than the use of tools, scientific instruments, and artist's materials. And on the other hand, while myths and ceremonies, invidious distinctions and exploitative privileges, are clearly traditional, so are tool uses, scientific formulas, and the techniques of painters and composers. That is, all are matters of cultural heritage, learned by apprenticeship as social accomplishments. The two traditions are different and the use each makes of intelligence is different; but they are not totally different. They are not separate realms of being; and the analytical distinction by which these differences are recognized is not a dualism, such as the metaphysical dualism of mind and body.

Once this has been established, the prevalence of dualism in the thinking of the past may perhaps be seen to be significant. Curiously enough, all the dualisms have something

[7] See Chapter VIII, below.

in common. All make unmistakable reference to the undeniable achievements and follies of the race. Can it be possible that all have been attempts, unsuccessful perhaps because of the limitations of the intellectual heritage of the past, to understand and characterize the distinction with which we are still concerned? The efforts of economists would seem to bear this interpretation. For the classical tradition in economics has given rise to a most pernicious dualism of the realms-of-being type. It was originally that of the "actual" and the "natural" or "normal," but during the last half-century these realms have been known as the "dynamic" and the "static." Contemporary economists maintain that the distinction is only an analytical device, but it is certainly more than that. Under both sets of names one of these states is existential and the other is ideal in both metaphysical and moral senses. If one be defined as the realm in which change is occurring and the other as a "stationary state," it is at once apparent that change is regarded as something of a nuisance and as an essentially transitory condition. How otherwise could the analysis of imaginary "stationary states" be regarded as a useful analytical device? It is useful only on the supposition that the static world is the real world and the dynamic world phenomenal in the metaphysical sense. The distinction is between "universals" and "particulars."

Nevertheless this distinction signalizes something more than the durability of medieval metaphysics. The modern economy is in fact both a triumph and a tragedy. The "restraints" of which it affords so many instances are by no means "unnatural." Alas, the entire history of civilization is one of grueling restraints. The attempt to identify the achievements of modern economic life with the forces of "nature," and its follies and cruelties with circumstances of a local and temporary character has been mistaken; but the efforts to distinguish between different sets of forces and their different sets of effects is a sound and necessary one. The differences are there. It remains to be seen whether the progress of knowledge has been sufficient to make possible another and more successful effort to deal with the perennial problem.

Chapter VI

TECHNOLOGY AND PROGRESS

TECHNOLOGY is organized skill. As a definition this formula is both inadequate and misleading, but there is no better way to explore and clarify the meaning of technology than by discovering the inadequacies of common-sense conceptions such as this one. All skill is organized, of course, and all behavior skilled in some sense or other. We commonly distinguish between the skill of the artisan and the mastery of the scientist or the "creative" artist, and these distinctions are important. But do they distinguish between skill and non-skill? We do not ordinarily think of the scientist or the artist as "unskilled."

However important they may be, such distinctions are between kinds of skill. An artisan is one who performs operations which a scientist has devised. Much the same distinction is made between the artist who is a "mere" performer and one who is a "creator." But differences appear even within the field of creation. In one of his later essays Roger Fry retracted his earlier declaration that Sargent was not an artist but repeated his earlier judgment in this form, that Sargent was an "applied" artist. The distinction was more than a slight. What Fry meant was that Sargent had adopted the color chords which the Impressionists had "created" (or discovered, or invented), and had used them in painting portraits of rich sitters. Whereas Sargent, according to Fry, had "learned something" from the Impressionists, later painters stood to learn nothing from his canvases.

A similar distinction is made between pure and applied science. A man who knows no mathematics is only a mechanic, however good a mechanic he may be. If he knows and uses the common branches of mathematics, he is an engineer. If his scientific training is sufficient to enable him to understand and reproduce the experiments of scientists, putting them to use in the fashion in which Sargent used the palette of the Impressionists in painting portraits, he is an applied scientist. If he masters the work of earlier scientists in such a way as to be able to carry it on, putting their discoveries to the same sort of use to which they in turn had put the discoveries of still earlier scientists, then he is a scientist, too, in the same sense as they. Considerations of social prestige enter into these distinctions and give feeling-tone to judgments such as Fry passed upon Sargent, but they are irrelevant to the analysis of technology. The distinctions exist independently of the invidiousness which has been associated with them.

But they are not distinctions between skill and non-skill. What they distinguish is types of skill. The word "technique" is generally employed by musicians and other artists to refer to the finger-dexterity of the instrumentalist or the hand-and-brush dexterity with which the painter applies his pigments to the canvas. Such technique is a more or less indispensable part of the equipment of every artist; but it is often mentioned sneeringly, and for this reason. A player may have acquired great finger-dexterity and still be musically illiterate. Nearly all the great composers were at one time eminent performers, but most of them let their "techniques" run down as they became increasingly absorbed in composition. Does this mean that playing the piano is a matter of skill but that composing music is not? By no means. At another level of generalization it is customary to speak of "the techniques of the composer," meaning such things as skill in using scores. Many a musician who has acquired great skill in reading music, that is, in thinking from printed notes to sounds, would experience the greatest difficulty in writing out the notes even of a quite simple tune which he had just heard for the first time. Mozart's celebrated feat of writing out in full an unpublished and closely guarded "Miserere" after hearing it once in the Sistine Chapel was not only an act of "sheer genius"; it was a technical achievement which was possible at all only because even at the age of fourteen Mozart was master of the techniques of the composer. He was indeed "very good at it"; but what he was good at must not be overlooked.

The conclusion toward which all these reflections lead is that all acts of skill involve the use of tools of one sort or another. Such distinctions as we have been considering are made in terms of the differences between these tools. An artisan is not a person of inferior dexterity. He is a person whose tools, however dextrously they may be used, are commonplace. But the skills of scientists and artists—even pure scientists and creative artists—are no less contingent on the use of tools. A mathematician or a composer may "have an inspiration" when he is wandering in the woods or (as in the case of Henri Poincaré) when he is catching a train. At the moment he has in his hands nothing which could be identified as a tool of his profession. Nevertheless his profession is a tool-using profession, and his "inspiration" could never have occurred to a man who had never used those tools. In the case of the composer they are such things as the diatonic scale, musical notation, existing instruments, and the like; but even more important to the particular inspiration of the individual composer is the literature of music: the works of other composers existing as physical objects in the form of printed scores over which he has pored most of his life. The same is true of the mathematician. At any given moment he may be without paper and pencil and not need them. But mathematics as a science could not have come into existence in the absence of paper and pencils (or any substitutes). Teachers of mathematics try from the beginning to impress upon their pupils that a "point" is not a chalk-mark on a blackboard. (In *Mr. Fortune's Maggot* Sylvia Townsend Warner has written a very amusing account of the efforts of a lover of mathematics to convey this distinction to an aborigine.) Mathematicians have been able to define a point as "that which has" neither length nor breadth nor thickness, whatever "that which has" may mean in such a formula; but they could never have done so without using physical objects as tools. More important for present-day mathematics are of course the symbols which have been devised as the notation of complex mathematical operations. Here also the symbols are not themselves the operations; but here also it is still true that the operations could not be conducted without symbols, and that no one could learn to think mathematically without having spent years poring over the printed record of the symbolically denoted operations of earlier mathematicians. The current issues of the mathematical journals are perhaps the most important tools of the trade of the practicing mathematician, and they are physical objects which must be used with skill, no less than wrenches and hammers.

This absolute mutual contingency of skills and tools is of supreme importance for an understanding of technology as a function of human behavior for two reasons. In the first place, technical activity can be identified in no other way than by its uniform, unvarying association with tools. In some cases identification is easy. When a primitive community is fashioning a dugout canoe, we observe that two sorts of activity are going on. While a number of men are engaged in hollowing out the log, one rattles sharks' teeth, and roars what are obviously incantations. We identify the former as technological activity and the latter as something else. But the distinction is not so apparent to the tribesmen, since they recognize all these practitioners as members of the same "holy order" of canoe-builders and know that all are following the sacred liturgy of their order, the "workers" no less than the roarer. To us hollowing out logs is a secular activity, but "intoning" is something else; and we apply our own distinctions as an a priori classification to the other people.

Other cases are not so easy. We recognize astrology and alchemy as pre-sciences; but the whole activity in which their practitioners engaged was that of necromancy. Furthermore, as we have learned to our sorrow, certain ways of thinking have been carried over from the earlier activity into what we have regarded as the age of reason, so that our own science at least in its early stages has been contaminated by foreign elements. How are these to be distinguished? Categories such as "truth" and "knowledge" are disconcertingly inconclusive. It is precisely the "knowledge" of early modern times that is most dubious. The only reliable distinction is provided by what we call "experimental techniques," that is to say the tools of science. Even the necromancers employed "laboratory" techniques and were scientists insofar as they did so, in spite of the romantic names they gave their instruments and operations.

The case of the fine arts is even more confusing. Like science, all the arts were originally sacerdotal. All design and pictorial representation was at first cabalistic; all rhythm and tone patterns, all the gestures and postures of dance and drama, were at first the literal enactment of mystic rites. Modern anthropological studies have left no doubt on this score. And in this case we have emerged from the savage state only very incompletely. The arts are still associated with ecclesiastical activities and their contemplation and creation are still generally regarded as "spiritual" experiences in a sense that is not true even of science. The effect of works of art is still generally conceived to be a sort of "seizure," and the creation of "masterworks" is still attributed to "inspiration" of a sort that is not vouchsafed to even the greatest of scientists. People repeat Wagner's hyperbole about "God and Beethoven" as though it were a literal transfiguration—and all this in spite of the constant insistence of practicing artists that their achievements are the result of "taking pains."

In this case also there is only one solution to the enigma: that provided by technical analysis. Popular reputations wax and wane. The "seizures" people feel in the presence of great "masterworks" are of the nature of self-hypnosis induced by expectation. Their subjects are usually awe-struck by such things as "the marvelous colors," although the actual pigments may have been renewed half-a-dozen times by quite mediocre and anonymous restorers. To the annoyance of musicians the enthusiastic public admires Mozart for his "quaintness" and Bach for the intricacy of his counterpoint, although what they call Mozart's quaintness was a characteristic of all eighteenth-century music, while Bach's great distinction was that he added to the contrapuntal intricacies of his day a harmonic richness which music had never known before. The achievements of the great creative artists are genuine achievements, but they are technical achievements which can be understood and genuinely appreciated only by a certain amount of study, a certain amount of knowledge of what is actually, technically going on. This understanding and appreciation is understanding of the tools—color and design, tonal structure and texture, and the like—with which artists actually work. In the tangled web of human life, technical activities are almost inextricably blended with activities of another sort. The enthusiasm which they merit is almost indistinguishable from religious ecstasy. Nevertheless all tool-using activities have something in common which can be understood by virtue of the tools.

It is the peculiar character of all technology, from chipped flints to Boulder Dam and Beethoven's quartets, that it is progressive. It is inherently developmental. This circumstance which gives technology its peculiar importance in the analysis of culture—and most of all for economists—also can be understood only in terms of tools. If we limit the conception of technology to "skill," we are at once subject to great risk of conceiving technological development as the growth of skills; and since skill is a "faculty" of "individuals," we are pre-conditioned to think of the growth of skill as in some sense an increase of this faculty on the party of individuals. But we know nothing of any such increase.

That is what makes it so hard for economists of the traditional way of thinking to understand the technological principle. They understand the crucial importance of the issue. Since Veblen first began to write, it has been apparent that some sort of claim was being made for technology as a master-principle of economic analysis. This claim was seen to rest on the peculiarly dynamic character of technology as itself inherently progressive and the agent of social change, in particular the agent of industrial revolution. As one of the most thoughtful of contemporary economists has remarked, this whole way of thinking "assumes for technology some kind of inner law of progress of an absolute and inscrutable character," as well as "some equally absolute and inscrutable type of 'causality' by which technology drags behind it and 'determines' other phases of social change." [1] The whole issue between old and new ways of thinking in economics comes to focus here. The new way of thinking

[1] Frank H. Knight, "Intellectual Confusion in Morals and Economics," *International Journal of Ethics*, XLV, 208-9.

does indeed rest on some kind of inner law of progress. But there is nothing absolute or inscrutable about it. What makes it seem inscrutable is the inveterate predisposition of orthodox economists to think in terms of a conception of human nature as that of the uniquely individual "spirit." Thinking so, they think of technology as a skill-faculty of the individual spirit; and thinking so, they find the principle of technological development quite inscrutable—as indeed they must. For the developmental character of technology is implicit not in the skill-faculty of the human individual but in character of tools. The whole analysis must proceed on the level of generalization of culture rather than of individuality in order for the principle of technological progress to be understood at all.

On that level it is perfectly obvious. As a result of the rapid advance of machine technology in recent years, the process of invention has attracted general attention and has become the subject of a considerable literature.[2] These studies have given the *coup de grâce* to the "heroic" theory of invention—the myth which attributes inventions to the sheer magnitude of soul of the "Gifted Ones." It is now generally agreed that all inventions are combinations of previously existing devices. Thus the airplane is a combination of a kite and an internal combustion engine. An automobile is a combination of a buggy with an internal combustion engine. The internal combustion engine itself is a combination of the steam engine with a gaseous fuel which is substituted for the steam and exploded by the further combination of the electric spark. This is speaking broadly, of course. In actual practice the combinations are for the most part much more detailed. What is presented to the public as a "new" invention is usually itself the end-product of a long series of inventions.

[2] Outstanding in this literature for clarity and cogency is a little book by S. C. Gilfillan, *The Sociology of Invention* (Chicago, 1935).

In this process, materials—what economists have so misleadingly designated as "natural" resources—function as devices. According to the principle of indestructibility of matter there is no such thing as a "new" material. Helium gas must have been present in the earth of the Texas panhandle geologic ages before man first invaded the Western hemisphere some thousands of years ago. Nevertheless helium was not a "natural resource" of the republic of Texas, inasmuch as helium was not identified in the sun for many years after the end of the republic, nor isolated from the earth's atmosphere for many years after that, nor discovered to be a component of Texas natural gas until still later, nor treated as a resource until it was used in balloons only a few years ago. The history of every material is the same. It is one of novel combination of existing devices and materials in such a fashion as to constitute a new device or a new material or both. This is what it means to say that natural resources are defined by the prevailing technology, a practice which is now becoming quite general among economists to the further confusion of old ways of thinking (since it involves a complete revision of the concept of "scarcity" which must now be regarded as also defined by technology and not by "nature").

Furthermore, as regards the nature of the process there is no difference between "mechanical" invention and "scientific" discovery. Scientific discoveries also result from the combination of previously existing devices and materials, laboratory instruments and techniques. It was by combining a magnet with a Crookes tube, for example, that J. J. Thomson discovered that the stream of incandescence in the tube was in fact a stream of physical particles and was even able to calculate the mass of the electrons. It was by combining a prism with a telescope that astronomers were able to identify elements (such as helium) in the sun. Even in the fine arts "creation" comes about in the same way. Leonardo's great achievement illustrated by the famous Mona Lisa, about which so much nonsense has been talked,[3] was that he applied techniques which the monks had devised for the portrayal of angels to the portraiture of living subjects. Cézanne characterized his achievement as resulting from the application of Pissarro's studio technique to painting from nature. In every innovation analysis reveals the combination of previously existing devices. That is what the achievement is which in different fields we call invention or discovery or creation.

This principle of combination is important by virtue of the light it throws on previous obscurities. One of these is the role of chance in discovery and invention. An extraordinary number of the most significant discoveries have been made by chance. Columbus discovered America by accident. Ostensibly he was sailing toward the Indies. The discovery of the X-ray resulted from the exposure of sealed photographic plates by their accidental juxtaposition to a Crookes tube. Ehrlich's "magic bullet" treatment for syphilis eventuated from the accidental relation between the spirochete of that disease and the trypanosome which Ehrlich had much earlier selected for experimental purposes because it was easily identified under the microscope and could be bred in laboratory animals. In the case of mechanical inventions the role of chance is even more notorious. Adam Smith relates the tale of the invention of the automatic valves by which the steam engine operates from the trick of a lazy boy who tied the control string to a moving part which then opened and closed the valve automatically.

But what do we mean by "chance" or "accident"? These words are of course relational. In a sense nothing occurs by chance, but some events are less relevant than others to any given point of reference. In all these cases the point of

[3] See Rockwell Kent's comments on this work in *World Famous Paintings* (New York, 1939).

reference is the previous activities of some individual. The discovery of America was "accidental" with reference to the intentions of Columbus; but it was not accidental that it should have occurred in 1492. The arts of shipbuilding, seamanship, and navigation being what they were by the end of the fifteenth century, somebody was "bound" to have "discovered America" within a decade or so; and this also is true of inventions and discoveries generally. The lore of science and mechanics is full of simultaneous discoveries, often by several agents and as a result of strikingly similar combinations. The simultaneous development of the infinitesimal calculus out of the same mathematical material by Newton and Leibnitz is a case in point. So is the simultaneous enunciation of the theory of biological evolution by Darwin and Wallace. In this case the identity of the materials which entered into combination and the extreme separation of the agents of discovery are equally striking. Although Darwin thought out his statement in England and Wallace in Malaysia on the opposite side of the world, both were practicing naturalists concerned with the problem of species, and both received definite stimulation to this particular formula from reading Malthus' *Essay on the Principle of Population.* Instances could be multiplied indefinitely. The Patent Office is engaged in a perpetual struggle with the problem of simultaneity. But what seems utterly mysterious so long as invention is regarded as an act of individual inspiration is easily explained in terms of the principle of combination.

These combinations are physical not less than ideational. To be sure they are achieved by men, usually by men of great ability. But the things they put together are physical objects. The coexistence of these objects constitutes a possibility of combination which transcends the acts of any individual. It is in this sense that inventions seem "bound" to occur. Granted a working steam engine, the steam-propelled locomotive was bound to follow. Granted the much lighter internal combustion engine, its application to the buggy and the kite was bound to result—almost simultaneously—in the automobile and the airplane. It is no disparagement of genius to recognize that certain combinations would almost necessarily have occurred in somebody's hands sooner or later. Individual genius not only places its possessor in the front rank of pioneers; it also determines when a discovery is made. Often this happens "before its time." That is, some inspired Mendel works out a given combination, the laws of inheritance among sweet peas, years before other combinations have occurred in the field of cytology to which those laws are supremely relevant. The over-all determinant which defines the universe of discourse within which genius is at play is an objective actuality—the tool pattern.

Another anomaly of the inventive process which also is resolved by the tool-combination principle is the extraordinary role of tyros and amateurs in science and mechanics and even the fine arts. The number of important discoveries and inventions which have been made by juveniles and by such people as lawyers and clergymen whose professional training is wholly unrelated to the field in question is strikingly large—too large to be attributed to the peculiar talents of the individuals concerned, who in many cases have done little or nothing else to attract attention. In mathematical physics, for example, the Nobel prize has been given to so many men of such extreme youth as to give rise to the saying that in this field a man has passed his peak by twenty-eight. Why is this? Doubtless precocity has something to do with it in certain cases. Children learn languages easily, including the special languages of mathematics and music; but it is notorious that most prodigies peter out, and in any case the prodigy theory does not explain the discoveries of the clergyman, Joseph Priestley, or the paintings of the stockbroker, Paul Gauguin.

The explanation which follows directly from the tool-combination analysis of invention is the one which accounts for the annoying facility with which an intruder often finds a solution almost instantaneously for a jigsaw puzzle with which the player has been struggling for hours. Where the solution is a matter of putting together existing pieces, it may be impeded by fixed ideas, preoccupations, and other behavior "sets," on the part of the regular player from which the intruder is free. Consequently he sees at once the possible combination which has been hidden from the player by his own intense preoccupation. Innovations are often made by people who are so innocent as not to realize how outrageously novel they are. It is even said that important scientific discoveries have been made as a direct result of ignorance on the part of a discoverer who simply did not "know" that the thing he did "could not be done," and so just went ahead and did it. This is the explanation of the importance of detachment for scientific research and other creative achievement, what Veblen called "idle" curiosity. Obviously (though it has not been obvious to hostile critics, perhaps because they lacked detachment) he meant "detached" and not "indolent." Excessive preoccupation of any kind—pious, financial, uxorious, or even professional—is inimical to the "free play" of the imagination in the course of which combinations somehow occur. Discoveries are not made by punching timeclocks, and closing laboratories and libraries on Sunday is an excellent way to inhibit creative activity.

These corollaries of the analysis of invention in terms of the combination of existing devices, in which Mr. Gilfillan and his colleagues are interested for their own sake, assume increasingly great theoretical importance as they proceed from the particular to the general. If technological development results from the combination of existing tool-material devices, and if such combinations follow the pattern of existing devices and often do so in the hands of people whose peculiar advantage it is to be free from inhibiting preoccupations, then it would also seem to follow that innovations are likely to occur at any time and in any region in which devices are brought together which have hitherto existed in separate regions. This is an observed fact. The diffusion of culture traits from one culture area to another is quite generally accompanied by innovation. Indeed, so striking is the stimulus which results from culture contacts that it has been called the "cross-fertilization" of cultures. But it is the tools themselves, not the people, that have been hybridized. Such innovations—and they include some of the most important technological advances in history[4]—are not to be explained by any special excitation of the imaginations of the people among whom they occur. As a matter of fact the people most directly concerned are usually quite unaware of the importance of what is going on; and furthermore, once the mutually conditioning devices have been brought together, no sublime inspiration is necessary to the recognition of the pattern. The combination occurs almost "of itself," often quite anonymously. That is one reason why the history of mechanical inventions is so difficult to trace. No one has bothered to record the event because no one is aware that an act of "heroism" has been committed. It remains for later historians gradually to become aware of the transcendent importance of these almost surreptitious developments. Regarding them, as it is their habit to regard all history, as the sum of the acts of individual men, they are at a loss for an adequate explanation. But on the cultural level of generalization, regarded as combinations of physically existing devices, these innovations are not only explicable but inevitable. Where cultures meet, cross-fertilization is to be expected. It is a direct result of the physical embodiment of technical behavior patterns in tools and physical materials.

[4] See Chapter VII, below.

We have here the explanation of the "inscrutable" propensity of all technological devices to proliferate. This "propensity" is a characteristic not of men but of tools. Granted that tools are always tools of men who have the capacity to use tools and therefore the capacity to use them together, combinations are bound to occur. Furthermore it follows that the more tools there are, the greater is the number of potential combinations. If we knew nothing of history but had somehow come to understand the nature of our tools, we could infer that technological development must have been an accelerating process, almost imperceptibly slow in its earlier stages and vertiginously fast in its most recent phase. This is, of course, the observed fact. Mr. H. G. Wells, with his gift for dramatizing history, has remarked that the entire development of civilization (as distinguished from "savagery") has occurred within roughly one hundred generations, which is perhaps not more than one one-hundredth part of the experience of the race. The machine age occupies not more than one-tenth part of this period; the mass-production age, one one-hundredth. The old stone age was of prodigious length; the new stone age much shorter but still many times longer than the whole of subsequent history. Archeologists and historians are well aware of this fact. Indeed, it is one of their persistent puzzles. But it is a puzzle to which the analysis of mechanical invention now provides a key. The tool itself is the key to the great mystery.

For the tool-combination principle is indeed a law of progress. If we suppose that tool-combinations occur in the same fashion as that in which digits are combined in the mathematical theory of permutations, then the resulting series is a progressive one in the mathematical sense of a series each member of which is derived from each preceding member by the same operation. In such a case it would be sharply progressive in the sense that the number of combinations would increase very rapidly, that is by squares:

$$x;\ x^2;\ (x^2)^2;\ ((x^2)^2)^2 \ldots \text{ or } x;\ x^2;\ x^4;\ x^8;\ x^{16} \ldots$$

Obviously this supposition at once calls for a number of reservations. We do not know that tool-combinations occur according to the mathematical law of permutations. Indeed we have no way of knowing for any given set of tools, devices, or materials, how many combinations are possible. We know only the ones that actually occur, and even these present a problem of enumeration which is perhaps insoluble, as is the initial enumeration of the given set. The mathematical analogy also takes no account of time, although time is of the essence of an actual historical sequence. Does the completion of each stage of the progressive series represent a year or a thousand years? Does the time-span increase for successive stages as the magnitude of the sets increases? Clearly the mathematical representation of the actual process of technological combination can be nothing more than illustrative, and illustrative only of one aspect of the process, that of increasing magnitude.

Nevertheless the analogy is highly suggestive. Although no one supposes that history conforms to any simple mathematical series, the idea that the actual technological process is progressive and accelerating has occurred to a number of students in widely separated fields of investigation.[5] This

[5] For example, Alfred (Count) Korzybski, *The Manhood of Humanity* (New York, 1922), p. 20: "...the spectacle we behold is that of advancement in scientific knowledge and technical power according to the law and at the rate of a rapidly increasing geometric progression or logarithmic function"; R. D. Carmichael, *The Logic of Discovery* (London and Chicago, 1930), pp. 144-45: "[Man's] law of progress seems to be that of the geometrical ratio. As equal intervals of time are added to his experience he seems to increase his wealth of thought in an approximately fixed ratio.... The recent rapid development of mathematical science gives support to the law of geometrical progression as the law of man's growth. This body of doctrine has increased at a rate which itself has an increasing rate so that the

principle is not teleological, any more than the physical principles of gravitation or centrifugence. It need not be supposed that any given invention is "bound" to occur. Certainly it will not occur if the solar system is obliterated by the collision of the sun with a wandering comet, nor will it occur if the human species is suddenly and completely obliterated by disease. It will not occur at any given time in any given community if all technological development, or even that particular strain of technological developments, is inhibited by contrary forces at work in that community at that time. No one supposes that the technological process is the whole of culture, any more than anyone supposes that centrifugence is the only physical force to which inhabitants of the surface of the earth are subject. On the contrary, all students of technology have recognized that it is but one aspect of culture and that culture exhibits another aspect which is inhibitory to the technological process just as gravitation inhibits centrifugence.[6] In some communities, apparently, technological progress has been totally arrested. Stone-age culture is still extant in certain regions. There is no community whose history does not reveal periods in which technology has been virtually stationary for long periods of time. But these facts do not deny the existence of technology nor invalidate the analysis of technological development in terms of a continuous, cumulative, progressive process, any more than the fact that we do not fly off at a tangent to the earth's surface invalidates the principle of centrifugence. It means that other forces also are at work, not that technological progress is an illusion.

Granting all this, some students of the social sciences hesi-

---

total body of it in our day has become larger than anyone two generations ago could have contemplated as possible"; George Sarton, *The Study of the History of Science* (Cambridge, Mass., 1936), p. 20: "... the progress of science is constantly accelerated, and hence ... more and more is accomplished in shorter and shorter periods."

[6] See Chapter VIII, below.

tate to identify technological development with progress for another reason. The concept of progress is in bad odor at the present time, and rightly so. In the past, progress has been conceived in terms of the prevailing transcendentalism as movement toward a preconceived "end" or consummatory state. This consummatory state, as we now realize, has always been a projection, or "collective representation," of prevailing culture. That is, every people has conceived "heaven," or perfection, as the pure essence of its own prevailing institutions or mores, just as Dante pictured Paradise and Purgatory in terms of his own (community engendered) preferences and prejudices. We know today—it is a ground-principle of modern social science—that such conceptions have no general validity, and students of the social sciences are therefore chary of any assumption which embodies them.

But when they insist that any conception of progress "must" be transcendental, they go beyond scientific caution. Why "must" it? What does "must" mean in this connection? It cannot mean that no other conception is possible, since another actually exists. It has been employed in mathematics since ancient times without demur. It is entirely clear and definite. Why, then, should its employment in the analysis of technology arouse resistance? But social progress, we are told, "must" be movement toward a preconceived "end." Why "must" it? There is only one answer to this question. Although modern social studies have convinced us that human behavior exhibits no such "end" and therefore no such movement, we are still sufficiently obsessed by traditional ways of thinking to retain the conviction that if we are to think about social progress at all, we must do so in terms of transcendental "ends." We "must" because that is the traditional way of thinking.

This sense of intellectual compulsion to follow traditional ways of thinking is bound up with our whole conception of value, and our emancipation will certainly not be complete until it has included that category.[7] But the analysis of technological process by students of mechanical invention and of the history of science and the arts is already sufficient to indicate the existence in all culture of a dynamic force, a phase of culture which is in itself and of its own character innovational, one in which change is continuous and cumulative and always in the same direction, that of more numerous and more complex technological devices. It may be objected that the very word "direction" implies an "end," but this is not so. Direction is implicit in the nature of a series. The series of cardinal numbers is directional, since the numbers continually grow larger as we count. It would be ridiculous to say that in counting we are striving to approximate infinity, or that counting is meaningless except as infinity is preconceived to be its "end," and it is just as ridiculous to insist that no continuous process can be conceived in the realm of culture except in terms of a preconceived "end."

Indeed, the restoration of the concept of progress is one of the crying needs of contemporary social science. The truth is, our agnosticism has gone too far. In ridding our minds of the naïve collective representations of the past, we have gone so far as to deny the intelligibility of any sort of pattern in cultural development. But the development of culture exhibits pattern. The successive layers of artifacts which are laid bare by the digging of the archeologists are not a sheer hodge-podge conglomeration. Each successive layer is somehow related to the ones below and the ones above, and the relationship exhibits some sort of continuous process. Whatever the function be called which differentiates one from another, it is a continuous function and still further differentiates the second layer above from the second layer below.

To economists this problem of pattern is presented in the form of industrialization. It is a real problem. Something or

[7] See Chapter X, below.

other has been going on continuously. Whether good or bad, purgatorial or paradise-approximating, it is the same process in each generation. What is this process? For reasons which have already been discussed, traditional economic thinking has attributed this continuous development to the agency of business enterprise, and this attribution has been one of the basic postulates of that way of thinking. But its technological character has been suspected all along by intellectual mavericks. It is now strongly substantiated by all the studies which have contributed to our present understanding of the technological process. Students of economics are therefore confronted by a challenge. In spite of traditional assumptions, the origin and development of the industrial economy remains a mystery. Can the technological principle of explanation resolve this mystery? It is to this challenge that we must now address ourselves.

Chapter VII

INDUSTRIAL EVOLUTION

In the present state of historical knowledge, any solution of the enigma of industrial society must be largely conjectural. This means that it must be subject to revision, perhaps total revision, as our knowledge is extended by further historical research. It does not mean that one conjecture is no better than another. That it rested on a sandy foundation of "conjectural history" was one of Veblen's favorite jibes at the classical tradition, and in this case as in so many others the criticism is implied but not developed. The same is true of the jibe at the "taxonomy" of orthodox price theory. A taxonomy is a classification, and there is nothing bad a priori about classification. The point is that the word "taxonomy" has been most extensively used by botanists among whom it is understood to refer particularly to the taxonomic exercises of Linnaeus and his predecessors whose classification of the plants has had to be almost totally revised in the light of modern knowledge of the morphology and physiology of plants because it was based on external observations of gross structures. Veblen made his meaning clear to the perspicacious reader by other jibes of an even more explicitly botanical and Linnaean character, but these also have been shrugged off as mere epithets. In the case of "conjectural history," the fault, obviously, was not with the fact that the historical reconstructions of the classical economists were conjectural. With his conjectures on the "savage" and "barbarous" stages of culture and on the role of the "dolicho-blond" in history—bad guesses, based on nineteenth-century anthropology, by which sympathetic students have been embarrassed ever since—Veblen was least qualified to object to the use of conjecture in historical reconstruction. The real basis of his jibe at the "conjectural history" with which classical political economy was buttressed was not that it was guesswork but that it was bad guesswork, based not on historical knowledge however fragmentary but on assumptions with regard to the price system, the role of capital, and the order of nature including human nature, for which a historical background was invented *ad hoc.* Or rather it was a legend dressed up in scientific language—a tribal myth, glorifying the ancestors, and on that account, perhaps, surviving undetected into the Age of Reason.

We are still unable to state as a matter of scientifically demonstrated fact just what the forces were which resulted in the appearance of an industrial economy, first in western Europe and then in America and so throughout the world. In the field of history, indeed, scientific demonstration is extremely limited and consists largely in establishing the authenticity of contemporary records, reducing the discrepancies among them with regard to dates, names, and to a still more limited extent the nature of the recorded events, and so on. This is why historians declare that it is not their business as scientists to assign causes to any social developments nor even perhaps to characterize such developments. Nevertheless it is with regard to social developments, their nature and causes, that we seek enlightenment; and if we can obtain answers to our insistent questions only by conjecture, then with conjecture we are obliged to deal.

Even so, our conjectures need not be wholly uninformed. Though certain historical knowledge is still extremely limited, it is vastly ampler today than two centuries ago. This is notably the case in the field of economic history. More work has been done in this field during the past generation than resulted from all previous efforts put together, in part certainly because of general dissatisfaction with the conjectures of the past; and with surprising unanimity modern researches testify to the extraordinary magnitude of the industrial revolution. History, it seems, has a way of disconcerting social dogmas. When Arnold Toynbee first popularized the phrase "industrial revolution," he was a very young man and he was lecturing not to academic classes but to audiences of workingmen. More orthodox economists have done their best to qualify the importance of industry as a prime-mover in economic change by limiting the industrial revolution to a brief moment between a supposed "commercial" revolution and a conjectural later stage of "finance capitalism"; but more and more research exhibits more and more convincing evidence of an industrial process identical and continuous with that described by Toynbee and extending at least throughout modern times. This body of fact is something with which any conjectural reconstruction must now reckon.

Another has resulted from the labors of the medievalists. The civilization of medieval Europe used to be described as static. The institutions of feudal society were thought to have crystallized into a stable, not to say rigid, structure; and the medieval mind was conceived to have been fixed in a groove of dogma, utterly subservient to the pronouncements of Aristotle and the doctrines of the Church. This was the view of the humanists who were engaged by the end of the fifteenth century in a struggle to free themselves from medieval shackles, a view which later generations, sympathizing with this effort, have therefore perpetuated. But it is a view which we now know to have been false.[1] Why, after all, were those shackles so easily cast off? Apparently they were not so strong as was supposed in early modern times. Even chronology betrays the conventional belief. This epoch during which for so long a time European society was thought to be stable was briefer than the occupancy of North America by European peoples; and during this brief period tremendous changes occurred. Most important of all, this age in which European society was so fully "integrated" and "self-realized" was immediately followed by the greatest convulsion in the whole of history, a strange outcome for a period of such complete stability. The truth is—and it is a scientifically demonstrated fact if there is any such thing anywhere in the field of history—the middle age was a period of ferment, pregnant with imminent and fundamental change; in short, the true parent of the industrial revolution.

Even pre-history is much better known at present than it was in Veblen's day. Not only is the continuity of the ancient civilizations of the Mediterranean region much more fully known today than half a century ago, primitive culture also is far better understood, including the continuity of ancient civilization with neolithic culture. What Veblen saw, through all the imperfections of the anthropology of his youth, that modern civilization is necessarily continuous with that of primitive man and is not understood until that continuity has been appreciated, is now far more completely substantiated than it was in the nineteenth century. To a far greater extent than ever before, anthropological studies enable us to see why and how later civilization is conditioned by earlier civilization, how the industrial revolution itself extends back to include even primeval man.

Indeed, the mystery of industrial revolution resolves itself

[1] See, for example, C. H. Haskins, *The Renaissance of the Twelfth Century* (Cambridge, Mass., 1927), pp. 3 ff.; Lynn Thorndike, *Science and Thought in the Fifteenth Century* (New York, 1929), pp. 10 ff.

into three related enigmas which must all be solved together or not at all. The first and most immediate is the question, why did the industrial revolution occur in western Europe and in modern times? Why not in China, or in ancient Greece? What forces were operative in the modern European situation which were not operative elsewhere and at other times? Granted that inventions occurred which altered the material framework of society, why did they so occur? This first question—for it is a single question—assumes another. It assumes that something or other was going on in western Europe, or perhaps the world, by virtue of which pre-industrial European society was the matrix of industrial revolution. What was this? To external appearance the civilization of medieval Europe was not utterly unlike those of China or of the ancient world; nevertheless it must have been effectively different in some respect directly related to the later burgeoning of industrial revolution. What was this difference? In what way was pre-industrial European society endowed with the capacity of parenthood of industrialism? Behind these questions there lies still another. In our speculation concerning other possible routes of industrialization we raise the question of China or ancient Greece. Why not the Dyak culture of central Borneo, or the Ainu culture of northern Japan, or that of the Andaman islanders? Apparently the parent civilization from which industrial society later sprang was itself of a very special character, one of but few in the history of civilization. What was this character, and how was it related to the development of that condition which we have called the "parenthood" of industrialism? When and why and how did the first cleavage occur in the development of culture of which industrial society was the end product?

Whether these questions can ever be answered with scientific certainty, our reflections concerning them are greatly assisted by the knowledge which modern researches have afforded, and this is true with regard to each of the three. If we proceed chronologically and deal first with the one which goes farthest back, we find that the anthropologists have a technological answer to the question why a certain type of civilization should have appeared in certain areas which was capable of becoming the matrix of later industrial developments as other cultures were not. It must not be assumed that there is any manifest destiny by which all cultural development is guided in this direction. Such an assumption would run afoul of the drift fence which anthropologists have set up to guard against just such teleological ways of thinking. There is no one line of cultural evolution along which all peoples are moving. We must not and need not assume that life in settled communities is "natural" to man. It would be just as reasonable to make a contrary assumption on the basis of the persistence with which men in settled communities seek to "return to nature" when opportunity affords. Rather it was a specific event in the lives of certain peoples which had this result for better or worse.

This event was the discovery or invention of agriculture. Even here we must not assume too much. As Thurnwald has pointed out,[2] there is an indefinite number of different kinds of agriculture and agricultural communities. It was the discovery of wheat, twelve to fifteen thousand years ago, and the development of the practice of cultivating cereal food which had the significant effect of stabilizing settled communities. The effect was not primarily spiritual or even social in any vague and general sense. It has been remarked that agricultural peoples seem quite commonly to develop characteristic superstitions and magic rites based on the reproductive cycle of the grains on which they are so dependent, and that these seem to produce theocratic social systems of a singularly onerous kind. But it can hardly

[2] R. Thurnwald, *Economics in Primitive Communities* (Oxford, 1932), pp. 4 ff.

be supposed that these practices formed the basis of the later developments which we seek to trace. Nor should it be supposed that the practice of agriculture stimulates the technological "faculty." What it does lead to is the accumulation of technical materials. When people stay put in any particular locality things accumulate, and the accumulation of the physical instruments and materials of living constitutes a forcing bed of technological development.

No doubt this tendency is at work everywhere. But there are certain regions in which the configuration of the earth has made continued occupancy possible over very long periods of time with correspondingly formidable technological development. It has long been apparent that certain areas have been the scene of such developments: the Nile and Mesopotamian valleys; the Indus and Ganges valleys; the Yangtse and Huang-Ho valleys; and the valleys of Central America and the Andes. In other regions agricultural occupancy has been more intermittent and more limited; in still others, virtually nonexistent. Thus the European plain was not the scene of development of any "great" (*i.e.*, continuous and extensive) civilization contemporaneously with these other regions, although it is one of the most fertile areas on earth, probably because it was not protected by natural barriers of mountain and desert and jungle as the others were. It is not that the geographical character of the "cradles of civilization" in any positive sense "determined" the cultural developments which took place there. Certainly it need not be supposed that neolithic man, foreseeing the future over thousands of years, cannily selected the regions in which great civilizations might materialize. Rather the geographical configuration of the different localities acted as a limiting factor. In some regions, like the European plain, exposure inhibited development; in others the unearned increment of natural barriers permitted development to occur. What occurred—the substance of the process—was a long-continued accumulation of technical contrivances and materials with the development, inevitable under such circumstances, of the progressive series of techniques which we call civilization.

This development was of course continuous with the technical achievements of primeval man, upon which the discovery of agriculture itself was posited. In this sense the industrial revolution is continuous and goes back to the *coup de poing,* not to mention the techniques of using fire, the domestication of animals, and all the rest. But however continuous, the emergence of the industrial economy has not been without event; and perhaps the first great cleavage by virtue of which the possibility of later development was narrowed down to not more than four great culture areas was the one here under discussion; and if so it is significant that this first cleavage has already been interpreted in technological terms.

The next problem is that of the circumstances which further narrowed the field not only to one of these four areas but to a particular region within the general field of Mediterranean civilization, that of western Europe. What is it in the culture-history of western Europe that is unique? This region was the residuary legatee of thousands of years of civilization in the Mediterranean area, but so were many others. The Nile and Mesopotamian valleys are still inhabited. Wherein does western Europe differ from them? When the question is put in terms of these alternatives part of the answer is obvious at once. Of all the regions in which Mediterranean civilization flourished in ancient times, Egypt and Mesopotamia are the oldest and western Europe the youngest. Indeed the difference in age is so great—running to thousands of years, or several times the age of the younger member—as to demand consideration. But although the solution to the problem may be a function of age, it is not a mere matter of chronology.

Western Europe was in the most literal sense the frontier region of Mediterranean civilization. This has been seen most clearly, perhaps, by the great Belgian historian, Henri Pirenne.[3] A frontier is a penetration phenomenon. It is a region into which people come from another and older center of civilization, bringing with them the tools and materials of their older life, their cereal plants and vines and fruit trees, their domestic animals and accouterments, their techniques of working stone and wood and their architectural designs and all the rest. They also bring their immemorial beliefs and "values," their mores and folkways. But it is notorious that the latter invariably suffer some reduction in importance under the conditions of frontier life. Existence on the frontier is, as we say, free and easy. Meticulous observance of the Sabbath and the rules of grammar are somehow less important on the frontier than "back home."

While this is true of all frontiers, the difference is greatly accentuated by the presence of a considerable population, indigenous to the region, to whom the whole culture-system of the invaders is more or less completely foreign. The discrepancy between the civilization of Caesar's Rome and that of pre-Roman Gaul was not as great as that between Winthrop's England and pre-British Massachusetts, and perhaps as a consequence the Franks were assimilated whereas the North American Indians were not. But we must guard against supposing that Frankish assimilation was complete. Modern Europeans are accustomed to think of ancient civilization as "their" civilization at an earlier stage; but this is true only with great reservations. Neither "Hellenism" nor "Hebraism" was indigenous to western Europe. Both were foreign importations, doubtfully assimilated by the "natives" for many centuries. For example, throughout the "dark" ages of western Europe when literacy was extremely rare and the

[3] In *Economic and Social History of Medieval Europe* (London, 1936).

ancient classics were almost unknown, the education of upper-class children of Byzantine civilization included memorizing the *Iliad* and the *Odyssey*. Modern educators may rejoice in this "emancipation," and as we shall see there may be good grounds, at least from the point of view of industrial revolution, for general rejoicing. The point is that western Europe was a frontier in which ancient culture was only partially installed.

The importance of this reservation is even further emphasized if we consider it in terms of the religion of the Western peoples. Ever since the Crusades the Western nations have considered themselves the defenders of the faith until it has been forgotten that it was not originally their faith. Of the many cultural elements which have been blended in Christian theology—the original Hebraism, the trinitarian syncretism and neo-Platonic mysticism of Egypt, Indo-Persian Mithraism, and all the rest—none originated in western Europe. Furthermore the conversion of some of the Western peoples to Christianity was so tardy and the persistence of pagan elements, such as the spring fertility rites of the May-pole and the Gothic cult of the tannenbaum, was so strong that the church continued to be greatly exercised over the residue of paganism in its midst until quite recently. This, it is now established, is the reason for the singular asperity, continuing even in the American colonies, of the measures taken against witchcraft. In addition it must be recalled that Mohammedanism was securely established in Europe itself, just across the Pyrenees, throughout the middle ages; and that it was much more a world religion and a vehicle of culture than Christianity.

To recall these facts is not to question the importance of Christianity in the history of the Western peoples. Historians have always made much of the church as a unifying element in feudal society, and justly so. But for this unifying element the Western peoples might not have achieved any sort of cultural unity. But our concern is with industrial evolution, and from this point of view the church must be recognized as the spearhead of institutional resistance to technological change.[4] Under the leadership of the church, feudal society opposed and interdicted all the great innovations of which industrial society is the outgrowth; but that opposition was ineffective—from the point of view of industrial evolution, happily so—and its ineffectiveness was due not to any pronounced difference of temper and intent which might be conceived to distinguish Christianity from other creeds but rather to the fact that it was after all an alien creed which bore much less heavily upon the Western peoples than did Islam upon the Arabs, Hinduism upon India, or Confucianism upon China. When we are tempted to think of the church as the quintessence of medieval civilization we should stop and ask ourselves which, after all, was the more significant symbol of European culture, Saint Thomas or his contemporary, the Emperor Frederick II?

This aspect of the case of European civilization comes to focus in the popular enigma of the fall of Rome, that favorite topic of moralists and debating societies. In his most famous phrase Gibbon attributed it to "the triumph of barbarism and religion"; the French and Russian revolutions have inclined others to explain it in terms of the spread of "Bolshevism"; and all the while the truth is that the Roman Empire did not fall. As J. B. Bury succinctly pointed out,[5] the empire of which Rome had for a time been the capital persisted without a break for a thousand years after the date which Western historians have agreed to consider as its end. Throughout this time it was what it had always been, the Hellenic empire of the Mediterranean culture area. The amazing perversion of the plainest of historical evidence by

[4] For a discussion of institutional resistance, see Chapter IX, below.

[5] In *A History of the Later Roman Empire* (London and New York, 1889), pp. v ff.

which Western historians have represented Odoacer as having brought the ancient empire to an end is a compound of two characteristically European provincialisms. One is the habit of regarding western Europe as the sole successor and inheritor of "the glory that was Greece and the grandeur that was Rome," and the other is a historic aversion to Byzantine civilization carried ultimately to the point of refusing to credit its existence. It was western Europe that fell, not Rome. Modern historical scholarship has at last recognized this fact and so has made it possible for us to understand the two respects in which the civilization of western Europe was unique.

The culture of western Europe was technologically continuous with that of the whole Mediterranean area, and it was also institutionally discontinuous. Gaul was a fully occupied Roman province for a period as long as that during which Europeans have inhabited North America, and during this time the whole technological accretion of thousands of years of ancient agricultural civilization was introduced into western Europe. At the end of this time—the date is of course indefinite since the process was very gradual—the tie of empire was severed. Never again was western Europe brought under the aegis of Mediterranean empire. The institutional deposit of ancient civilization was not completely obliterated. But historians are now generally agreed that the severance was all but complete. The feudal system which emerged from the institutional chaos of early centuries was in large measure a native growth, and even the Christian church underwent a very substantial transmutation from the proletarian cult of early Roman days to the feudal hierarchy of the papacy. Most of the Hellenism by which later European culture has been suffused and most of the influence of Roman law upon later European jurisconsults were medieval importations, "rediscoveries" of our cultural ancestors made with the help of Byzantine codifiers and Mohammedan philosophers. The actual experience of the European peoples was that of a frontier community endowed with a full complement of tools and materials derived from a parent culture and then almost completely severed from the institutional power system of its parent. The result was unique. It is doubtful if history affords another instance of any comparable area and population so richly endowed and so completely severed. That western Europe was the seat of a great civilization in the centuries that followed was due altogether to that endowment no important part of which was ever lost; that it was of all the great civilizations of the time incomparably the youngest, the least rigid, less stifled than any other by age-long accumulations of institutional dust, more susceptible by far than any other to change and innovation, was due to that unique severance. Almost certainly it was this composite character which made the civilization of medieval Europe the parent of industrial revolution.

The actual process was a true case of cross-fertilization. The fault line between medieval and modern European civilization is marked by a series of immense cultural eruptions. This fact and even its importance have always been recognized. In spite of the inhibition of their scientific methodology historians have never been able wholly to resist the temptation to rhapsodize over the series of world-shaking innovations by which the transition from medieval to modern times is punctuated. No list is definitive, and it is entirely possible that innovations of the first magnitude still escape our observation. But some are so obvious as to appear on every list. Thus no one doubts the importance of the invention of printing, of gunpowder, of the compass and astrolabe, of the symbol for zero, of the mill wheel and the clock. It was this series of inventions and discoveries and an indefinitely long series of lesser but related ones that set up the process of which industrial revolution was the consummation.

These master inventions and discoveries signalize a third process without which in all probabilty the industrial revolution could not have occurred. For the analysis of this process the case of printing is most serviceable for a number of reasons. No other innovation outranks printing in the importance of its effects; in its actual history no other is better known; and no other presents a clearer case of cultural cross-fertilization.

The actual invention of printing from movable types took place in one of the industrial towns of northern Europe—perhaps Mainz, perhaps Haarlem, perhaps both and also others—about five centuries ago. The specific device with which Gutenberg and the other contestants for the honor are credited was that of type-molds for casting metal types to be used interchangeably. Considered as a manifestation of inventive genius this device is so very simple as to constitute something of a mystery. Why should the invention of so simple an apparatus be regarded as a turning point of history? The obvious answer to this question is in terms of its effects, and this is the one that is most commonly given. But this only multiplies the mystery. Why should such a trifling invention have had such prodigious effects? If we say only that it made printed material available on a much larger scale than previously, we run the risk of imputing modern habits and motives to the fifteenth century. Who wanted printing to be available on such a scale? Should we imagine the thirteenth and fourteenth centuries to have eked out a miserable existence complaining bitterly all the while over the injustice which deferred the invention of printing to the fifteenth? Clearly something more than availability is at issue; and that something is related to a further mystery. If the type-mold was such a simple device (as it was), why should it not have been invented very much earlier, even in ancient times, perhaps. The ancients cast metal—why not types? To be sure, the art of printing did not exist in any form in the ancient world. It was developed in China over a period of many centuries and introduced into Europe probably in the thirteenth century (that time which was so singularly free from cataclysmic disturbances!) probably by the agency of Mongol conquest [6] (that military exploit which was so utterly devoid of cultural significance). But why did the Chinese, ingenious as they were and familiar with the arts of casting metal, nevertheless fail to invent type-molds? It will hardly do to attribute this failure to the ancestor-worshiping stupidity of the Chinese at the very moment when we are crediting them with the development and perfection, within certain limits, of an art which all the philosophers and scientists of the Western world had failed to achieve at all.

The answer, it is now generally agreed, is to be found not in Chinese character but in the Chinese language. That language, or family of languages, is non-alphabetical. In recent years, under the insistent pressure of the industrial West, a sort of "basic" Chinese has been developed; but classical Chinese involves the use of a vast number of distinct ideographs, a number so large as to make interchangeable types of doubtful value. Without doubt this is the reason why Chinese printers have continued to carve their texts from wooden blocks even down to the present time.

In this connection it is interesting to speculate on the possible relation between the Chinese written language and the origin of printing. The problem of textual purity is peculiarly acute for the Chinese. During the Han dynasty, which was contemporaneous with the Roman emperors, an organized effort was made to establish correct readings of the then ancient classics, and these were carved on stone blocks to which ever after scholars would refer for authentic versions of disputed passages. It became customary to assure

[6] Thomas F. Carter, *The Invention of Printing in China and Its Spread Westward* (New York, 1925), pp. 116 ff.

authenticity by taking pressings, an elementary form of the practice of modern archeologists of taking photographs of every inscription. This practice was one, at least, of the forerunners of printing, perhaps the chief one; and if so, the character of the Chinese language may have played a crucial part in the development of an art in China for which the West produced no counterpart.

In the West, however, the character of the written language was utterly different. It is supposed that the Phoenicians may have been the first to use a phonetic alphabet, but the practice spread in very early times to all the written languages of the Mediterranean culture area. Western Europe having been colonized by the Romans, its languages were reduced to the Latin alphabet (with Procrustean effects from which school children still suffer). Thus the region into which the Chinese art of printing was introduced in the thirteenth century was one in which only a small number of graphic symbols were made to serve all the needs of literature. Such being the case it was inevitable that the types for these symbols should be used interchangeably. The invention of Gutenberg was "bound" to occur sooner or later as a function not of Western inventive genius but of the character of the things which had thus been brought together. The two centuries or so which elapsed before the invention did actually occur may be taken as an index of the apparent triviality of the Chinese art. The Western world was at this time not unliterary. It had its own methods of recording and transmitting worthy writings, methods with which (our feelings to the contrary notwithstanding) it felt no general dissatisfaction. Paper had been introduced into the Western world from China some time before and by a different route, and its availability to the printers of the fifteenth century is another tool-combination of vast importance; but its importance was not felt by the scholars of the medieval world who regarded it as a distinctly inferior material. Hence the first uses of printing were of a singularly frivolous character, not at all indicative of any felt need for the improvement of the art. The invention of printing from movable types—whatever its consequences may have been—was itself the result of the conjunction of the technology of duplication with that of phonetic symbolism, and this conjunction was the result of a culture-contact which occurred as an incident to Mongol conquest in the thirteenth century.

But however striking, the case of printing is by no means unique. The same process is also illustrated almost as dramatically by the development of the sailing ship. Here, too, the consequences are prodigious. At one moment Europeans are no more involved in the affairs of other peoples than other peoples are in theirs. (This, it may be noted in passing, is probably the reason for the present disposition, of people who find the modern world disturbing, to idealize the medieval world as one in which these disturbances were happily absent. It is true, for whatever it may be worth, that medieval society was more completely self-contained than European society has been since that time.) At the next moment Europeans are circumnavigating the globe, intruding upon every continent and to a continually increasing degree meddling with the affairs of every other people.

Here, too, the actual process is singularly obscure and subject to outrageous misinterpretation. Just as in the case of printing we are a little inclined to think of the invention as the necessary preliminary to the dissemination of economics textbooks, or the *Saturday Evening Post,* in that of shipbuilding we have been very much inclined to explain "the age of voyage and discovery" as the necessary preliminary to world trade, in the first instance with the Indies. Because the Turks captured Constantinople in 1453 and because Columbus is known to have cajoled Isabella with talk of the riches of the Indies half a century later, we have concluded that trade with the Indies was an economic necessity and that the Turks had interrupted it. Only recently has it been demonstrated that the Turks did no such thing. Apparently the explanation of those exploits of voyage and discovery which has been taught to several generations of school children was a sheer fabrication, a case of historical conjecture of the sort historians have learned to shun.

Even more preposterous is the supposition that fifteenth-century mariners were the first who were bold enough to sail out of sight of land, since we know that Phoenician sailors brought tin from Cornwall before the time of Homer and that their tales of Scylla and Charybdis represent a conspiracy in restraint of trade; but in this case an important fact lies behind the legend. The Mediterranean is a sea to be treated with extreme circumspection not because of navigational difficulties (we forget that even the ancients could read the stars, as our word "cynosure" ought to be a perpetual reminder) but because it is subject to sudden and sometimes prolonged calms. Consequently a sailing vessel runs great risk. This is why sail was supplemented by oars from ancient times continuously right down to the nineteenth century and the introduction of steam power.

It was this circumstance which dictated the design of Mediterranean shipbuilding. The Mediterranean Sea dictated the use of oars, and the use of oars dictated shallow draft (except for warships which did not carry cargoes). The arts of shipbuilding and fitting underwent continuous development in the Mediterranean culture area from very ancient times right on down through the middle ages, with the result that the ships which plied this sea were the largest and sturdiest and best rigged in the world. But they were virtually confined to the Mediterranean not only by the short voyages which the use of oars and consequent necessity of carrying stores for a large crew necessarily imposed but by the fact that their shallow-draft design ruled them off the oceans. Such ships were unfit for voyages exclusively under sail because for this purpose a ship must be able to sail into the wind. Mediterranean ships were unable to do this. The reason for this limitation, it has been pointed out, was not ignorance of the art of tacking but the propensity of shallow-draft ships to make leeway when sailing into the wind. On this account Mediterranean mariners were perfectly justified in their fear of venturing out upon the stormy Atlantic.

Meantime, however, the Vikings were crossing the Atlantic in ships much smaller and, excellent as they were, much less sturdy than those which prevailed throughout the Mediterranean. This was possible because their ships had been evolved for use on a stormy sea and were therefore clinker-built and of (relatively) deep draft. Their sails and rigging were rudimentary compared with standard Mediterranean equipment; but lacking oars they developed the "steer-board," which was quite unnecessary to the oar-propelled galleys of the Mediterranean.

The ships which began to cross the oceans toward the end of the fifteenth century were a combination of these two types. We do not know exactly how or when or where combination occurred. Perhaps it was in the shipyards of the coast of the Bay of Biscay, where Viking culture flowing down met Mediterranean culture flowing up.[7] Even so, a considerable time elapsed before the meeting was fruitful; but this may serve to emphasize two points: that the combination was not deliberate and had no special "end" in view (such as the Indies), and that a ship is not one simple device but rather a mass of culture traits, so that combination would almost inevitably be the slow function of a general cultural amalgamation and general technological development. But it seems to be a fairly safe conjecture that the age of voyage and discovery was a function of ships, that the

[7] See, for instance, S. C. Gilfillan, *Inventing the Ship* (Chicago, 1935), pp. 49 ff.

ocean-sailing ships were the result of a combination of different types of earlier devices, and that the combination occurred as a result of culture contact.

Similar analysis of other notable discoveries and inventions of this early modern period produces similar results. The magnetic needle was introduced from China but combined with navigation in Europe.[8] The astrolabe, forerunner of the sextant and quite as important as the compass whether or not Columbus used it in 1492, was introduced from Islam but adapted to navigational use in Europe in 1485. Historians have always recognized the importance of gunpowder as an agent of social change. Some even say point-blank that gunpowder destroyed feudalism. The history of this invention is more than usually obscure. It may have been an independent product of the alchemy of Roger Bacon. But since an identical substance is known to have been used many centuries earlier in China for ceremonial purposes (and on that account perhaps never combined with the techniques of war), and since the Byzantines had developed the war-technique of pouring mixtures of sulfur, quicklime, and other materials from a siphon, it is possible to conjecture that the Chinese ceremonial powder became gunpowder when it was combined with the Byzantine siphon, which thereupon became a cannon. Certainly the Hindu-Arabic numerals including the symbol for zero, invention of which has been called the most important innovation of the age, were introduced from Islam, presumably by Leonardo Fibonacci of Pisa in 1202. The clock has been called the master-pattern of all subsequent expedients in the field of power-driven machinery,[9] but it was probably an adaptation and development of a still more elementary power trans-

[8] Apparently the first mention of its use in navigation is by Alexander of Neckham in *De Utensilibus,* about 1189.

[9] Thorndike, *Science and Thought in the Fifteenth Century,* p. 19; Lewis Mumford, *Technics and Civilization* (New York, 1934), pp. 14 ff.

mission, that of the windmill and water wheel, probably introduced from Asia Minor by the crusaders.

It is the analysis of cases such as these that supports a third conjecture with regard to the inception of the industrial revolution in Europe. Not only was western Europe the recipient of the technological accumulations of thousands of years of ancient agricultural civilization, the development of an independent culture on the European frontier of ancient society coincided with a period of old-world culture-contact and culture-diffusion which was equally unique. Even in ancient times some slight contact existed between the Mediterranean area and the civilizations of India and China, but these contacts were inconsequential in comparison with the eruptions of the middle ages. The rise of Islam effected contacts along the southern water route from China to Spain from which Europe obtained paper, the decimal system, a renewed acquaintance with the ancient classics, Arabian science, and how much else we can only conjecture. The Crusades have always been known to have had a secular and even economic importance probably outweighing their religious significance. But that importance cannot be measured in trade. If, as seems to be the case, the windmill and water wheel were introduced into Europe by returning crusaders, the whole subsequent development of Europe was affected. The eruption of the Vikings was almost certainly responsible for the development which ushered in the age of voyage and discovery. Mongol conquest brought printing from China.

These contacts multiply the importance of the frontier character of European civilization. Had they been deferred for another thousand years, those qualities of feudal society which the humanists so greatly emphasized—the tendency to institutional rigidity and cultural ancestor-worship—might very possibly have prevailed to such an extent as to render Europe as impervious to contact-stimulation as were the other great civilizations of the day. For all these contacts were necessarily bilateral, or multilateral. To note the most specific and perhaps the most significant instance, Islam also had its chance to develop Chinese printing. But whereas in Europe the fulminations of divines against the heathen art were without important effect, in Islam the prohibition of any "graven image" contained in the Mosaic code which Islam shares with Christianity was taken so literally as to exclude even the Chinese style of printing from carved wooden blocks. It was this state of mind and feeling which, prevailing all along the line, inhibited the free use of "heathen" arts in each of the older civilizations and so prevented the occurrence of tool-combinations which was potential in each culture area. Modern Europeans have inclined to take great credit to themselves for not being ancestor-worshipers as so many other peoples are. The truth is that the disposition to venerate the ancestors is endemic in all civilization and is felt most strongly by those who have the most ancestors, such as the Chinese and the Byzantines (who, perhaps, died of it). It is felt least by frontiersmen: Australians, western Americans, and in their day medieval Europeans.

In medieval Europe it was felt least by townsmen not because of any peculiar spiritual quality of urban residence but because the townsmen had sloughed off their ancestors. As Pirenne so graphically puts it, they were *déracinés,* uprooted men. This is the paradox of the medieval towns: they grew up *in* feudal society but they were never *of* it. Pirenne remarks in one of his most luminous passages that the towns were from the first a function not of local society but of world trade.[10] As such they were the inevitable medium of Jews and Syrians as well as European foreigners; but in spite of this the greater part of their population was always drawn from the local countryside. They were of course de-

[10] *Economic and Social History of Medieval Europe,* p. 142.

pendent for their living chiefly on the produce of the local countryside, and they were centers of manufacture and craftsmanship upon which the local countryside depended. In emphasizing this point in another passage Pirenne seems almost to contradict his earlier declaration.[11] But such is the nature of the paradox. The runaway serfs who populated the medieval towns ceased to be feudal serfs and became *déclassés,* eventually a "middle" class, not a part of the feudal order at all. It is another significant case of technological continuity and institutional discontinuity. Technologically, the medieval towns were a functional part of the community; institutionally, they were distinct.[12] Their closest ties were with each other and with the outside world.

Hence the effect of culture contact was concentrated in the towns. There, where representatives of all the arts and crafts were closely assembled and where all the apparatus of all the trades was concentrated, new devices from the outside world were brought into close contact with all the tools of the Mediterranean tradition. Nothing could have been more favorable to combination. It has already been noted that the invention of type-molds for printing from movable types could have been made only with the conjunction of the arts of the metal worker. Such instances could be indefinitely extended. For example, the use of metal types requires a change of ink. Throughout the ages the Chinese have used a water-medium ink for printing from wood blocks; but water will not spread evenly on metal surfaces. Little note is taken of this crisis in European civilization in the conventional histories of printing, the writers of which only remark that this circumstance led to the use of an oil-medium ink. But how did it lead? Such a statement recalls a remark which appears in a well-known manual of European economic history to the effect that the early European villagers found

[11] *Ibid.,* p. 179.

[12] This institutional situation is discussed in Chapter IX, below.

the long-shared plow best adapted to breaking the tough sod. Where did they find it—out in the woods? The truth seems to be that other contemporary denizens of the same north-European towns, Van Eyck by name, fine artisans in paint, had invented "a new method of painting" which at first they had closely guarded, so that it was just beginning to be known in the northern towns by Gutenberg's time. This "new method" was the use of linseed oil as a medium. The use of flax reaches back to the very earliest periods of civilization, but apparently the use of the oil of the flaxseed as a medium for paint, and so for printer's ink, began with the Van Eycks. This incident is a beautiful illustration of the technological continuity of the "fine" and the "useful" arts, and an equally clear case of the function of the medieval towns as forcing beds of technological development. For the performance of this function the towns of medieval Europe were qualified by three interrelated sets of circumstances: they were technological concentration points; they were semidetached from the institutional structure of feudal society; and they were in the most direct contact with the outside world where a process of hemispheric culture diffusion was going on.

From this point onward the character of the industrial revolution is unmistakable. Modern European society is an outgrowth of the process which was going on in the medieval towns. It is urban and "middle class" in that functional sense, and the whole process is one of social change induced by technological development. Since Arnold Toynbee's analysis of the dramatic events of the late eighteenth and early nineteenth centuries no one has ventured to deny that the steam engine and the power loom were vehicles of social change; but is this any less true of gunpowder and movable type? What does one mean by saying that gunpowder destroyed feudalism? Cannon made feudal castles obsolete; and since cannon and their ammunition are direct products of heavy industry, they brought the supreme coercive power of the modern state to focus in the centers of heavy industry, as it has been ever since. Furthermore the development of musketry and small arms shifted the center of gravity of a whole society by putting a weapon more lethal than the noble's sword into the hands of the common man, one which can be used with deadly effect by persons who have not spent their entire youth mastering the art of homicide. We have forgotten what firearms meant to common citizens because we have almost forgotten feudal aristocracy; but our ancestors remembered. Not for nothing does the American Bill of Rights guarantee to all citizens "the right to bear arms." Rights are governmental; but before any such right could exist there must have been bearable arms; that is, firearms.

The case of printing is the clearest possible exemplar of industrial revolution. The invention of printing from movable type had the immediate effect of extending the art of reading and writing to the whole community. Written languages which employ phonetic symbols are relatively easy to learn, incomparably easier than the Chinese written language. Throughout the ages the only barrier to general literacy in the West was the scarcity of materials. The invention of printing made written-language materials not only cheap but very common. The output of the presses in the six decades between Gutenberg's invention and the close of the fifteenth century has been estimated in millions. This can mean only one thing. In the course of two generations a whole community had learned to read.

The importance of the invention of printing derives from this result. It was by no means limited to the field of literature. The spread of literacy did greatly facilitate the spread of ideas, and this may well have been one of its most important effects; but it was by no means the whole effect. That was nothing less than the transformation of the essential character of the community, a transformation which had its incidence upon every aspect of life. Certainly its political effects are beyond exaggeration. No doubt Mr. H. G. Wells has exaggerated the political importance of newspapers, but in doing so he has only made the newspaper the symbol of a much more general intercommunication of which democracy is perhaps the political expression—without which, certainly, popular government is limited to units the size of the Greek city-state or the New England town meeting.

Democracy is of course more than intercommunication. It involves enlightenment; and enlightenment is more than the transmission of information. It involves subtle changes of attitude. Such changes of attitude were among the most portentous consequences of general literacy. Much has been made of the fact that the Bible was among the first products of Gutenberg's establishment. This is a fact of very great importance, but its significance is quite different from what is generally supposed. To the community at large the Bible had been a mystery throughout the ages. The veneration in which it was held was due in large part to this circumstance, as the doctors of the church well understood. Its publication was opposed by the church for this reason, and rightly —as events have amply proved. From publication it was but a step to higher criticism. The separation of church and state, which is one of the most fundamental expressions of the democratic attitude, was itself a consequence of the progressive secularization of Western civilization of which the printing press has been far and away the most important agent. It is easy to maintain sacred fictions in a community to whom every letter is an occult symbol; in a community to whom the printed word has become a common tool, no fiction is shielded from the scrutiny of the people, not even the divinity which hedges kings.

But the importance of literacy goes far beyond even the political life of the Western peoples. It is a commonplace of economic history that business enterprise was transformed. This change has been imputed to the "spirit" of modern capitalism which in turn has been attributed by Sombart and others to an access of "rationality" on the part of early modern business men. But the business men of early modern times can hardly be supposed to have experienced an access either of cupidity or of intelligence. The only demonstrable change was one of tools. At this point as at many others—for example, in the development of science—language and ciphering cross-fertilized each other. Bookkeeping involves both. The invention of double-entry bookkeeping—another great technical innovation of the time—constituted a tremendous advance in the technology of business organization. Their mastery of this instrument of strategy and tactics gave business men an enormous advantage in the struggle for power in which they were engaged. It even provided them with the ideology of the financial power-system. The concept of capital itself is only a sublimation of the system of notation in which every aspect of the life of the community can be reduced to an entry in a ledger. The "spirit" of modern capitalism was itself a product not of printing alone but of the industrial revolution of which printing was so significant a feature.

Most important of all, however, was the effect of printing upon industry. For purposes of "total war" what is called "functional literacy" has only recently been defined as "ability to read simple printed directions." [13] This is the most important kind of literacy because it conditions the industrial effectiveness of the whole community. The most important inscriptions of modern industrial civilization are those which read, "Danger: Live Wires," and things of similar import. That is, written language is a tool which combines with all other tools fundamentally modifying their accessibility and functioning effectiveness. The functional illiterate is ex-

[13] *Time*, July 13, 1942, p. 42.

cluded from the whole industrial process. He remains a vestigial peasant in an industrial community. Or, to put it the other way, literacy transformed a community of peasants into a community of industrial workers.

The case of printing thus illustrates the climactic characteristic of industrial revolution. It has often been remarked that the difference between industrial and pre-industrial civilization is not a matter of using mechanical devices but rather of the use of machines to make machines. Or the same thing is put in terms of invention, thus: it is not the occurrence of inventions that distinguishes modern civilization but the organization of society to bring this about. The primary instrument for such organization is literacy. If anything so subtle can be dated at all, it should be dated with reference not to the steam engine but to printing.

This transformation of the community includes much more than literacy. Among other things it includes the physical framework of existence. One of the most important—and most neglected—aspects of the industrial revolution is the revolution in housing which took place in early modern times. Economic historians have much to say about "the domestic system" of manufacture, but with their usual pertinacity they conceive this system almost exclusively in terms of ownership and control, not in terms of physical shelter. But industrial operations require shelter, not only because the tools and materials of industry suffer by exposure to the elements but even more because the level of efficiency which even the simplest handicraft operations exact from their workers is higher than that required of peasants and can be obtained only by provision of a certain degree of shelter. The general introduction of stockings and night clothes is often cited as indicative of the changes brought by industrialization, and in this connection such things are usually treated merely as comforts or even perquisites. The sheer energy-sapping brutalization of medieval (and earlier) life has now so far been forgotten that we no longer realize that perpetual chill and improper sleep are crippling. It is in this sense that the domestic revolution of early modern times made an indispensable contribution to the general industrial process.

We know little about it, but we do know that three innovations in domestic architecture distinguished the houses which became the scene of "the domestic system" of manufacture: flues, glazed windows, and closed plumbing. None of these existed in any pre-industrial community except in rudimentary forms. Each had its own industrial background of stone masonry, glass manufacture, and metalworking; and each had its remoter cultural sources in earlier and more rudimentary devices. All were developed by the artisans of the medieval and early modern towns so as eventually to make possible the predominantly indoors civilization of the industrial economy.

Little as we know about the transformation of Western civilization, there are many elements in the process which are as well known and as significant as those which have been mentioned, of which, however, the present discussion can take no account. For it is in no sense a history but rather an analysis of the nature of the process of industrial revolution. But enough has been said to indicate that what we know of this process clearly identifies it as an industrial revolution in the strictest interpretation of the phrase: a series of social changes, affecting every aspect of life, in which "mechanical invention" plays a decisive part.

We know that the meaning of the conventional phrase "mechanical invention" must be broad enough to include pure science and fine art, both of which interact continuously with mechanical invention in the narrower sense, and we know that such interaction is no new thing. The introduction of the Hindu-Arabic numerals, for example, was surely no less important to science than to business and to craftsmanship. Indeed, scientists almost begrudge Leonardo Fibonacci his commercial interests. Science (astronomy) endowed industry (navigation) with the astrolabe; but industry (optical glass) presented the same science with the telescope.

We also know that this process—the series of social changes in which technological innovation plays a decisive part—has been going on in essentially the same fashion throughout modern times. The "revolution in coal and iron" and the "revolution in textiles," to cite the familiar phrases, were no more industrial than the invention of printing or the building of ocean-going ships; nor were the social consequences of these earlier innovations less significant or far-reaching than those of the steam engine and the power loom. The French antiquarian, Lefebvre des Noëttes, is credited by Pirenne with having established that a "revolution in transport" occurred in western Europe in the eleventh and twelfth centuries to which the conventional phrase is no less applicable than to railway building.

Thinking in terms of the classical tradition, economists have done their best to attribute this whole process to the institutions of capitalism. But that beautiful hypothesis is now being upset by brutal facts. An understanding of technological process is sufficient to establish the reverse. It is already clear that technological innovation played the decisive part in establishing the institutions of capitalism. By making industry paramount in modern life, the industrial revolution has made the captains of industry powerful. Power is certainly important. The process of institutional adaptation to technological change is therefore tremendously important as well as subtle and complicated, and special attention must therefore be given to it. But before this can be done it will be necessary to consider the nature of that other, ceremonial, aspect of behavior in terms of which the institutional system and its changes must be understood.

Chapter VIII

CEREMONIAL PATTERNS

In the attempt to analyze that aspect of behavior from which technology is to be distinguished, the student is at once confronted with terminological difficulties. Although a great many writers have made the distinction more or less clearly and consistently, no single term has come into anything like general use to refer to nontechnological behavior as a whole.[1] Veblen used the word "ceremonial" in this

[1] Thus, for example, Dewey's *Quest for Certainty* (New York, 1929), is a full-length analysis of the nontechnological way of thinking; but the book offers no general designation of the behavior function of which "the quest for certainty" is an expression such as would then parallel Dewey's own designation of the "instrumental" function. Incidentally, the designation "instrumental" has two important advantages over the synonym, "technological," which is in more general use among students of the social sciences: (1) the latter term suffers from popular association with the most crudely mechanical "techniques," an association from which the term "instrumental" escapes by virtue of its suggestion of "instruments of precision"; and (2) there is no abstract noun corresponding to "instrumentalism" by which the technological theory of economic progress might be designated. "Technology" means something else, and "technologism" is barbarous. Such a term is very much needed. As a designation of a way of thinking in economics the term "institutionalism" is singularly unfortunate, since it points only at that from which an escape is being sought. Prop-

connection, and it will have to serve for the present. But it must be used with caution from the outset. In particular the student must guard against the identification of "ceremonial behavior" with the vestigial ceremonies of which modern life affords so many instances, "mere" ceremonies which have lost the greater part of their original meaning and are now carried on for no particular reason by force of social habit. Academic life affords many instances of vestigial ceremonies of this sort. For example, commencement ceremonies are recognized by the academic community as "a lot of mumbo-jumbo" inherited from a remote past and carried on for no more important reason than to "give dignity" to a certain event by recalling its past associations. Pursued with caution, however, the analysis even of "mere" ceremonies may have valuable results.

Thus it is quite evident that even the most vestigial ceremony contains an element of "make-believe." We pretend that a person upon whom the degree has been conferred is in some subtle qualitative sense a different individual. He is now a "doctor of philosophy," entitled to all the advantages and emoluments which that rank confers as well as subject to its duties and responsibilities. No one really supposes that the commencement ceremony has made this difference. All it does is to "celebrate" the successful completion of the candidate's studies and researches, an event which has been effectively marked by examinations presumably of an explicitly technological character corresponding to the "workmanlike" activities which have preceded them. To be sure, ceremonial elements do creep into these activities and even into the examinations which are presumed to test only the

---

erly speaking, it is the classical tradition that is "institutionalism," since it is a way of thinking which expresses a certain set of institutions. As a designation of the way of thinking which recognizes the decisive part played by technology in economic life the term "instrumentalism" is far more satisfactory.

technical adequacy of the preparation, a circumstance which is of great importance for the further analysis of ceremonial patterns. But the avowedly ceremonial character of the commencement exercises does not prevent their being taken seriously. However brilliant a young scholar may be and however genuine his contributions to the sum of human knowledge, the fact that he has not "taken his doctor's degree" is accounted a blemish on his character. As a well-known American sociologist once remarked, "It's easier to take the degree than to spend the rest of your life explaining why you didn't!"

Behind such a ceremony there looms the phenomenon of status. As we continually explain to the impatient young, that is the way the world is, and we are all bound by it willy-nilly. Each of us knows, as a scholar, that the quality of scholarship is all that counts. But not only is the world at large ignorant of such matters, its thinking is dominated by considerations of status to which each of us as an individual is therefore obliged to conform. The schools and colleges and even the industrial research organizations to the staffs of which young scholars naturally aspire are all under the necessity of "putting up a front." It is not enough for them to make a sincere effort to engage competent scientists and scholars; they must be able to boast that possession of a Ph.D. degree is a condition of membership in their organizations. That is what the community expects. Trustees and executive vice-presidents are impressed by considerations of rank; and consequently the universities are obliged to co-operate by conferring rank, and the young scholar must coöperate by achieving the rank which will enable college presidents and industrial executive officers to engage him without embarrassment.

Obviously this phenomenon of rank and status is a universal one. We sometimes call it "feudal," and so it is in the sense that feudal society was permeated by considerations of rank and status. But this is only the most general characterization of the feudal order. In this sense and to some degree all societies are "feudal." What distinguishes the feudal system of medieval Europe is the peculiar character of the particular system of status of which it was the manifestation. Modern Western society still contains many vestiges of those specific status relationships. But the organization of society in terms of some sort of system of rank is a universal phenomenon. All societies exhibit cases of it. The investigation of kinship systems and of divisions of rank and status along the lines of age, sex, occupation, and the rest, is one of the principal concerns of anthropologists and sociologists. In our own society the system is so bewilderingly complex and multifarious as to constitute one of the chief concerns of all individuals throughout their lives. The informal education of children, of which we often say that it is much more important after all than formal education, consists largely in learning who are the "right" people and why; but this concern is by no means limited to childhood. The first difficulty with which the young scholar will be confronted when he becomes a member of the staff to which he aspires, apparently in good standing since he has conformed to the requirement that he be a doctor of philosophy, is that of determining the source of the special influence exerted on the organization by certain of its older members, an influence which he sees at once can have no relation to scholarly achievement. This influence, he may eventually learn, derives from their descent from one of the "old families" of the region, or from their possession of large private means, circumstances which perhaps lead the trustees or executive vice-presidents to regard their beneficiaries as "one of themselves" in a sense that may not be true even of the president.

In contemplating these familiar aspects of our social life, many people cherish the belief that such cases are only minor deviations from "actual merit" which still remains the prevailing basis for discriminations of rank. After all, however spurious certain academic reputations may turn out to be, it still remains true that the scholarly attainments of Ph.D.'s as a group are greater than those of non-Ph.D.'s as a group. This belief is probably stronger in our own society than in any other, and it may have more justification in our own than in any other society. If so, the difference is very significant indeed for the future of industrial society and challenges serious investigation.[2] But to some degree it prevails quite generally and exemplifies two universal features of the ceremonial pattern of behavior. One is the "make-believe" character of ceremonial behavior by virtue of which distinctions of rank and status ape differences of technological competence. There is no people and no individual to whom technological competence is not a genuine reality. Consequently the greatest possible genuineness that can be imputed to any distinction of rank is the supposition that it coincides with technological reality. Anthropologists report that if a member of a primitive community be asked why the members of the community regard the cultivation of crops as "women's work," he will invariably reply that women are the only ones who can make crops grow. This state of mind is universal. Our own community cherishes the belief that only men can drive nails and only women can boil water without burning it, that only business men and generals can make decisions. Furthermore these are beliefs for which we are prepared to die. Vilhjalmur Stefansson reports that until quite recently European explorers in the arctic have believed so firmly that only a born Eskimo can build a snow igloo that in the absence of Eskimos they have shivered and died in oiled silk tents, apparently without even making the attempt to master this esoteric art which he offers to teach any boy of twelve by mail.

Such beliefs are not actuated by technological reality.

[2] See Chapter XI, below.

They pay reality the compliment of imputing it to ceremonial status, but they do so for the purpose of validating status, not that of achieving technological efficiency. The belief in the substantial identity of rank with actual competency implies, and means to imply, that it was considerations of actual competency which in the first place led to the recognition of the distinction of rank. But this is certainly not the case. Obviously the designation of Eskimos to build igloos and women to raise crops could never have resulted from any genuine trial in which Eskimos and women demonstrated their superior efficiency. The precise contrary is the case. The distinction of status was established first, and it was thereafter assumed to coincide with actual technological competency.

This is what Veblen called "ceremonial adequacy," meaning the determination of competence not by (technological) demonstration but by ritual. This second characteristic of status is also illustrated by the commencement ceremony. Such a ceremony is not merely a bit of pageantry, it is a particular kind of pageantry; or rather it is a pageant so directly inherited from the past and so fully preserved in its original form as to exhibit clearly the peculiar character of all pageantry. Clearly the commencement ceremony is an investiture—a quasi-sacrament. If we ask ourselves which of the seven sacraments of the Christian church it most closely resembles, there can be no doubt about the answer. It is a close approximation of the consecration of the priesthood, to which in historic fact it is closely related. The wearing of academic vestments, the recitation of a Latin liturgy, and the laying-on of the doctoral hood—all are clearly suggestive of the sacrament.

This is an extreme case, perhaps, and in view of its insignificance almost a frivolous one. Many distinctions of status which are of far greater importance in the life of the community are not accompanied by such a ceremony, or at least do not appear to be. The status of parents with reference to children, the "color line" by which Negro and white are distinguished, even the property distinction between owner and non-owner, and many other matters of rank and station, are of far greater moment than any academic degree, since they affect the whole community and in some cases all the activities of those who are affected. Outside the classroom and the laboratory a doctor of philosophy is just a common citizen; whereas children are children and Negroes are Negroes in all their affairs. Nevertheless students of the social sciences have long since recognized the ceremonial character of all these distinctions. Parents are not proved to be wiser than their children; they are so *de jure*. Negroes are not distinguished by any objective test of mind or body, not even color. Many Negroes are lighter than many "white" people. A Negro is by social definition a person either of whose parents was a Negro, likewise by social definition. An owner is not distinguished by intelligence, executive skill, or social conscience, but rather by legal investiture.

Moreover the ceremonial character of these distinctions is no mere invention of sociologists. In virtually every case it is in literal fact a matter of legal record. The registration of births, and marriages, and deeds, and of contracts generally, is the social mechanism by which distinctions of status are ceremonially established in modern society. This sort of thing may seem to be a far cry from the mystic rites of earlier societies, but the two ceremonial systems are in fact historically related. In a celebrated formula the great legal historian, Sir Henry Maine, declared that the whole movement of Western society has been "from status to contract." The difference is real and immensely significant; [3] but the continuity which underlies the change is no less real and significant. It was not flint-chipping from which contract evolved but status. The substance which is perpetuated

[3] See Chapter IX, below.

with modifications in the legal system of industrial society is that of status. Furthermore, the public records in which these distinctions are preserved are modifications of and substitutions for the sacraments. We have only to run over the original sacraments to see that what they consecrated was the ultimate basis of the distinctions which have since become secularized by the public record office and the civil law. This is true even of property, of which the original (feudal) basis of investiture was by birth, marriage, and death, each of which was the occasion of a sacrament by force of which alone the physical event became ceremonially adequate.

Lay readers and elementary students often get the impression from discussions of this sort that the purpose and to some extent the actual effect of scientific analysis of ceremonial patterns of behavior is only to "debunk" the distinctions under discussion; and this is especially true of a second major aspect of the ceremonial behavior function, that which is now generally identified, in America at least, by Sumner's term, "mores." But this is very far from being the case. The fact that distinctions of status are ceremonial does not mean that they do not exist nor that they are of negligible importance; and the fact that the prohibitions (and injunctions) by which all social life is ruled derive their sanction from tradition and their force from "public opinion" does not mean at all that such sanction and such force are of no effect in the behavior of "enlightened" people. Recognizing the very great force of community tradition, it is the object of social analysis to try to understand the nature of this force and the fashion in which it operates in the life of any given community and even more in the process of social change to which modern Western society is subject to such a notable degree.

In particular it is the object of social analysis to try to understand the relation between the different aspects or functions of social behavior. In *The Theory of the Leisure Class* Veblen was primarily concerned with status. In *Folkways* Sumner was primarily concerned with "mores." What is the relation between these matters each of which was the concern of a great modern classic? Neither Veblen nor Sumner raised this question, Sumner because he did not make a clear distinction between technological and ceremonial behavior functions,[4] and Veblen because he failed to recognize the "mores" as a universal characteristic of ceremonial behavior.[5] But once the question is raised its answer is seen to be close at hand. The "mores" of course follow the pattern of the system of status—follow not in the temporal sense (status first and then mores) but in the analytical sense of a behavior pattern which is in one of its aspects a system of status and in another a corresponding system of mores. The mores, according to Sumner, define what is "right" and what is "wrong," what one must do and what one must not do. But these distinctions differ for different people; that is, the mores define for any given person in any given station in life what such a person in such a station must do and must not do.[6]

What is important here is not merely the reduction of the

[4] This distinction is implicit in certain passages of *Folkways* in which Sumner was concerned to distinguish between "mores" and "folkways"; but it never becomes explicit and as a basis for distinction between "folkways" and "mores" it is contradicted by other passages.

[5] Indeed Veblen's (conjectural) derivation of status from the "warlike" and "predatory" bent of "the barbarian culture" suggests that he did not conceive it to have been a feature of the earlier and "peaceful" society of "the savage level of culture" and so did not regard it as universal. In this he was misled in part by mid-nineteenth-century anthropology (in which Rousseau's "noble savage" was still kept alive), and in part perhaps by the Marxian doctrine of class struggle. (Throughout Veblen's work there runs an implication that the common man is somewhat less addicted to ceremonial behavior than his masters, dynastic and capitalistic—an implication which contemporary social scientists would judge to be contrary to fact.)

[6] In the language of George H. Mead, they define the "role."

larger status-structures to mores-atoms; it is rather the character of the ceremonial-status behavior function which is still further revealed in the analysis of the mores by which status is defined. In recent years anthropologists have adopted two words from the Polynesian language to refer to the prohibitions and injunctions which Sumner lumped together. One of these, taboo, has come into general use. Common usage has even dulled the edges of taboo by using it with reference to the mild prohibitions of everyday life, but the word still retains some of the original connotation of horror and disgust. Thus we say that incest is taboo, using another person's toothbrush is taboo, and nude bathing is taboo on public beaches even for little boys. Few people view nude bathing by little boys with horror and disgust (the "ole swimmin' hole" is a distinctly romantic memory); but the use of another person's toothbrush is more or less disgusting. We rationalize these feelings by talk of hygiene, as we do also in the case of incest, but it is not the medical aspect of the case which gives rise to our feelings. We do not wait for the appearance of communicable disease before condemning the promiscuous use of toothbrushes, and we recognize nudity as an affront to decency even while we agree that the affront is mitigated by juvenility. The difference after all is one of degree.[7]

Degree of what? We should agree that in every case there is a loss of virtue, or of moral quality, but of different degrees in different cases; and these words also may serve as guides to social analysis. For both of them and all their

[7] This difference of degrees of heinousness is what confused Sumner's attempt to distinguish the "folkways" from the "mores." "Folkways" are traditional ways of doing things which are not "mores"; but some such acts, such as the instances cited above, differ from mores only in degree of heinousness, whereas others, such as swinging a hammer by the end of the handle, have no flavor of heinousness at all. In some passages Sumner seems to think of "folkways" as lesser "mores"; in others he seems to think of them as different in kind—*i.e.*, technological traditions. He never cleared up this confusion.

synonyms have the meaning not only of the distinction of right and wrong but also of moral character ("morale") and metaphysically unique individuality ("virtu"). We resent contamination of our toothbrushes as an infringement of personality. What we feel as a result of unceremonious exposure is a loss of personal integrity, even of force of character. After such an experience (say, accidental discovery in the nude) we feel that we "can't face" people. The oriental expression, "loss of face," is a graphic description of a universal experience, one which Polynesians would identify as of the essence of taboo; and the same is true of the Western phrase, "to feel small." It is as though individual personality or force of character were a quantitative matter, a mystic potency capable of being reduced by infractions of taboo. This is indeed the literal meaning of the mores. The whole ceremonial conception of life is one not merely of a distinction between what is and what is not to be done; it is also a conception of human personality in terms of mystic potency capable of being diminished by transgressions of the code.

This mystic potency is also capable of being increased. We gain in moral stature by scrupulous observance of the code and most particularly by "virtue" of ceremonial investiture. This is what the Polynesians call "mana," a word which has come into general use by anthropologists,[8] though not as yet by the lay public. "Mana" is the affirmative of that of which "taboo" is the negative. There are certain things which we are expected to do, the doing of which results in an access of virtue. Most specifically "mana" is the mystic potency which is thereby increased. It is literally absorbed from contact with the virtuous who (and which) are thus also said to possess "mana." In ceremonial investiture "mana" flows from the person of the shaman or from the sacred stone into the person of the chief, just as one "takes courage" from

[8] Chiefly through the influence of R. R. Marett. See especially *The Threshold of Religion* (London, 1914).

association with persons of superior courage. Among some primitive peoples the successful warrior appropriates to himself the mystic potency of his fallen enemy by cutting out his heart and eating it.

This sort of thing may seem at first to be utterly remote from modern life, but students of the social sciences are agreed that it is not. Modern society has inherited these ways of thinking and acting from ancient society, and they comprise a very large part of ordinary social behavior. The evidence of this is by no means limited to ceremonial expressions such as that of the public official who prefaces his declarations with the words, "By virtue of the authority vested in me." The whole system of status rests on the assumption that the different orders of society possess different degrees of mystic potency. It would be quite intolerable otherwise. A belief on the part of both whites and Negroes in some sort of ineffable difference is essential to the maintenance of the color line and unquestionably will continue so long as the line exists. The difference is one of mystic potency to which the investigations of geneticists, ethnologists, sociologists, and others, are quite irrelevant; and the same is true of the rich and the poor. Nothing is more touching to the sensibilities of the whole community, poor as well as rich, than the spectacle of a "gentlewoman" reduced to the necessity of manual labor; and nothing is more outrageous than that the unemployed should go to the movies or the "new rich" (current sarcasm for defense workers) employ servants.[9] Both instances are "out of character."

[9] "New Orleans matrons, hard put to find servants, laughed last week at the story of a housewife who went to the Negro slums to look for a cook. She asked two Negro women sitting on a rickety porch if they knew of one, was told: 'No, ma'am; we're looking for one ourselves.'" —*Time,* July 20, 1942, p. 13. The article continues, editorially, "In the U. S. conscience, with its original tincture of Puritanism, such things were troubling last week. . . . Somewhere in the thoughts of those who reveled and of those who stood aghast was probably the same thought. . . ."

In modern civilization the dependence of the whole system of status upon the mystic potencies of mana and taboo is concealed from common observation by the state and the law. Since all rights and obligations are defined by law, and since all titles to property, citizenship, and the like, derive ultimately from the state, this is ordinarily the end of the matter, especially in democratic communities where the state has come to be conceived as the will of the people. But social philosophers and students of jurisprudence must face the question, Why should the people will such things? What is the nature of exclusive possession, for example? How did it originate? Why has it become a feature of the legal systems of all peoples? These were the questions with which John Locke tried to deal in his celebrated *Treatises on Government*. It was his thesis that property relationships are "natural" and therefore antecedent to civil government because exclusive possession is established when man first mixes his labor with the soil. But just how is this done? In modern society a trespasser establishes no rights by raising crops on fields that are not his. Locke tried to extricate himself from this difficulty by distinguishing the "first" mixture as the determinant of a proprietorship which thereafter is transmitted in other ways; but of course the "original" appropriation is entirely supposititious. Furthermore the supposition is a suspiciously familiar one. Mixing one's labor with the soil is a kind of personality-projection of which students of primitive society find examples in every culture. Even today we speak of a person's "leaving the imprint of his personality" upon a room. The peculiar intimacy we impute to toothbrushes and to articles of clothing, especially those worn next the skin, is more than a matter of law. One's home has a more than legal significance. Indeed it is not at all uncommon for people to justify the institution of property in argument by reference to these personal intimacies as the ultimate essence of the relationship to which the law supplies only its institutional machinery.

Such justifications are essentially mystical—not so much natural as supernatural. What they exhibit is not rationality but "rationalization" as modern psychiatry understands that word. What they invoke is a spirit world of mystic potencies which act and react upon each other *as though* they were causal agents of the natural world. They can even be manipulated in quasi-causal fashion by magic rite and ceremony. It is in this fashion, of course, that transfer of title is effected. The potencies of the father flow into the son, in part at birth—as is evidenced by the mysterious but unmistakable resemblances between son and father—but in part at the father's death, on the occasion of which mana flows from father to son, actuated by the appropriate ceremonies, by virtue of which the son is empowered to buckle on his father's sword and "come into" his father's property.

All these ideas have indeed been watered down, in some cases almost to the vanishing point, by the institutional machinery of the modern state. Thus the transfer of property has become in modern law a matter of convenience adapted to and enforced by the exigencies of an industrial economy.[10] But if we inquire what it is that has been diluted, a ceremonial answer is inescapable. That is why Locke's analysis of property was unable to escape a paradoxical resemblance to the conception of divine right which had been presented by his antagonist, Sir Robert Filmer. Inevitably both are couched in terms of mystic potencies.

Under the influence of Sumner, modern social thinking has showed a disposition to identify all such matters as "conventional fictions" and to let it go at that. This misses the essential point. It is the most essential characteristic of fictions of every kind that they *seem* to be true. Ceremonial gains and losses of potency by virtue of which the status-

[10] See Chapter IX, below.

relations of all members of the community to each other are established seem to be effected by a series of causally effective acts. These magic rites and ceremonial investitures in every case simulate the materially effective causal sequences of the world of tools and materials. They are not merely non-technological; they are pseudo-technological. In his chapter on the "musical banks," in *Erewhon,* Samuel Butler described two currencies both of which were used in every business transaction, one the work-a-day currency in terms of which Erewhonians did business, and the other the musical bank currency some of which was always exchanged in connection with every transaction and which the people pretended was the real and effective medium of exchange. The difference is one of primacy. It is not a case of distinguishing between distinct entities, *a* and *b,* but of identifying the *a* with respect to which the other entity is *a′*. When this issue is raised, there can be no question about the answer. No one supposes that tool-using is effective because it simulates the goings-on of the spirit-world. On the contrary, it is the spirit-world in which the causal nexus of tool and material is simulated. It is not the examinations for the Ph.D. degree which pretend to the effectiveness of the commencement ceremony; it is the ceremony which pretends to the effectiveness of the examinations.[11]

This issue is fundamental to an understanding of economic process. It is the one posed by Professor Knight, that of "some . . . absolute and inscrutable type of 'causality' by which technology drags behind it and 'determines' other phases of social change." The study of technology has already exhibited the "absolute and inscrutable character" of technology to be a function of tools; and the analysis of

[11] Students of economics to whom this universe of discourse is unfamiliar would do well to read Hans Vaihinger's *The Philosophy of "As If"* (London and New York, 1924) and Dewey's *The Quest for Certainty.*

ceremonial behavior patterns clearly shows not that technology "drags" ceremonial behavior along in its wake but that ceremonial behavior of its own character invariably simulates, and in this sense follows, technological activity. In the process of social change a "drag" of some sort is a matter of common observation. Sociologists quite commonly employ the word "lag" to refer to this phenomenon. Far from being inscrutable, this also is an objectively verifiable feature of ceremonial behavior, quite as objective as a tool. Not only does ceremonial behavior determine status by the ritualistic transfer of mystic potencies; it does so by virtue of a set of beliefs of which all "ceremonial adequacy" is an expression, or in which the whole power-system of status and mores finds its supposed justification. The universally observed "archaism" of the ceremonial behavior function is an inevitable consequence of this third aspect of ceremonialism.

It is precisely because myths, legends, and beliefs are objective social phenomena that their existence has seemed enigmatic. Since they are objective phenomena, students of ancient cultures and simple peoples have been able to collect them, to arrange and classify and publish them much as anthropologists collect and arrange and exhibit primitive artifacts in museums. Moreover these legends have a sort of nostalgic charm, since they are after all relics of our own more or less distant past. In many cases their perpetuation has enlisted the most distinguished literary talent, so that they have thundered down the ages in the epic hexameters of the classic bards. Consequently they challenge explanation as a phenomenon in their own right.

But the attempts to explain the growth of legend as a distinct phenomenon have been embarrassingly fatuous. Since the legends themselves purport to be accounts of the creation of the universe and of the origin and history of the people whose legends they are, we have quite generally made the mistake of accepting them at face value as the genuinely intellectual attempts of simple peoples to "explain" themselves and the universe around them. In this we have been greatly aided by the condescension with which we have regarded "primitive mentality." By assuming that our ancestors were utter fools, we have been able to explain at the same time both the fantastic flights of imagination which these supposed attempts at explanation exemplify and also the stupid indifference of these peoples to the intellectual challenge of their own recent history and of the physical phenomena with which they are most closely surrounded. Thus we say that their mythology exhibits their intellectual curiosity with regard to the creation of the heavens and the earth, while their failure to ascertain whether putting fish in a bucket of water makes it heavier or not by weighing both procedures is due to their complete lack of intellectual curiosity.

Meantime all explanations of the "mythopoeic" faculty in terms of restless intellectuality overlook what is after all the most striking feature of all superstitious lore: its indissociability from the current ceremonial practices of the community. Myths, legends, and superstitious beliefs of every kind are invariably tied up with "mores" of which they are the purported explanation. So impressed was Sumner with this organic relationship that he made the existence of supporting legend one of the stigmata of the "mores" by which they are to be distinguished from mere "folkways." Unfortunately this also involved him in an enigma. If the "mores" be regarded as the primary phenomenon, beginning as community habits which eventually achieve the character of "mores" as a result of embodiment in legend, the question then arises, How and when are legends invented for the sanctification of habits? Sumner left this question unanswered (and it is one of the major confusions of *Folkways*), for of course it is unanswerable. Neither mores nor legends can be explained in isolation. Both are aspects of one behavior function. Ceremonial behavior implies the existence of a legend and a legend implies the existence of ceremonial behavior patterns.

This is what Emile Durkheim saw and expounded in his great book, *The Elementary Forms of the Religious Life.* Human behavior is collective behavior, and the whole conceptuology of legend and belief is "collective representation." Neither precedes and actuates the other or can possibly do so, since each is a function of the other. This functional relationship is one which the present generation is far better prepared to understand than that for which Durkheim wrote, thanks to the great advances which have been made during the past generation in the field of psychopathology. As we now appreciate, the psychopath is a myth-maker on his own account, and the mythopoeia of primitive peoples is a phenomenon of psychopathology in the most literal sense. Primitive communities frighten themselves into paroxysms; they warp and distort their conduct of life in the most fantastic fashion; and all the while they invent for themselves a conception of life and the world in terms of which their utmost extravagances seem to be a reasonable and efficacious organization of the affairs of life.[12]

The temptation is strong to speculate on the physical basis of ceremonial behavior, and especially on the role of emotion in status, mores, and mythology. Human beings are uniquely sensitive to each other's presence and emotional attitudes, so much so as to seem frequently to be in the grip of outside forces in the presence of which their own "wills" are virtu-

[12] Following the lead of Freud's pioneer essay, *Totem and Taboo,* a number of studies have appeared in which leading psychopathologists have applied their principles to the interpretation of ceremonial behavior and especially its legendary aspect. But perhaps the most thoughtful and temperate—least afflicted by the conjectural excesses to which psychoanalysts are liable—is by a layman, Everett Dean Martin (*The Mystery of Religion,* London and New York, 1924).

ally powerless. We still speak of emotional "seizures," and this sense of being overpowered by an outside force which it is futile to oppose is an accompaniment not only of rage and fear but also of love. The romantic novels of the present day talk about love very much as primitive peoples do, with only this important difference, that the savages act on their beliefs with philtres and incantations. Moreover they have this justification: strangely enough these emotional "seizures" can indeed be produced by the action of drugs and also by the mass-suggestion and autointoxication and hypnosis of dance and chant. We know that both drugs and incantation produce their effect by their action on the autonomic nervous and endocrine systems; but since the savages do not know this, it is after all small wonder that they should have conceptualized this whole complex of experiences quite universally in terms of an etiology of occult forces and a therapeutics of magic rite. In doing so they are only applying their intelligence to disturbances to which all human flesh is heir.

It is even possible to conjecture that the whole ceremonial behavior function by which human beings have made so much trouble for themselves throughout the ages is an organically inevitable joint-product of the same evolutionary process, the same refinement of the nervous (and perhaps endocrine) system which made speech and tool-using possible; that we could not have had these without at the same time becoming more susceptible to emotional disturbances (which, we must note, the lower animals also share in lesser degree). And at the same time the development of speech made it inevitable that we should give tongue to our emotions—an activity from which the lower animals are saved by their speechlessness, which also however excludes them from tool-using. In such an interpretation technological and ceremonial behavior would stand as in the most literal sense obverse and reverse of each other, both equally a consequence of evolutionary refinement of nervous organization, and both equally attributable to articulacy and so to intelligence, memory, imagination, and all the other most distinctively human "faculties." But this still does not mean that the two are one. As constructs—organized behavior systems—they are nevertheless distinct and opposed.

It is this opposition which is our primary concern, and especially as it affects the development and conduct of the industrial economy. In that process the ceremonial behavior system is opposed to technological activity in this sense, that whereas technology is of its own character developmental the ceremonial function is static, resistant to and inhibitory of change. We still know very little of the origin either of speech and tool-use or of legend, ritual, and status; but we know a great deal about their history. In particular, we know that they have a history, and this is most especially true of the mythopoeic aspect of the ceremonial function. The very objectivity of legend, which has so confused our attempts to understand the nature of this activity as such, has greatly assisted our study of its history. Because legends have an objective existence and can be collected and arranged, students of folklore have been able to learn a great deal about their history.

All legends derive from the past. The arts of the poet and the dramatist embellish them, but their narrative and ideational content is given and inalterable. This is what makes it possible to trace folk history through legend, and this is what makes the ceremonial behavior system, of which legend is an indissociable part, of its own character "archaic," backward-looking, static, change-resisting. Legend recounts the drama of the ancestors, and the ancestors are dead-and-gone and therefore inalterably fixed. What the ancestors did and said, what was done and said in the creation of the heavens and the earth, is not subject to tinkering; and since it is the legends which motivate the mores and the mores which define all the roles of rank and status, it follows inevitably that the whole ceremonial behavior-complex is essentially static. It is so not because any single ceremonial act is soul-freezing—cataleptic—in any absolute and inscrutable fashion, but because the behavior-system of which any such act is a derivative is—as a system—past-preserving.

This does not mean that ceremonial behavior-systems do not change. We know they do. But the changes which occur do not originate in or derive from the legend-mores-status complex itself. The "Argonauts" of the Pacific sailed great distances from island-group to island-group because of the technological perfection of their outrigger canoes, on each occasion, probably, against the direst imprecations of the medicine men. Not being ideological revolutionaries, they took their ceremonial system with them. But their adoration of the banyan tree (or whatever it may have been) would necessarily suffer some modification in a habitat where there were no banyan trees. At the same time contact with other peoples would lead to partial assimilation of their ancestors and ceremonial system. Children of American immigrants from southeastern Europe learn Mrs. Hemens' poems in school and assimilate the "Pilgrim fathers" as their ancestors. This does not mean that the legends of southeastern Europe are in evolution in the direction of British Puritanism, nor that the latter is developing an affinity for the mores of southeast European peasantry. Both legendary backgrounds are rigid and stiff-kneed. But people move with technology, and ceremonial practices are changed by changing circumstances which are quite external to them. Of themselves they do not change. Whatever the complexion of the ceremonial system may be, following a technology-induced change of physical habitat, it is reminiscent of some *status quo ante;* and it is as resistant to further change, however ineffectively, as was the original from which, however fragmentarily, it was derived. The most tragic feature of American democracy today is the widespread determination of its adherents that it shall continue throughout an indefinite future to be precisely what it was to the "founding fathers."

The history of the human race is that of a perpetual opposition of these forces, the dynamic force of technology continually making for change, and the static force of ceremony—status, mores, and legendary belief—opposing change. Most of the time and in most parts of the world status has prevailed. In the whole history of the race there have been only a few world technological revolutions. One of these, perhaps, was the spread of neolithic culture. Another was the spread of agricultural civilization. The industrial revolution may be another, though its success and permanence are by no means assured. As Veblen remarked in a celebrated passage, it still remains to be proved whether machine technology will prevail or whether our civilization will provide another tragic instance of "the triumph of imbecile institutions over life and culture." [13]

[13] *The Instinct of Workmanship* (New York, 1914), p. 25. See also the concluding paragraph of Vol. III of J. H. Clapham's *Economic History of Modern Britain* (Cambridge, 1926-1938).

Chapter IX

TECHNOLOGY AND INSTITUTIONS

DID INSTITUTIONS such as those of business enterprise, democracy, Puritanism, and the like "make possible" the development of the industrial economy? That has been the traditional belief. There is a sense in which that belief is true. But there is a more important sense in which it is quite false. The difference is between active and passive agents. If the institutional structure which prevailed in western Europe prior to the industrial revolution of the past five centuries or so had been sufficiently solid and rigid to inhibit technological change, then it goes without saying that the change would not have occurred. Since the industrial revolution did occur, obviously the institutional structure which it confronted was insufficiently solid to prevent change. That structure was a causally significant part of the total situation; but its significance was —and consequently is still—permissive, not dynamic. To attribute the total process solely or even primarily to the agency of institutions is equivalent to attributing a crime wave to the weakness of the forces of law and order. There is, after all, a significant difference between committing a crime and failing to prevent its commission; and there is an equivalent difference between the permissive responsibility of the institutions of western Europe for the changes of the past five centuries and the active agency of technological development of which those changes were and still are the direct expression.

This difference can be understood only in terms of the nature of social institutions. No word is more frequently or more vaguely used in contemporary social science than "institution." Some such word is of course indispensable. All social behavior is continuous with all other social behavior, but the analysis of this whole must resolve it into parts of some sort. That is what analysis means. The whole is a complex of individual acts, or of "folkways and mores." But these are prodigiously numerous. To proceed from the social whole without any intermediate level of generalization to the vast ruck of particular folkways would be equivalent to proceeding from the organism as a whole to the level of generalization of cytology without any intermediate morphology. Some sort of division of the social whole into parts is inevitable, and for this the familiar "institutions" stand ready to hand. For many centuries the church, the state, and the family have been recognized as more or less distinct foci of social activity, and common parlance has always identified them as institutions. Modern social science has therefore—perhaps unavoidably—taken over these institutions as the basis of social morphology.

The list of course does not end here. Property has always been regarded as an institution, and the proliferation of social activities in the modern community has provided many instances of more or less clearly identifiable foci which are now quite distinct from family, church, and state, such as educational, recreational, and eleemosynary institutions. Proceeding in this fashion social scientists have come to regard an "institution" as any subdivision of the social whole and so to identify as institutions such different features of modern life as the city, science, divorce, machine technology.

In this fashion the meaning of the term "institution" has become progressively vague; for it is abundantly evident that the family, science, and the city, for example, are anything but co-ordinate. The family, the church, and the state are centers of activity in which virtually all members of the community participate, whereas the city is a category by which certain individuals, its residents, are distinguished from all others. The activities to which the terms "family," "church," and "state" make reference are more or less distinct in time and place in the lives of their participants. Family life centers in an edifice, the home, and is more or less concentrated into non-working hours. People go to (a) church (building) on Sunday. Educational and recreational activities are more or less co-ordinate in the sense that children also go to school (buildings) from nine to three, and in the evenings go to the "movie" (theater). But is "science" something that one does on certain days, something that one "goes to"? Or machine technology?

The confusion with regard to the nature of institutions would be less if the word were an exclusively scientific term invented *ad hoc* to designate any cluster of activities of whatever character. Such a term is sorely needed. Phrases such as "activity cluster," or "organizational structure," are both cumbersome and stilted, and in the absence of any other term it is not surprising that the word "institution" should have been overloaded. But it is unfortunate, nevertheless; for it is inevitable that this word should retain something of the meaning with which it was imbued through its original association with the family, the church, and the state, with the result that the designation of such "organizational structures" as the city, or machine technology, as "institutions" carries the quite unfortunate implication that they are just such structures as the family and the state, which is certainly not true.

These original or basic institutions are something more than structural subdivisions of the social whole. They also have functional peculiarities in common which give them their common tone and color, and mark them off, functionally as well as structurally, from the undifferentiated mass of social behavior. It is sometimes said that the family, for example, is an organizational structure which society has set up for the nurture and education of children. Such a description is clearly technological, since its reference is to medical, dietetic, and sanitary considerations, and to the intellectual techniques of language mastery, the use of elementary tools (buttons, safety pins, and the like). All this is quite false. The family was not "set up" in this sense at all, certainly not as an efficiency device for getting certain sorts of work done. On the contrary, it is notoriously inefficient—judged by technological standards—and in consequence of its inefficiency these activities have been organized in other ways to a steadily increasing degree.

The functional meaning of the family was never better described than in the much-quoted remark of Robert Frost's "hired man": "Home is where if you got to go there, they got to take you in." The family is a power-system through the medium of which rights and duties are defined: those of husbands with regard to wives, and vice versa; those of parents with regard to children, and vice versa; and to a less degree (at least in modern Western society) the privileges and obligations of an indefinite series of remoter relatives. Family life is a focus of mores to a notable degree—to such a degree, indeed, that we often use the word "immoral" to designate specifically sexual (that is to say, familial) infractions of the code. It is quite true that certain activities of a technological character, such as nurture and education, do occur under the auspices of the family; but they do so as a consequence of the rights of parents to the persons of their children and the rights of children to be supported according to their station in life. If anyone doubts this, let him apply to a court for the custody of some other person's child on the ground of a difference of opinion with regard to dietary or educational procedure. He will soon discover that it is the sacred right of parents to malnourish and miseducate their children.

The same is true of all the original or basic institutions. Property is sometimes described in textbooks as a device for the organization of the physical equipment of the community for purposes of production, in spite of the evidence of the vacant lot which the pupils habitually cross on their way to school. The conception of the state as having been "set up" for the organization of certain types of activity was once so widely held as to have earned a special designation: the theory of "social contract." But no modern political scientist adheres to that theory. On the contrary, it is now generally agreed among political scientists that the state is "the supreme coercive power," and that its origin is to be sought in the legends of mystic powers defining arbitrary status which go back to the very "beginning" of civilization.

Not only are these explicitly ceremonial functions of the original and basic institutions clearly recognized by all contemporary students of social organization; it is these functions which are imputed to all social activity by the indiscriminate use of the term "institution" to designate all subdivisions of the social whole. Because the institutional prototypes have a penumbra of legend, many sociologists proceed to speak of science as the legendary penumbra of modern Western civilization; and because the prototype institutions are clusters of mores, by which among other things occupations are defined, many sociologists speak of the division of labor in the modern industrial economy as though there were no qualitative difference between specialization in the use of tools and the mores-dedication of men to hunting and women to agriculture.

No doubt modern civilization merits a certain amount of cynicism. The jurisdictions of certain crafts have become "institutionalized," and in many respects modern society has indeed made a fetich of science. But to recognize these truths is only to emphasize the realities of which they are falsifications. It is outrageous that a carpenter should have to be called to bore a hole through which an electrician may then be (institutionally) empowered to pass a wire; and it is outrageous that the general belief in the achievements of the physiology of nutrition (combined with general ignorance) should make it possible for a scoundrel to market sea water at $1.25 a glass as a remedy for "mineral deficiencies."[1] Nevertheless no one would assert that such incidents tell the whole story of scientific research and technological specialization. Indeed, no careful analyst would attribute these practices to science and technology. If the public "legendizes" science, surely that is because of our age-old indoctrination with superstition; and if the craft unions "institutionalize" certain occupational procedures, surely that is a phenomenon of status rather than a function of tools and skills.

What is at issue here is more than a mere matter of terminology. The confusion of the structural with the functional significance of institutions in the current literature of the social sciences has led to a confusion of technological with ceremonial behavior functions, and this confusion has blocked our understanding of the process through which the institutions of modern industrial society have been undergoing modification. As organization structures, or (structurally conceived) segments of social behavior, "primary" institutions such as the family must be understood to contain tool-activities as well as ceremonial usages. But the peculiar quality of these particular foci of activity is unquestionably ceremonial. The family is a behavior complex in which the

[1] *Time,* June 29, 1942, p. 66.

nurture and education of children is subordinated to the mores of the husband-wife and parent-child relationships, as are all the other activities which the mores of any given community relegate to this particular status-system; and the same is true of the church, the state, the secret societies of primitive communities, and an educational system which makes instruction contingent upon saluting the flag and has as one of its principal functions the segregation of children between the conventional hours of nine to three.

In the same sense couvade, circumcision, and ownership are institutional in character since, although they are not co-ordinate with the "primary" institutions as major segments of community life, they are of the same character as the family-church-state complexes. Whether the city is an institution in this sense is extremely doubtful. Fustel de Coulanges undertook to treat the city as an organism, just as the sociologists of his time proposed to regard society as an organism; but most contemporary social scientists would agree that the metaphor was greatly overplayed in both cases. Does the city have the institutional character of family or state? To some degree, perhaps, city life has developed a characteristic set of mores and status relationships which do not prevail elsewhere and may therefore be regarded as institutionalized, but only to a very slight degree. The differences between one concourse of people and another are quite as marked as the resemblances. Are Altoona, Washington, and New York three instances of the same phenomenon? One may venture to doubt it.

Is science an institution? To some degree even science has become institutionalized as "something to conjure with" in modern society. Scientists as members of a profession have been institutionalized by advertising artists who always picture them vested in ceremonial robes of white and surrounded with occult paraphernalia—microscopes, test tubes, and Kjeldahl flasks. Some scientists have contributed to this process of institutionalization by the air of mystery and supernal authority which they assume on their public appearances. But do these performances derive from the nature of science, or from other and more explicitly institutional heritages? Individual scientists may behave like bullroarers outside the laboratory, and particular scientific procedures may become institutionalized in the community; but surely science as a mode of behavior is qualitatively different from respectable family life. And the same is true of technology. Particular techniques and individual artists or artisans may become institutionalized. But surely the institutionalization of agriculture, for example, as an occupation of women in primitive society is dictated by the mores of family life rather than by the nature of the tools and skills employed.

Words, too, are tools. We must not assume that the word "institution" *must* be used in any particular fashion. To do so would be to institutionalize it. But if it is to be a tool, it must cut. It must distinguish something or other from something else. To apply the word "institution" to every sort of activity and behavior function is to destroy its cutting edge altogether, and thereby to reduce its use to that of a much coarser word-tool such as "part" or "subdivision," with which we are already adequately equipped.

If we use the word "institution" to refer to those behavior structures which have the qualities of those structures with regard to the identification of which as institutions all students agree—family, church, and state—that is, segments of social behavior predominantly ceremonial in character, it becomes obvious at once why we persist in imputing so much potency to institutions. Not to do so is impious. As good parents and citizens, devout communicants and respectable property owners, we are obligated by the mores to believe that a separation of children from parents, or of property from owners, must be followed by disaster (probably a blight upon all the tribal crops), and that all good things result from the assiduous practice of the institutional mores. This is the institutional imperative. Members of the holy order of canoe-builders may use flint scrapers in hollowing out a log and they may know just what flint to use for every part of the job; but they must believe that it is their consecration to the order and most particularly the liturgy of the shark's teeth by virtue of which their technological efforts are ceremonially adequate.

It is in this spirit that we have attributed modern industrial progress to the institutions of Western society. In doing so we have overlooked none of the ancient shibboleths. Credit goes to property of course, but also to the family which provides the pattern of inheritance and employment and the incentive to industry and thrift, to the state which guarantees the titles to property and supplants feudal privilege, and even to the church which lends unprecedented dignity to the business man and for the first time sanctifies the accumulation of wealth. The phrase with which we do honor to the institutional structure of modern industrial society, "free private enterprise," recognizes all these sanctities. It is "free" by virtue of the state, "private" according to the familial pattern of ownership, and "enterprising" in the sense of the Christian parable of the talents.

Nevertheless it is a matter of common observation that all institutional ties and sanctions have been progressively weakened in modern Western society. Would anyone deny that the influence of the church has steadily diminished throughout modern times, or that the family is much less potent now than formerly? The cases of the state and property are not so clear, perhaps. To many students these seem to be the dominant institutions of the present age.[2] Nevertheless even these institutions, which do incontestably bestride the modern world, show many signs of having under-

[2] The role of these institutions in the present crisis is discussed in Chapter XIII, below.

gone internal modification—a process of secularization, as it were, in the course of which the original mystic sanctions have been overlaid with such a tremendous proliferation of administrative machinery as to effect a marked alteration in the character of the institutions themselves, an alteration of character which is also observable in church and family. Although authority and status have by no means disappeared from modern family life, it is certainly true that efficient teamwork plays a much larger part in the activities of the contemporary home than ever before. There is less insistence today than at any previous time upon status-determined rights and occupations and more concern for efficient co-operation. The church also has by no means abandoned its sacerdotal functions, and some church leaders are vehement in their insistence that these are the only true functions of the church; but the occasion for their insistence is the steady growth in importance and volume of quite another type of activity and interest, that of the community center and welfare agency.

These changes signalize the impact of technology upon the institutions of Western society. It is a mistake to think of this process as a direct challenge or even collision. The growth of technology is always surreptitious and apologetic. Thus, for example, scientists have always protested that they have no quarrel with religion. The astronomer only insists that the creation of the earth cannot be conceived to have occurred in six literal solar days, the geologist that a disturbance capable of parting the waters of the Red Sea would also have prevented the passage of the hosts of Israel; but each protests that he does so only in the interest of "true" religion and not in a spirit of antagonism at all. The same protests have been uttered all along the line. Historians inform us that the burghers of the early modern towns insisted that they had no thought of opposing, let alone destroying, the feudal system of medieval society; their only wish was to be allowed to live and to pursue their own interests in their own way. That change nevertheless comes about is due almost altogether to the alteration of the physical conditions of life which technology effects. If superstition plays less part in modern life than formerly, that is due not so much to the "conversion" of the mind of the community as to the incidence of sanitation by virtue of which modern life is less nasty, brutish, and short than formerly and hence somewhat less subject to superstitious mass hysteria. But even changes of mind are the result of a similar process. An invention which was made in order to facilitate the reproduction of religious tracts resulted in flooding Europe with books; and a community which learned to read in order to have direct access to Holy Writ ended by reading books on dietetics.

Thus technological development forces change upon the institutional structure by changing the material setting in which it operates. But the adaptation does not involve a change in the character of the ceremonial residue which survives the change. There is no such thing as an institution (or a set of institutions) that is "appropriate" to a given technology in any but a negative sense. The disappearance of armor may have resulted in the disappearance of the institution of chivalry. As G. G. Coulton remarks:

> When the Hundred Years' War brought a real national conflict between England and France, when archery became of supreme importance, and a large proportion even of the cavalry were mercenary soldiers, then the exigencies of serious warfare swept away much of that outward display and those class-conventions on which chivalry had rested.[3]

He also remarks in the same passage that "at least as early as the middle of the 13th century"—the time when European society is supposed by some of our contemporaries to have been so thoroughly integrated—"the commercial side

[3] *Encyclopædia Britannica,* 14th edition, XIII, 434.

of knighthood became very prominent," especially through the sale of well-born daughters. With the progress of the industrial revolution other forms of assets became more important and the family complex sloughed off much of its feudal substance, including the class-valuation of daughters. But inheritance remains as a feature of the modern institutional structure; and as such it is a sheer feudal vestige performing no useful (industrial) function whatever and "better adapted" to the present technological scene than chivalry only in the sense that is also true of the system of patronymics: it has not yet fallen so directly afoul industrial technology as to have become intolerable.

It is this process of dilution and attenuation to which the institutions of Western society have been subjected by the industrial revolution. The changes they have undergone signify in part a reduction of the importance of these institutions in modern life. By creating machinery for the more efficient performance of certain industrial operations technological development has resulted in the shift of those activities, for example, from the home to industry. This has the unintended but nevertheless considerable effect of diminishing the importance of the family as an institution. There has also been a reduction of the ceremonial content of the institutions themselves, accompanied by a proliferation of technical organizational mechanisms in the same area. Thus the reduction of the feudal substance of inheritance has been accompanied by a proliferation of organizational devices for the conveyancing of property by virtue of which industrial society has been able to tolerate a vestige of that institution without seriously affecting the continuous operation of industry. But the ceremonial content which is still retained must nevertheless be identified as pure atavism. The transmission of property from father to son, etc., is no more "adapted" to the exigencies of machine production than bull-roaring.

The discussion of the specific institutional changes which have accompanied the industrial revolution has been greatly hampered by the language which conventional usage has prescribed. Concepts such as "individualism," "freedom," "privacy," and "enterprise" are not only vague; they are tendentious and ambiguous. Each of these words has two sets of meanings one of which is regarded with general approval but is non-institutional in character, while the other is institutional in character but is not the object of general approval. Thus freedom, for example, is a splendid thing, if we mean by it the abolition of serfdom. But that is a negative condition. We often think of it in terms of seemingly affirmative "rights": equality before the law, habeas corpus, jury trial, and the like. But these rights, precious as they are, do not confer any positive benefit. As has so frequently been pointed out, freedom from serfdom or even chattel slavery may actually mean freedom to starve; while equality before the law is purely juridical in the sense that it does not by any means extend the law's reliefs on equal terms to all citizens. It only abolishes serfdom. This is a great boon for which much blood was shed in earlier centuries, and is therefore greatly to be cherished. But it is a relief from institutional tyrannies of the feudal past, and as such it is a result, not a cause, of industrial revolution.

There is another sort of freedom which is positive and substantial; but it also owes nothing to any institution. If we think of freedom in terms of freedom of movement, we may mean one or the other of two things. Serfs and slaves are not free in this respect. The abolition of the institutional restraints to which they have been subject in this respect may be a great relief, but it does not endow them with the faculty of movement. But this has been done, for example, by the invention of the automobile, and quite without benefit of any institutional sanction. That is, the automobile has in fact greatly increased the movement of virtually the whole community. This sort of expansion of the limits of possible action has been very considerable throughout modern times and has affected many aspects of life. Obviously it is not the result of any sort of institutional sanction. No authority has been extended to the twentieth-century community to move about. Movement has occurred because it is now technologically possible, and for no other reason. This sort of freedom, also, is highly prized. Few would care to return to the activity-limits of, say, colonial America. But what we prize in this regard also is institutionally negative in the sense that it is not owed in any direct and demonstrable sense to any institution.

There is another sort of freedom which is clearly institutional in origin. The rich enjoy degrees and qualities of freedom which are not shared by the poor. These advantages are positive and substantial. The rich are not merely freed from inhibitions; they are endowed with potentialities of actual experience which do not exist for the poor. They are free to spend their winters in Florida and their summers cruising in the Mediterranean. Over and above the negative equality before the law which all citizens enjoy, they are free to give bail and to employ astute counsel. In this sense of their ability to escape the consequences of their acts, they are even free to commit crimes. The reality and immensity of this freedom is beyond question. Furthermore it is obviously a perquisite of status. Conceived solely in terms of wealth without any reference to the historic class-division of society, it still flows directly from the institution of property. But it does not enjoy the approval of the community. When we sing hymns to freedom we are not rejoicing that the rich have advantages not shared by the poor. "My Country, 'tis of thee, sweet land of liberty," does not make reference to this phenomenon.

The concept of individualism is still further confused by metaphysical connotations. Since "individuality" partakes of the nature of the Ultimate Reality, whatever that may be, the highest accolade which any social order can receive is that it safeguards and develops "individuality," and the most damning criticism is the charge that the hated regime "sacrifices individuality" to some institutional Moloch. Thus the most grievous fault of National Socialism is said to be that it subordinates the individual to the state. In discussing other societies than their own, and their enemy's, students of the social sciences are agreed that all societies do this—indeed, that the distinction between the individual and society is artificial and invalid. Nevertheless, individualism, like freedom, has various concrete meanings which can be distinguished readily with results quite different from prevailing belief.

There is a concrete sense in which the Protestant Reformation may be discussed in terms of individualism. The vital issue between Protestantism and Catholicism is the one which used to be known among Protestants as "popery"; that is, the Protestant churches began by challenging the authority of the Church of Rome. Since they of course retained the Bible and the essential Christian beliefs in the messiahship of Christ, the vicarious atonement, etc., the (negative) elimination of papal authority could be and was stated affirmatively in terms of individual access to the Bible and to direct communion with God. But Protestantism added nothing to Christian liturgy or creed. It must not be supposed that Catholicism attached no importance to the Bible or to conscience. Indeed, the common belief that Christianity as such and throughout its history is pre-eminent among the religions of the world for its solicitude for (metaphysical) individuality stands as a contradiction to the supposition that solicitude for individuality began with Protestantism. What individualism means in the Protestant connotation is therefore wholly negative: it means the denial of the authority of the pope, or "Rome."

Conceived as a severance of institutional ties the Protestant Reformation was clearly an aspect of a much more general severance. It developed in those regions and among the people—the middle-class burghers of the late medieval towns—whom the early phases of the industrial revolution had placed in a position of confrontation to the feudal order generally. These citizens did not invent for themselves *de novo* a new culture, nor had they any thought of doing so. They were in origin and therefore in thought and feeling Europeans and Christians; but they were also, as Pirenne so graphically says, *déracinés,* and they found themselves in possession of an instrument of great power, the incipient machine technology. The assertion of their power in the face of challenge by feudally vested authority obliged them to challenge that authority and to detach themselves from it, ecclesiastically no less than politically. Thus the assertion by Protestants of the primacy of "individual conscience" in the religious life, however great and precious an achievement it may have been, was institutionally negative in the sense that it did not of itself enrich the lives of communicants; it only (however important this may have been) released them from previously prevailing institutional inhibitions.

Their lives were positively and substantially enriched, and in this quite different sense the individualities may be taken to have been expanded, by the same forces of industrial revolution of which the Reformation was one expression and the Bill of Rights another. That is, learning to read, getting more to eat, wearing stockings, living in heated and more or less decently ventilated houses, losing the dread of typhus, cholera, and even leprosy, may all be described as enrichment of personality. But it is enrichment of a very different kind from that represented by the Protestant Reformation, and to regard these two "individualisms" as identical in the sense that the whole enrichment was achieved once and for all when the authority of the pope was successfully challenged is simply to confuse the issues.

Both of these "individualisms" were the effects, negative and positive, of industrial revolution. But there is still another sense in which that term may be used to refer to a change which was clearly institutional. Just as the breakdown of papal authority left conscience and the Bible as the central realities of the religious life, so the breakdown of family and class left the institution of property as the central reality of economic and even political life; and in this case also the sanction which remained was exercised by persons. This may not be sheer coincidence. There may be some general law of institutional decomposition by virtue of which the collapse of a power-system always takes the course of decentralization. But whether this is true or not, it is certainly true that the power of wealth which followed and supplanted the feudal system (in which that power was merged with family ties, class structure, and all the rest) was not a creation of the Protestant way of religious life. It was a derivative of the feudal power-system, an institutional residue which remained when other aspects of that system had vanished and so occupied a central position in the resultant institutional structure.

The power of wealth is certainly a positive and substantial phenomenon, and it may be conceived as an expansion of "individuality." It is certainly institutional in character and origin, and related to the other institutional residues of modern society. But to regard Protestant "individualism" as the source, or cause, of wealth "individuality" is to misconceive the whole process of which both were exemplifications. No Christian needs to be persuaded that Christian theology has no special affinity for wealth, any more than the teachings of Jesus afford any special basis for the hierarchical power-system of feudal society. The medieval church was feudal not because it was Christian but because it was the church of feudal Europe; and the modern church is capitalistic, Catholic no less than Protestant, because it is the church of capitalism. The functional relationship between church and the other features of the institutional structure of society is older than capitalism and is neither the cause nor the result of the rise of money-power. Both owe their importance in modern society to the changes wrought by industrial revolution, and both derive their substance from an older institutional structure in which they also played a part though a somewhat different one.

The institution upon which by general agreement the institutional weight of the modern economy chiefly rests is that of property. Property is sometimes described as a modern innovation, but this is true only in a very limited and special sense. The institutional structures of all societies have a property aspect,[4] although it is nowhere else as fully separated from family, state, and church as in modern Western civilization. That is, the behavior-system of every community contains a cluster of mores which define the fashion in which certain articles and instruments are thought to be imbued with the personality of their "owner," as we would call him, specifying the powers he exercises with respect to them and the limits to be observed by others by which they are sometimes forbidden even to touch or see specified articles.[5]

These mores, it goes without saying, are most explicit and detailed in their specifications of patterns of behavior having to do with the tools upon the use of which the livelihood of the community chiefly depends, since the supreme coercive power is power over the essential instruments of production. In a locally self-sufficient agricultural economy such as that of feudal Europe, land is of course the most

[4] For an outstanding discussion of the universality of property, see R. H. Lowie's chapter on "Property," in *Primitive Society* (New York, 1920).

[5] Ernest Beaglehole, *Property: A Study in Social Psychology* (London, 1931).

essential instrument of production, control of which means power to exploit the whole community heritage, as Veblen said, of technological ways and means. This pattern of control coincided, as it always does, with the pattern of feudal relationships generally. Ownership is never absolute. The most exclusive pre-emptive rights may be qualified by inalienability. The "owner" may be authorized by the mores to prohibit any other person from any use whatever of a given article (as current mores justify one in refusing the use of a wedding ring even to the dearest friends and closest relatives) and at the same time the owner himself may lack the power to dispose of it (as is also the case with wedding rings). It is the fact that feudal property (that is, the essential property rights in land) was subject to entail that prompts some students to draw a hard and fast line between feudal fief and industrial property. This is the point at which the greatest change occurred between the mores of feudal and commercial society. But the change must not be allowed to obscure the continuity. Only the permanent changes! It would be impossible to define property even today exclusively in terms of conveyancing, since there must be something which is conveyed. If we go beyond the very great differences of transfer to the mores which define that which is transferred, the continuity of modern with feudal property rights is undeniable; and what is most continuous is the focus of each set of property mores upon the essential instruments of production.

The point is that the change in the alignment of property rights from feudal to commercial society followed a change in the instruments of production. If we are to suppose that it was the evolution of the modern pattern of property rights which "made possible" the development of machine technology, we must suppose that this development preceded the appearance of machine technology and worked itself out within the range of instruments of production of feudal society. But plainly such was not the case. What actually occurred was a development of industry and commerce by virtue of which new instruments and materials so progressively overshadowed the products of feudal agriculture and the manorial economy that the feudal community became increasingly dependent upon the newly burgeoning industry and commerce, with the result that feudal fief progressively diminished in importance until it ceased to represent "supreme coercive power." It was not the feudal instrument of production which was first freed from entail and made subject to conveyancing. On the contrary, entail has persisted even into the twentieth century. The property which passed from hand to hand in medieval and early modern commerce consisted of chattels, and the process of evolution was one in which the importance of chattels gradually superseded the importance of land as a consequence of the character and volume of the chattels, which in turn was a consequence not in the first instance of alterations in the mores but of technological development, a development which of course must be taken to include revolutions in the technology of transport such as the one pointed out by Lefebvre des Noëttes. As an instance of the impact of technology on institutions this change runs true to form. What resulted from the earliest stages of the industrial revolution was a change in the material conditions of life in the course of which a shift in the technological center of gravity inevitably occurred. A land economy became a chattel economy, with the result that chattel-mores became paramount and land-mores progressively inconsequential, until one had virtually absorbed the other.

But the mores even of chattel-transfer had the character of an institutional heritage. The medieval merchants did not "institute" transfer of property as an *ad hoc* invention "better adapted" to their activities than the institutions of feudalism. Chattel property had existed throughout feudal times, as it does in all societies. This is what the textbooks have reference to when they say that the institution of property existed but played only a minor role in feudal society. They can manage to ignore the property aspects of feudal fief, but they cannot altogether deny the existence of disposable objects even in the heyday of feudalism. However, the carry-over of institutional patterns from the feudal to the commercial power-system was by no means limited to chattel property. It is of the essence of modern property rights that "a man's home is his castle." This phrase has been repeated so often and for so long a time that it has lost its original and literal connotation, but its true meaning is contained in the literal significance of the constituent words. In medieval times fugitive serfs and uprooted men of every degree established themselves in faubourgs where they proceeded not to invent institutions "adapted" to their way of life but rather to arrogate to themselves as much of the feudal institutional order as could be invoked under the circumstances. In particular they sought to invest their burgher homes with all the inviolability of the feudal castle: the right of security from search and seizure, the right not to have soldiers quartered on them without their consent, the right to dictate the terms of employment which obtained beneath their roofs—that is, the rights of masters with reference to servants.

Far from relegating feudal property-mores to the dust-heap of superannuated things the modern institution of property derives its substance from the past and carries over into the machine age a quite surprising amount of feudal baggage. Since the faubourg home of the merchant and master-journeyman was not in fact a feudal fief, it was free from the outset of the feudal qualification of entail and so was quite as disposable as any chattel; and since it was nevertheless a home it was able to arrogate to itself the most inviolable sanctities of feudal fief, advantages which the feudal baronage had managed to establish only by force of arms. This happy combination of rights and privileges, sanctified by immemorial tradition and reaffirmed in modern law, has been perpetuated into the machine age in which the artificial and, as the French say, anonymous personalities of corporations exercise over vast industrial principalities a system of rights and authorities which had its immediate origin in the feudal castle. Indeed, the odor of the castle still pervades the corporate atmosphere.

But to do justice even to textbooks, it is not this system of rights which is commonly held to be the institutional foundation of machine industry, but rather the extraordinary flexibility of the modern institution of property and to an even greater degree of the modern corporation. As an organizational device unquestionably the modern corporation is far better adapted to the exigencies of large-scale machine production than individual proprietorship or partnership. But what makes it so is a matter of administrative technique. No time need be wasted in the discussion of the technical aspect of administration. In recent years it has become the subject of a large and highly specialized literature and is now recognized as a special field of study both by political scientists and by students of business administration. It is a machine phenomenon par excellence. The machinery of personnel administration, of stock-taking and inventory control, of efficiency management and cost accounting, of physical distribution and transportation, sales organization, bill collection—everything connected with the operation of a modern concern—is highly technical. A glance through the advertising pages of any magazine of general circulation reveals the extent to which modern business makes use of such instrumentalities as telephone, telegraph, and air mail; local intercommunications systems, both telephone and radio; air travel and transport, long- and short-haul trucking; research organizations of every kind—and so on indefinitely. The consolidation of management rests at every point upon the utilization of mechanical devices. Practices which have sometimes been thought to be purely financial, such as the "one price system" of modern retail merchandizing, are entirely dependent upon the technology of labelling, cash registers, filing systems, and the like; that is to say, business machines. Large organizations, of which the criticism is sometimes made that they effect no economies of mass production, nevertheless owe their existence to technological developments in other fields than manufacture. Some of the great distributing concerns, for example, are in effect fleets of trucks and strings of warehouses. The stock exchange itself is not the outgrowth merely of the instinct to truck, barter, and exchange; in its modern role it is a network of wire services.

So great has been the proliferation of technical instruments and skills in modern business that "management" has come to play a constantly increasing part in its conduct, and "ownership" a correspondingly decreasing part. Berle and Means have even gone so far as to suggest that corporate organization has displaced property, and Professor Burnham has declared that the change is revolutionary in character and proportions. No doubt it is; but it is a revolution within the institution of property, a differentiation of hitherto organically related functions: that of discretionary control and that of derivation of income. To an extraordinary degree wealth has come to be conceived in terms of command of income from property which has assumed the form of corporate securities and so has come to stand not so much for equities in any physical plant as for a "share" in corporate earning power. Veblen called attention to this aspect of the change many years ago, and since it has extended to every corner of modern business life affecting even the conception of what constitutes an asset and the whole meaning of valuation, Professor Commons held that Veblen's appreciation of this institutional phenomenon was his major achievement and the cornerstone of "institutionalist" economics.[6] Certainly it was quite typical.

But both of these functions are functions of ownership. The "right to income" derives from the immemorial sanctions by which the harvest was assured to the owner of the field; and "discretionary control" also derives from the same mores by which trespassers were excluded from the property and the owner vested with authority to till and tend and supervise. Hence their dissociation is fraught with consequences of the highest gravity. The right to income has been supported in the past by a whole complex of mores and status-relationships. Having become detached from its legendary background, will it continue to be honored? And, on the other hand, will *de facto* discretionary control which has been achieved through the exigencies of administrative technique continue to enjoy the immunity to "government interference" which was once thought to be implicit in the sacred rights of property? As Professor Burnham points out,[7] the modern corporation is not a substitute for the institution of property. Government also has been the scene of a managerial revolution. The regulatory commissions employ the same administrative techniques and devices which have given rise to the corporation and so are a joint product of the same technological development. In government, too, the proliferation of managerial machinery has overshadowed the ancient sanctions of sovereignty. The managerial revolution is more than the displacement of one ruling class by another ruling class, more than the displacement of recipients of income from discretionary control. It is perhaps an expression of the much more significant and far-reach-

[6] See especially his "Comment" in the *American Economic Review,* XXII, 265.

[7] See especially his discussion of Berle and Means, *The Modern Corporation and Private Property,* in *The Managerial Revolution* (New York, 1941), pp. 88 ff.

ing displacement of ceremonial by technological functions throughout society.[8]

Changes such as these do indeed affect the internal character and constitution of the primary institutions of Western society, and the resultant institutional situation is indeed much better adapted to the operation of the industrial economy than were the institutions of medieval or early modern times. And this development is of very great importance, as Veblen, Commons, Berle and Means, Burnham, and many others have pointed out. The dissociation of the functions of property and the subdivision of equities into infinitesimal increments which are both perpetual and completely interchangeable, all mirrors the continuity of the machine process in space and time. But these institutional changes did not precede and "make possible" the technological development with which they coincide. They were not derived from preexisting institutions by the proliferation of the legendary mores of rank and power. What brought them to pass was rather the elaboration of administrative techniques along distinctively instrumental lines, and the gradual atrophy of whatever institutional considerations of rank and power failed to take this line. To speak of this process as having made possible the development of machine technology is to misconceive completely the essentially technological character of the process.

One aspect of the economy of modern Western society is institutional in character and derivation. The power-system of the modern economy is still a matter of institutionally determined status. In spite of all the apparatus of administrative machinery, discretionary control is still a matter of ceremonially determined rights the sanction of which derives from the legendary past. It was the essential sanctity of the property relationship which continued to command respect

[8] This aspect of the process is discussed further in Chapter XI, below.

throughout the period when other feudal relations were decaying and so to retain the solicitude of the state and the blessings of the church which had formerly been bestowed upon the feudal system generally. It was the ceremonial character of property which inspired modern society to think of accumulated wealth as the primary instrument of industrial production, just as feudal fief had been regarded as the primary instrument of agricultural production, and so to elaborate the concept of capital and the whole classical interpretation of economic process.

This power-system and its legendary background, the system and theory of capitalism, is not the author of the industrial technology by which the modern community gets its living and on which it therefore completely depends. It is the residue of our ceremonial past, and as such it is an impediment to economic progress as ceremonial proprieties have always been. This does not mean that we may expect, or that we should intend, its speedy dissolution. But it does define the problem of value and welfare which industrial society has now to face.

VALUE AND WELFARE

Chapter X

THE MEANING OF VALUE

THERE IS a very general feeling at the present time that Western society, or perhaps the modern world, needs a new set of values or a new conception of value. This sense of the need for a new value-orientation transcends and includes economics, since according to the prevailing tradition of economic thinking the price system is a mechanism by which the values of the community are registered through the character and intensity of demand. A great many people seem to think that Western society (or the modern world) has valued the wrong things; that we have overvalued material comfort to the detriment of spiritual values such as freedom, which in consequence we are in a fair way to lose. But since we have never had any intention of relinquishing our freedom or spiritual integrity, the general dissatisfaction is to some extent directed at the social mechanisms through which our valuations take effect, dissatisfaction among other things with the economic mechanism and with traditional ways of economic thinking by which we seem somehow to have been tricked into valuing goods more than freedom and integrity. Could this have happened if our values had expressed deep and unswerving certainty? Perhaps the most disturbing feature of the whole situation is the fact that the values of Western society have lost their sanction. Whatever they may be—whether or not we have valued the wrong things—we seem no longer to value anything with "abiding faith." This, as so many commentators have pointed out, is the chief weakness of the democracies. Although we see no merit whatever in the beliefs of other peoples in the racial superiority of the "Herrenvolk" or the divine mission of the Mikado, we are obliged to confess that we believe nothing any longer with the intensity of conviction which they are able to muster for their preposterous superstitions.

There is a reason for this which must be understood before there can be any possibility of correcting the condition. Belief itself is at a discount in the modern Western world. The progress of science has undermined the sanctions upon which hitherto the values of all communities have been founded. The whole difficulty is implicit in Sumner's doctrine of the "mores." Values are determined by the mores; the mores are determined by immemorial tradition; and immemorial tradition "just grows." Science has been unable to identify any immanent principle of spiritual growth. Indeed, all the evidence points in the other direction. As Sumner declared with tedious reiteration, the mores can make anything right, or wrong. The physical universe obviously does impose certain limits on the absurdity and bestiality of social practices. The Hindu practice of suttee made suicide mandatory for widows, but mores which made suicide mandatory at the age of ten would not long continue to prevail. But short of the extinction of the community there is no limit to the variety of social practices and no general standard of value. Moreover, the intensity with which any value may be held is no index to its validity. We do not honor Hindu widows for the unflinching heroism with which they assume their position in their husbands' funeral pyres. Rather do we deplore the state of mind and culture which induces that sort of unthinking dedication to custom, however hallowed.

This is a position from which we cannot recede, for it is a direct consequence of the whole scientific way of thinking. Not only is the mores-principle one of the most widely held and securely established of all the categories of social analysis, one which underlies and conditions all the modern work in all the social sciences; it is a consequence of scientific method itself and as such would inevitably reappear even if all the work of all the social sciences were to be liquidated by some universal totalitarian regime. So long as the laboratory sciences persist—and no political regime, however benighted, could any longer fail to appreciate the dependence of its own mechanized might upon laboratory science—it is inevitable that laboratory techniques will be applied to the phenomena of human behavior, since there is no line of hard and fast demarcation between human and non-human phenomena. The control of subject peoples by the manipulation of calories and vitamins is a tacit admission that the superiority of the "Herrenvolk" derives not from "blood" but from digestion. Ministers of public "information" may suppress the dissemination of this truth; but they cannot prevent its existence and therefore its possible redissemination at some future time. Minerals are essential to mechanized might; prospecting is essential to obtaining minerals; geology is essential to prospecting; and archeology is instrumentally inseparable from geology. It is impossible to dig without turning up human remains, and such remains are in fact the raw materials of a science of society. Books can be burned; but unless the clock is turned back virtually to the stone age, they will inevitably be written again, since the materials from which the present books have drawn their facts will still exist and in even greater profusion. And these books will inevitably restore the mores theory, since that theory is only a generalization of the fact of the variety of cultures.

It is this impasse in contemporary social thinking of which the present public confusion is the consequence. We have established the relativity of mores, a principle to which we have been led by the convergence of analytical techniques which cannot be gainsaid, one from which therefore we cannot now recede. It seems to extend to every sort of social behavior, including all values whatsoever, and to result in a sort of intellectual nihilism which not only baulks further social thinking but entangles our present ideas in all sorts of contradictions. We seem even to be caught in the enigma of the Cretan who said that all Cretans are liars. If all values are relative, including intellectual values, then it would seem to follow that modern scientific thinking also is relative to the culture which accredits it, including social thinking, including the principle that all values are relative.

For economics in particular this impasse is disastrous. Economics is nothing if it is not a science of value. The founders of the classical tradition of political economy held the belief of the eighteenth and earlier centuries that genuine and stable, if not eternal, values do exist and are somehow knowable; that such values are registered in demand and therefore measured by price; and hence that the economic affairs of commercial society are meaningful, since they are organized by price which is the measure of value. The mores principle completely destroys this theory. If the things that people value are just the things those people happen to value, then demand means nothing beyond the bare fact that that is what is demanded, and price means nothing more than the particular money-ratio at which something or other happened to be bought and sold; and the whole economic "system" of modern society is no system at all and means nothing but that such is the way things happen to be wherever they happen to be that way.

Contemporary economists are only too well aware of this difficulty. They have responded to it, generally speaking, in two ways: by giving up economic "theory" as a bad job and devoting themselves to empirical studies of the tin-plate and cottonseed oil industries and such like things; and by reading the whole problem of value out of economics—referring it back to philosophy, whence it came—and devoting themselves with great assiduity and amazing ingenuity of mathematical technique to the analysis of "price relations." No sneer need be directed at empirical investigations. We very much need to know something of what is going on in the various industries. But price either means something or not. If not, what is the point to "price analysis"? If so, just what does it mean? The economist may determine to take wants as they come, to accept them as "given" and treat them as "primary data," but he is still under the necessity of assuming that they mean something to somebody, if not to him. If they mean nothing—and that is the corollary of the mores principle—then the whole of theoretical price analysis falls to the ground.[1]

The only possibility of escape from mores-nihilism is by the further prosecution of the analysis from which that principle itself has been derived. If all judgments are relative to the ceremonial practices and traditional beliefs of the communities which make them, as we know some judgments are—if, for example, the analysis of social behavior in which we are now engaged is qualitatively indistinguishable from the myth-making of savage society—then our civilization is probably doomed. Loss of conviction is without doubt a very grave disaster. But is modern science no different from savage myth-making? Is Sumner's identification of mores the

[1] For a remarkably clear and prescient analysis of the consequences of this impasse for economic theory, see J. M. Clark, "Economics and Modern Psychology," *Journal of Political Economy,* XXVI, 1-30, reprinted in *Preface to Social Economics* (New York, 1936).

last word in social analysis? Or is it possible that by pursuing the investigation we may learn still more about the forces which are at work in human behavior and social development, and that further understanding may resolve the impasse which partial knowledge seems to have created? Surely these questions are self-answering. We have come to realize, not without dismay, that many of the values which our society has inherited are of dubious validity; but the assurance with which we pronounce this judgment offers a marked contrast to the disenchantment with which we view even our own legendary heritage. We no longer believe ourselves to be a "chosen people"; but our doubt in this regard is posited on our comparative certainty with regard to the theorems of science of which this negative judgment is one. Our doubt is born of certainty.

We do in fact make a distinction of kind between science and mythology, and social investigation did not come to an end with William Graham Sumner. Archeological exploration, the comparative study of existing cultures, the first-hand examination of the human animal, and theoretical analysis of social behavior, all have flourished more luxuriantly during the last few decades than ever before, and we have learned a very great deal. What we have learned does not invalidate Sumner's conception of mores, but it does quite definitely establish the existence of another sort of behavior quite distinct from that with which Sumner was primarily concerned and quite different from it in every respect.

In a word, we have learned to distinguish technological from ceremonial behavior functions. We have learned that ceremonial purity, such as results from having "kept all the commandments," is indissociable from the system of relationships of rank and status and is in effect a matter of "knowing one's place" in the "well-established order of society"; and we have learned that this whole scheme of things derives its sanction from tribal legends and is therefore unamenable to change, since the legends from which all ceremonial sanctions come are a purportedly true account of what actually happened in the past—the divine descent of the tribal ancestor, and all the rest—which is accordingly inalterable. Such practices are nevertheless altered. They are altered by changes in the material setting of community life which result from the development of technical innovations, tools and skills such as boats and seamanship by use of which people travel from the old habitat to a new one in which, perhaps, the fact that there are no volcanoes to be appeased by human sacrifice means that the practice of human sacrifice disappears. We have learned that such technical innovations come about as a result of the physical character of tools which, like all physical objects, are capable of being combined. We know with certainty that inventions and discoveries are combinations of tools, instruments, and instrumentally manipulated materials; and that the more tools there are, the greater is the potentiality of technical invention and discovery. Thus we have learned that this process of technological innovation is the dynamic force in social change.

But is it "good"? This is a question of the nature of value. Is "value," that is to say distinctions of "good" and "bad," exclusively ceremonial in character? If so—if distinctions of good and bad are necessarily determined by the mores—then technological development, however dynamic, is without moral significance and offers no avenue of escape from mores-nihilism. But if the technological process is itself the locus of value, the case is very different. This is a question of fact. What in fact is the nature of value? What do we actually mean by value? What is it that we are trying to say—not what should we think and say, but what in fact are we thinking and saying when we talk about values? How do we actually evaluate?

It is one of our immemorial traditions that values are

unique phenomena, *sui generis,* different from everything else in heaven and earth. Thus "choosing" between virtue and transgression, or between lemon and strawberry, is thought to be a unique act, different from every other sort of act of which man is capable. The "decision" between right and wrong, or between present consumption and the accumulation of capital, is thought to be a unique sort of decision; and the same is true of value "judgment." Other words are also used with reference to the act of valuation, but it is unnecessary to extend the list. The point is that all are used with other connotations from which however the value-connotation is in all cases thought to be quite distinct. The question is, Is this distinction valid? Is value in fact the unique phenomenon it has been traditionally held to be? Is choice, decision, or judgment between values a different sort of choice, decision, or judgment from other choices, decisions, or judgments?

There is a sense in which every act is a choice, a decision, and a judgment. A mechanic reaches for a tool, or a housewife for a pan. Neither one takes what comes at random. The mechanic selects a wrench which he "judges" to be suitable. He "decides" which of two will more exactly fit his bolt and "chooses" that one. Clearly this issue is one of fact; that is, it is capable of being instrumentally verified. If both wrenches are actually tried, it can be established beyond argument which one fits the bolt and which does not. Here is a situation in which, apparently, there is no room for those differences of taste for which there is no accounting except in terms of unique value-judgments. And yet a bystander may remark, "I like to use a pipe wrench for all those jobs"; or even, "We Joneses prefer pipe wrenches." The mechanic might well reply, "In that case you Joneses are fools," and might proceed to document his "judgment" by pointing out the fact that a pipe wrench cuts the head of the bolt and therefore prevents the use at any future time of a wrench which exactly fits it; and continued use of the pipe wrench may so cut the bolt that even the teeth of the pipe wrench will no longer take hold of it. To this Mr. Jones may reply that he nevertheless prefers to use a pipe wrench "because he likes it," because it gives him "satisfaction"; but the only effect of these remarks is to establish him as a fool who is ignorant even of his own folly.

Wherein is this case different from any other choice or decision? There are situations, to be sure, in which instrumental verification of a given judgment or choice is extremely difficult owing to the complexity of the materials involved, or even momentarily impossible owing to the absence of the materials that are essential for complete demonstration. This is true to a notable degree of judgments in the field of the fine arts. People whose knowledge of painting, for example, is confessedly limited nevertheless do not hesitate to express preferences and to insist not only that they know what they like but also that what they like is good. The eminent British critic (and painter), Mr. R. H. Wilenski, arguing that judgments of paintings are valid to the degree to which they are based on intimate and detailed knowledge, insists strongly that a judgment such as this one is not judgment at all but autobiography. "For when a man says, 'This picture gives me a thrill and that does not,' he is not talking about the pictures, he is merely talking about himself. When he has confessed to the thrill in fifty different cases we begin to know something about him." [2] But even so, it is his previous experience of pictures, his knowledge such as it is, which this man's judgment is revealing, as Mr. Wilenski himself declares in other passages.

In part this knowledge and experience are instrumental and make the same appeal to instrumental verification as do bolt and wrench. People frequently express their delight in a certain type of landscape painting. This means in the first

[2] *The Modern Movement in Art* (London, 1927), p. 4.

place that they are at least aware that landscapes have been painted for many years and by many painters of the highest reputation, and hence are "picturesque." More specifically it may perhaps mean that the landscape under consideration bears some resemblance to the work of Corot's "middle period" with which the market was flooded in the latter part of the nineteenth century, with the result that many people's childhood recollections are of prints and debased imitations of Corot's (poorer) work. They may never have known Corot's name; and yet if the present work could be hung alongside samples of the work of Watteau, Constable, Cézanne, Dali, and Corot's popular style, they would unhesitatingly identify the Corot as sharing with the present work the qualities which make a picture "what they like." This is what Mr. Wilenski calls an "emotive fragment."[3] Its presence and identity are capable of instrumental verification, given adequate materials; and its recognition can thus be proved to be the substance of the judgment and "choice" of the present picture, precisely as judgment of fit determines the choice of a wrench. The question is, Precisely what picture fits our emotional experience?

But judgment of a picture is affected in considerable degree by other considerations which, although they are never entirely absent even from the machine shop and the laboratory, play a much less conspicuous part in those situations. Asked which of two pieces of electrical apparatus will work more effectively in a given mechanism, many people will excuse themselves from expressing a "choice," or judgment, on grounds of ignorance; but few people ever go through an art museum without expressing any preference. Here there is a moral imperative. Whereas mechanics is a mere craft of which anyone may without shame confess his ignorance, to be wholly unresponsive to art is definitely shameful. For art is "a fine thing" by common consent, that is,

[3] *Ibid.*, p. 14 and *passim.*

by rule of mores; and the mores, having placed us all under necessity of "admiring" works of art, proceed to supply us with simple rules for identifying proper objects of admiration. The good pictures are the ones the right people admire.

It is this quality, of course, which distinguishes moral as well as esthetic "choices" and "judgments." If few people decline to choose among objects of beauty, nobody ever declines to give advice; for nobody can confess to ignorance of "right" and "wrong." Not only do the mores forbid such a thing; they also provide simple rules well within the comprehension of all. Right is what the right people do publicly, and vice versa.

Judgments of this kind may become a bit complicated; but they are still objective and verifiable, and in this sense identical with the judgment which determines the choice of a tool. Who are the right people and what is actually done by them are matters of fact. An apprentice might be advised to watch a skilled mechanic and use the same tools he uses, just as a child is advised to follow the example of the right people in all things. If there is a difference, it is only one of meretriciousness.

As this word suggests, esthetic judgment may be serviceable material for analysis at this point also. We frequently identify works of art as meretricious, meaning that they are in some sense false. In what sense this is the case can often be stated accurately and in detail. For a supposedly original artist to represent a copy of another painter's picture as his own would be a fraud, as would also be the case if he were to represent as an original what is really a duplicate of an earlier picture of his own. Furthermore pictures may be copies in different degrees. A given canvas may be original and unique as regards its subject. That is, it may be an unmistakable likeness of a sitter of whom no other portrait exists. And yet as regards treatment—color scheme, composition, manner of applying paint to canvas, etc., etc.—it may be a deliberate and slavish imitation of some other painter's work. It is this criticism which has so often been directed at the work of Sargent, for example, of which Mr. Wilenski remarks that "... in his landscapes his technique was the photographic naturalistic yellow and purple parody of the French Impressionist's spectrum palette," and "Occasionally Sargent left his naturalistic techniques in his wardrobe and made a successful imitation of a portrait by Van Dyck."[4] Or a painter may imitate himself, as Corot did from 1850 to 1870, turning out hundreds of canvases all exactly alike.[5] Such work is meretricious in the sense that it purports to represent original creative effort but in fact does not.

The conception of moral value in terms of conformity is meretricious in precisely the same sense. A "choice" or "decision" which is really a sidelong imitation of the behavior of somebody else certainly is not a genuine decision or choice, just as an apprentice's imitation of a master mechanic does not represent genuine skill. Social scientists declare that moral behavior is one hundred per cent imitative, and copybook moralizing (like copybook art) bears them out; but not one of the great moral leaders of mankind whose sincerity is universally acknowledged has ever been satisfied with conformity. Nor has any moral leader been content to accept the mores; for the mores, too, are meretricious.

Social scientists have always hesitated to make unequivocal pronouncement of the baselessness of the mores and the falsehood of the superstitions from which they derive their supposed sanction. Perhaps this reluctance to be unequivocally clear is due in part to realization of the calamitousness of their moral nihilism were it to be shared by the

[4] *Ibid.*, pp. 119, 115.

[5] When a series of reproductions of the work of a very popular contemporary American painter of seascapes appeared in a magazine a year or two ago, the editor called attention to the identity of treatment by appending this remark to one of them: "In this one the rocks are on the left."

whole community.[6] Or it may be due to the scientists' conscientious realization of the limitations of present knowledge. Falsehood is necessarily relative to truth. Before it is possible to declare that superstition is false, some standard of comparison must exist; and prior to recent studies of technology this seemed not to be the case. With the recognition of the continuity of science and technology, however, such a standard of comparison has now been provided. Consequently it is now quite evident that all myths are quasi-scientific explanations of the phenomena of group behavior, just as all dreams, even the waking dreams of disordered minds, are projections of the physical universe in which we work with tools. Jove's thunderbolts are quasi-tools, and so are the simulacra into which witches insert pins as quasi-weapons. The blight which will afflict the crops as a result of an outrage to the mores is a real, physical, affliction brought on by a series of quasi-mechanical causes and effects. Knowing something about electrical discharges, we now declare Jove and his thunderbolts to have been wholly imaginary, just as we declare without equivocation that phlogiston was a lamentable error; and in doing so we unhesitatingly subject Jove to the test of continuity with the tool-activities of mankind, just as we do with phlogiston.

Mores are inevitably subject to the same test. Always the mores have purported to be a true—that is, quasi-technological—account of what would happen "if." Even conformity has this significance. To assume that all will be well if one walks uprightly in the eyes of the community is to predicate that the community is literally indestructible; and this is a matter of fact, subject to instrumental test. In this sense no system of mores has ever been "other-worldly." Always it is

[6] Sir James Frazer produced the *reductio ad absurdum* of this way of thinking in *Psyche's Task* (London, 1909), in which he argued that superstition must be a good thing since our own civilization is founded on it.

the preservation and salvation of mankind here and now that is at issue. It is to be presumed that Jesus advocated turning the other cheek as a measure conducive to immediate human welfare, here and now. The master-pattern of all prayer is, "Thy kingdom come, Thy will be done, *on earth* as it is in Heaven." The Buddhist may contemplate extinction as the highest good; but this is a conception of the meaning of the universe, analogous to the scientific conception of a "contracting" universe, and no more postulates the inefficacy of Buddhism in the present affairs of man than such an astronomical theory by forecasting ultimate extinction postulates the inefficacy of science.

To put the linkage of traditional belief to instrumental fact another way, no creed has ever represented itself as incredible. The definition of faith as "Believin' things you know ain't so," or "*Credo quia impossibilis,*" is that of small boys and small minds, one which the church and the community necessarily reject. Throughout the ages the unanimous effort of spiritual, moral, and intellectual leaders has been to bring the mysteries of life into effective relation with the commonplaces. That is why such leaders have again and again sought to free their communities from incrustation by ideas and action-patterns which the advancement of material knowledge and instrumental skills has at length revealed to be without effect. Always the constructive effort of such leadership has been in the direction of some sort of integration of the "spiritual" ideals and truths with the physical realities of existence. The integration may now seem to have been the other way around, and to have been a flight from the commonplace to the transcendental. But the rain maker never carries occultism to the point of declaring that his rain is falling when none is actually in evidence, and the sophisticated transcendentalism by which modern thought has sought to integrate the two aspects of the universe does not offer itself as a substitute for machine technology as a means of subsistence. In declaring that science as a whole falls short of Absolute Truth modern transcendentalism in effect admits the efficacy of science and technology at every particular point as working guides to ordinary living. We are now free to follow science in all things provided only that out of respect to immemorial tradition we deny that we are doing so.

With the clear recognition of the meretriciousness of mores which comes of an understanding of the role of technology in social behavior we are for the first time in a position to resolve the dualism by which all civilization has been plagued and to recognize that all acts of choice, judgment, and decision are identical at least in their intent. By intent every judgment is a determination of fact. Every decision intends to take account of facts, and every choice has as its prototype the mechanic's choice of the right tool.[7]

[7] This thesis is generally identified with John Dewey, and quite properly, since he has devoted virtually his whole working life to its development. However, he would be the first to insist that it is not his creation in any unique sense, that it owes nothing to the "authority" of his intellectual "leadership," and that its claim to consideration does not derive from the cogency of his reasoning. On the contrary, it is implicit in all the modern sciences, especially those which touch human behavior most directly. See, for example, his celebrated essay on "The Influence of Darwin on Philosophy," in the volume by that title. Dewey's "influence" has been widely and bitterly deplored. But it can be said with certainty, and should be said without equivocation, that what these critics deplore goes far beyond the personality and achievements of John Dewey. They deplore the whole trend of modern science. This is clearly, though negatively, indicated also by their usual appeal from "Deweyism" to "the great thinkers of the past." But it is the future, not the past, which will determine the issue. If civilization turns back from science, then "Dewey's influence" will no doubt disappear, and a great deal more besides. But if science continues to be cultivated, the "integration" of our culture for which so much solicitude has been expressed in recent years will inevitably result from the unity of science—which, of course, is the basis of the whole idea of integration. Earlier civilizations have not been "integrated," current supposition to the contrary notwithstanding; they have been split wide open by the continual conflict between the

It is the technological continuum which is, and has always been, the locus of value; and it has this meaning because of its continuity. This continuum is identical with what John Dewey has called "the continuum of inquiry," and its significance as the locus of value—including economic value—may be understood in terms of the logical significance of the instrumental continuum.

Logicians have always conceived truth in terms of the process of "verification," which is to say "true-making." A proposition is true if the conclusions it implies, or the predictions which it makes, are "verified." What sort of act is a "verification"? We sometimes talk as though prediction in this scientific sense were synonymous with prophecy; as though it were a peculiarly meritorious achievement on the part of astronomers to predict eclipses years ahead; and as though the social sciences stood self-condemned by their inability to predict the outcome of an election just a few months off. But this is a sad misconception of the scientific process. Physical scientists are no better able to predict the weather on election day than social scientists are to forecast the vote, and no astronomer is in a position to guarantee any eclipse. For all we know to the contrary the sun may collide with an unknown comet next week. All scientific prediction

---

(technological) evidence of the senses and the (ceremonial) beliefs of the ancestors. Such a development may not continue to employ Dewey's terminology, and many of his formulations may be superseded; but the unity of science will inevitably prevail over the dualisms of "mind" and "body," of instrumental values and "moral" values, to correct which he has labored so long and valiantly.

The application of Dewey's theory of valuation to an understanding of the meaning of value in the field of economics, toward which the present discussion is attempting to move, goes beyond Dewey's published works. But surely it is implicit in his essay on the "Theory of Valuation" (1939), contributed to the *International Encyclopedia of Unified Science,* and published as a separate pamphlet. And equally surely the application is bound to be made, in a world in which the published works of Dewey and Veblen, for example, co-exist and are bound to be read occasionally by the same people.

is essentially instrumental. Using certain specified apparatus a scientist gets certain results, and he announces these results with the implied "prediction" that if any other scientist performs the same operation with the same apparatus he will get the same results. Following such an announcement other scientists do assemble apparatus according to the specifications and try it out. If they do then get the same results, this is considered to be a "verification" of the original research.

This kind of "prediction" and "verification" extends not only to all the sciences, social as well as physical; it is the common experience of the race. A housewife, following a familiar recipe for producing a cake, gets an unexpected result; and straightway she invites her neighbor to try out the same procedure. If she also gets the same result, this "verifies" the original operation, the result of which is thus "proved" to be due not to any lack of skill or mistake in following the recipe but to some other factor as yet unknown. When Sumner, for example, announced that his lifelong collection of data indicated a very wide variety of social practices, in effect he invited others to collect data of the same kind. This has of course been done, and Sumner's results have been copiously verified.

What we call truth is a function of this procedure. That is, it derives from the use of instruments, tools, and instrumentally manipulated materials. The very word, "truth," is in effect a synonym for continuity, and the continuity it postulates is that of instruments and tools—that is to say, technology. Deny this continuity by assuming the impossibility of repeating instrumental procedures, and truth itself straightway disappears.

Such is also the meaning of value. In the same sense the word "value" is a synonym for continuity, and the continuity of which it is a synonym is technological continuity. "Value" means continuity, literally; and that is its sole meaning. If anyone doubts this, let him try the simple experiment of substituting the word "continuity" for "value" in as many situations as he can. He will make two discoveries. One is the extreme vagueness, or scope, of the word "value," which is actually used in an indefinitely wide variety of situations; and the other is the discovery that in all these situations it is used as a relational term to point to some particular stream of relationships. The one meaning all these situations have in common is this stream-nexus, or continuity. In this sense truth itself is but one kind of value, as indeed logicians have often noted. But whatever the differences of emphasis in all these value-situations, there is still an underlying identity. Philosophers speak of "the true, the good, and the beautiful," and always the assumption is that logical values, moral values, and esthetic values have something in common. What they have in common is the technological (or instrumental) continuum to which all make reference and from which all derive their meaning.

Mankind is a tool-using species. All that man has done and thought and felt has been achieved by the use of tools. The continuity of civilization is the continuity of tools. All the arts, all the sciences, and the whole elaboration of organized activity by which "the great society," as Graham Wallas called it, has come to be, together owe their existence and derive their substance from the continuity which links the surrealist's pigments to the clays with which the Aurignacian caves were daubed, and in terms of which the cyclotron is but a continuation of Neanderthal experiments in chipping flint.

Economic value is no exception to this rule. Throughout the ages every community has owed its existence to its heritage of tools and apparatus, the "know-how" which is a function of the tools, and the materials which owe their significance to the tools with which they are manipulated. It is by carrying on this instrumentally organized activity that every community—and each separate individual—"makes a living." Whatever contributes to carrying on this activity is economically valuable, and whatever arrests or even hinders this activity is therefore economically deleterious. In the last analysis every economic choice or decision, from the shopper's choice between two brands of patent breakfast food to decisions of state upon matters of general economic policy, involves a judgment as to which of the alternatives presented will in fact contribute most to the continued efficient working of the technological system upon which all life depends.

The criterion of every economic judgment is "keeping the machines running." Such a phrase may have an ugly sound to conventional ears. But it must be remembered that keeping machines running is a complex business. It used to be thought (by some) that the way to keep machines running is to chain children to them, and that literature, painting, and music exist only for the delectation of the rich; but surely no one thinks so any longer. Surely no one supposes today that a community produces poetry and maintains symphony orchestras at the expense of its working efficiency. Does it detract from the dignity or the importance of "the finer things of life" to recognize that people do better work by virtue of living with them? Even in the midst of their great war effort—perhaps because of it!—the British have found that "Music While You Work" programs originating in the government's own studios and transmitted to the actual work-rooms of munitions factories have in fact heightened industrial effort; and if "Deep in the Heart of Texas" has proved more popular than the symphonies of William Walton and Vaughan Williams, is this a judgment upon "serious" music or upon a frivolous and antiquated educational system and a social order which allows symphonic music still to remain outside the common experience of the majority of the people? Is it a condemnation of Mr. Walter

Damrosch that as a result of his efforts millions of school children are now growing up in America who have listened weekly to the greatest masterpieces of musical literature throughout their school careers and may therefore some day run the machines better for listening to Bach and Beethoven?

"But machines are only a means!" Are they? Deeply rooted in our thinking is the idea of a metaphysical dualism which bifurcates all human experience and even the universe itself. The supposed bifurcation of experience into "means" and "ends" is a manifestation of this dualism. As such it has been a chief object of attack in all of Dewey's discussions of value and related problems. It should be quite unnecessary to recapitulate his analysis here.[8] "Means" and "ends" are no more distinct orders of phenomena than causes and effects. It is now, one hopes, universally understood that all causes and all effects are such relatively to each other; that no substance or event is of its own character inherently a cause, or an effect; but that every cause is so designated with reference to some particular inquiry in terms of which something has been taken as a given effect, or vice versa. In similar fashion we do distinguish the particular means by which a given end is to be arrived at, understanding all the while that what is the end in view of certain means (as eating lunch may be the end to which trudging home may be the means) is not on that account the "end and aim" of all existence but is itself the means to something else. It is not from this working distinction that we have educed the metaphysical principle of the primacy of "ends" but from immemorial traditions of ceremony and superstition in which an imaginary universe has always been represented as the "real" one, the "first cause" of which the work-a-day world is only an effect, and the "end" to which common existence is but the "means."

[8] Moreover the notion of "ends" will be discussed with reference to the concept of progress in Chapter XI, below.

Economists who repeat the familar adage to the effect that consumption is the end for which all economic activity is carried on may protest that they have no such metaphysical principle in mind. But what do they have in mind? Students commonly declare that "it stands to reason" that consumption is an "end" and production a "means." But why does it stand to reason? No particular act of consumption has any such significance. Indeed, as economists well know, the subsistence of the worker is one of the conventional "costs of production." Is consumption a state of grace in the spiritual sense, one which like salvation may be regarded as a consummatory state at which one arrives by (productive) penance and divine intercession? Without question that is the set of ideas which gave meaning to the adage in the mind of Adam Smith, and that is the background in terms of which such a proposition still seems to "stand to reason." What it stands to is not reason but tradition.

To challenge this tradition is not to assert that production is the "end"; it is rather to dismiss the whole dualism of metaphysically distinct states of grace in favor of the continuity of technological process. To speak of keeping the machines running is not to subordinate "human life" to "mere machines." What that phrase has reference to is the whole life-activity in which mankind has always been engaged. It is literally co-extensive with life itself, identical with the existence and continuance of the species, and it is the locus of value because of this integral continuity. To speak of value is to speak of the relation of any single act—choice, preference, decision, or judgment—to the whole life-process.

To all those who are accustomed to think of price as the "measure" of economic value it will seem to be a great defect of the conception of economic value in terms of technological process that it lacks the quantitative certainty of price. But the quantitative certainty of price is an illusion, the very illusion from which economic thinking is now struggling to free itself. So accustomed have we become to thinking that in the field of economics values are known, definitely and quantitatively, that we have lost all sense of what a prodigious anomaly this is. In no other field of human experience does value make itself known in any such definite and quantitative way. Shall we say that moral and esthetic judgments are utterly defective so long as they fail to follow an accounting system in which units of beauty and virtue are enumerated? Moral and esthetic judgments are difficult. They are subject to error. Are they therefore in all cases utterly invalid? Few of us are prepared to make any such admission.

On the contrary it is the great defect of the price theory of economic value and the great embarrassment of orthodox economic thinking that price makes economic value seem very much more definite and quantitative than it is. There are three notable respects in which this is the case. For one thing, price as we say "sets a value" on goods and services which by other and less quantitative standards of value we do not hesitate to designate as "anti-social." These, we have become accustomed to say, are economic values but not moral values. Just what does this mean? Does it mean that economic values are not real values? But the whole point to the price theory of value is that price is a social mechanism by virtue of which the community achieves some sort of value-economy of real significance. Or is it only a value-mechanism, without real significance, a maximization of satisfactions whatever they may be, in the Mandevillian sense, public virtue being the summation of private vices? There is no escape from the paradox that price quantifies vice quite as readily as virtue except total escape, by pushing the whole problem out the back door with the declaration that for economics (with its majesty certainty) "wants are primary data."

Price also quantifies mistakes. Price can be supposed to measure value only inasmuch as it achieves a common denominator of "wants" registered in purchases. But purchases are acts of folly as well as of good judgment. This has been obvious all along, and has been the basis of one of the most familiar and persistent criticisms of the price theory of value. That theory, so runs the saying, endows the "economic man" with a degree of skill in managing his affairs which would make his fortune as a professional purchasing agent or a certified public accountant. That is, prices can be assumed to "measure value" only on the assumption that the people whose "wants" and other business judgments they summarize are all endowed with the wisdom of Solomon. Since they are not so endowed, prices do not measure real values but only quantify the judgments people make antecedent to their price transactions. Whether those judgments are wise or foolish is determined not by the pricing mechanism but by their relation to the technological life-stream.

Furthermore all the transactions which the pricing mechanism quantifies are conducted within the limits of the prevailing distribution of financial means. Economists are well aware of this limitation, and when they are speaking of the economic welfare of the community as a whole, they usually take account of it in some such fashion as this: the price system brings about the greatest sum of satisfactions that is possible in view of the prevailing distribution of income. With regard to the welfare of the community this is as much as to say that slavery is the happiest arrangement that is possible consonant with the existence of slavery. With regard to value what it means is that price registers the limitations which are imposed upon the choices, preferences, decisions, and judgments of the members of the community by existing financial arrangements. But this also is as much as to say that real value is antecedent to price and is registered in price only to a very limited degree.

The certainty which price quantification seems to impute to economic values is the chief illusion under which economic thinking has labored throughout the period of dominance of the classical tradition. It is not the purpose of these paragraphs to rehearse again all the intellectual shortcomings of that tradition, but only to point out how indissociable they are from the quantitative rigidity of price. The apprehension of value, no less than the apprehension of truth and beauty, is a difficult and complicated business, subject to continual error and significant only by virtue of continuing verification and correction; and this is true of the valuation of the materials and activities of everyday living no less than of the highest and finest things of life. If economic value means anything at all, its meaning is that of a gradual and continuous realization of a more effective organization of the technological life-process.

The price system is not altogether unrelated to this process. Indeed, if it were, it could never have gained ascendency over the economic thinking of the modern community. But it has the same relation to the actual life-process which the moving picture has. In the course of the continuous experiment of living we do make purchases, and those purchases —like the opening of the shutter of the moving-picture camera—take instantaneous photographs of the real process at isolated and widely separated moments. It is these fragmentary snapshots of reality which are registered in price. Because wants change and because successive price transactions do register the change, just as successive photographs do give evidence of movements which have occurred in the interval between snapshots, some proponents of the price theory of economic value have declared that the price system is true democracy, a democracy in which a vote is cast every time a purchase is made.[9] This comparison is indeed significant, since it identifies the illusion of economic

[9] Ludwig von Mises, *Socialism* (London, 1936), pp. 442 ff.

certainty with the illusion of political certainty. Is voting the essence of democracy? We sometimes say that every people enjoys the government it deserves; but this is a singularly retributive conception of government. Surely the essence of democracy is to be seen not in the succession of electoral accidents but in the process of public information and discussion and resolution by which the accidents of the ballot box are mitigated. As Dewey would say, the essence of democracy is education, the continuous process of public enlightenment: and this is true of economic no less than of political life. The quantitative certainty of price is a misrepresentation of the realities of economic life just as the quantitative certainty of election returns is a cynical misrepresentation of political reality. In both situations we have a singular disposition to shirk the continuous effort of judgment by appeal to these spurious certainties. No political thinking need be done between elections, we sometimes say in effect, because the last election is a mandate which must prevail until another ballot is recorded; and no more economic thinking need ever be done than what is recorded in the price system. This is always a welcome relief, one which we have sought to enjoy throughout modern times. As Professor Heckscher has remarked of the triumph of laissez faire over mercantilism, "Not the least reason for adherence to laissez-faire principles was the fact that they offered a very welcome pretext for doing nothing when nobody knew what to do." [10] In appearance, at least, confusion is greater than ever today. Whereas in the eighteenth century no one knew what to do about the industrial system, today no one knows what to do about anything; and in the moral vacuum of the twentieth century we still find it very comforting to reflect that although wants have no general significance, they are at least brought to quantitative exactitude by price.

But nature abhors a vacuum, moral no less than physical,

[10] Eli Heckscher, *Mercantilism* (London, 1935), I, 472.

and the twentieth century is not the last. Social analysis has not stopped with the discovery of the diversity of ceremonial practices and conventional evaluations. There is also the continuity of tools, in terms of which—in spite of ceremonial diversities—a basic continuity of judgment has always prevailed. This continuity still prevails and is the basis of valid judgment today as it has always been. For every man the real and valid judgments of economic value are those he makes between purchases, judgments of value in use as economists once said, tested and verified by the way things work in the continuous effort of existence. It is to this test that all economic values are in fact submitted, those of public policy affecting the industrial system as a whole no less than those of private life. For every individual and for the community the criterion of value is the continuation of the life-process—keeping the machines running. That is what we have in fact been doing throughout the ages, and that is what we must continue to do and do continually better—technologically better—if we are to continue and exceed the achievements of the past.

Chapter XI

THE PATH OF PROGRESS

ECONOMIC THINKING has always embodied some conception of progress and must always do so; for the concept of value is the chief concern of economic thinking, and progress is indissociable from value. Agnosticism with regard to value implies agnosticism with regard to progress. It may be a gay agnosticism like that of the old American folk song, "We don't know where we're going, but we're on our way!" As Professor Walton Hamilton once pointed out, this refrain is a remarkably apt characterization of the state of mind into which some contemporary economists have got themselves. But gay or not, the state of mind which is described by this characteristically Hamiltonian irony is one of complete and stultifying agnosticism. Value may also be conceived to be known but unattainable, in which case progress also is unattainable. But if value is knowable and attainable, then progress also is knowable and attainable. If the technological process is the locus of value, the continuous development of the technological arts and crafts and the accompanying recession of superstition and ceremonially invested status is progress.

If the industrial revolution is itself the vehicle of progress, then Condorcet and the other optimists of the "age of reason" were not so far wrong as subsequent generations have believed. This does not mean that perfection is "just around the corner." But the authors of the idea of "infinite perfectability" really made no such rash promise. In attributing the disorders and violence of the times to bad institutions Condorcet was speaking the language of Veblen and Dewey more than a century before them; and in declaring that we are now entering a period of "neo-technics," he was only anticipating Patrick Geddes and Lewis Mumford.[1] The fact that we have not yet fully realized the possibilities of science and technology—possibilities of emancipation from the follies of the past and of attainment of an "economy of abundance"—is of secondary importance. The primary consideration is the fact that we do now realize these possibilities more clearly and more generally than ever before. The disorders of the present age are more widespread and more cataclysmic than those even in which Condorcet himself was "liquidated." But no one any longer believes that disorder and destruction are inevitable or necessary. The "demonstration" that increase of population necessarily and inevitably nullifies all the achievements of advancing technology, by which the Reverend T. R. Malthus, avowed spokesman of the landed gentry, undertook the final refutation of Condorcet's revolutionary optimism, was abandoned even by its author in the second and subsequent editions of his celebrated *Essay* and is now completely discredited. No one any longer doubts the physical and technological possibility of a world-wide economy of abundance.

Far more than in the time of Condorcet the twentieth century has accepted the machine. No serious student attributes the evils of the age to its machines. Popular essayists sometimes write as though tanks and airplanes were responsible for the bloodshed which is now going on, and

[1] See Mumford, *Technics and Civilization, passim.*

novelists occasionally draw pictures of the horrors of a future in which life will have become wholly mechanized, with babies germinating in test tubes, "scientifically" maimed for the "more efficient" performance of industrial tasks. But this of course is literary nonsense, two kinds of nonsense. One kind portrays the devices of the future as horrible perversions, just as traveling in stagecoaches at the vertiginous speed of fifteen miles an hour was once thought to be. Extracorporal gestation might well be a great improvement on nature, just as the extraction of the mammary secretion of the cow is a great improvement and one to which we have been able to reconcile our sentiments of decency, though it must have seemed a horrible perversion to the stalwart moralists of primitive society. As Mr. J. B. S. Haldane pointed out many years ago, all biological inventions seem disgusting at first.[2] But this is nonsense. If science can reduce infant mortality by establishing an "unnatural" relation between a human baby and a lactating quadruped, then by all means let it be done. Such, happily, is now the prevailing attitude.

To represent schemes of mutilation as the teaching of science for the attainment of efficiency is nonsense of quite another kind; it simply is not true. Mutilation is neither scientific nor efficient. If we can credit science at all, we must know that any community in which any sort of mutilation is practiced is a mutilated community. Modern industry demands the full powers of all its participants. Its development has all along been coincident with the expansion of the powers of a continually larger part of the community. Any deviation from this procedure is contrary to science and to industrial efficiency. It is said that the control of subject populations has recently been attempted by the withholding of certain vitamins from their diet; but no one has ever claimed that such a procedure enhances the effi-

[2] *Daedalus* (London, 1924), p. 44.

ciency of its victims, and no one who knows anything about science has ever seriously supposed that it is the discovery of the vitamins which has brought about such practices. After all, this is not the first time that victors have maimed the vanquished, as every good Bible reader knows.

There is nothing wrong with the machines. Nevertheless many people whose minds are entirely free from nonsensical aversions are still unable to think of progress in terms of the advancement of science and the arts, chiefly for this reason. The traditional conception of progress is that of movement toward the attainment of an "end." Within the limits of day to day activity finite and provisional ends are of course set up. Thus one may speak of progress toward the attainment of an academic degree. In a much more general but still limited sense one may even speak of the advancement of science as progress toward knowledge, or something of the sort. But the idea still persists that the attainment of such limited objectives constitutes "real" progress only insofar as these limited objectives contain some particularization of the universal "end."

This is also true of value, which has likewise been traditionally conceived in terms of ultimate value, the *summum bonum* of the philosophers. Thus the difficulty with regard to "ends" is a major obstacle to a technological (or instrumental) understanding of the whole value-progress complex. It is frequently expressed in simple and direct language such as this. A machine is neither good nor bad in itself. The question is, What is it for? What does it do? What end does it serve? A machine (or instrumental technique) may serve desirable ends. It may save life or enrich personality. But a machine may also serve the ends of destruction and debasement. Machines are used in war, and scientific knowledge may be employed in the commission of crime. How then can we speak of machines, or even of the arts and crafts and instrumental procedures as a whole, as being good in themselves, irrespective of the ends for which they are employed? How can we speak of the advancement of science and technology as progress except with reference to some conception of the end to the attainment of which all human efforts are directed?

It is by virtue of this way of thinking that consumption plays its unique role in economic theory. Consumption is the "end" for which all other economic activities are carried on, by definition. Textbook writers have fallen into the habit of explaining consumption to their readers as the process in which goods are "used up"; and this involves them in difficulties, since many things—such as diamonds, or even books—are not used up by their consumers, whereas many other things—such as fuel—are used up in processes otherwise identified as production. The truth is, the other meaning of this root, by which it is linked to "consummatory" and "consummation," is the only one by which it can be clearly distinguished from production and is in fact the meaning which its earlier users definitely intended to invoke, as any student can demonstrate for himself by substituting the word "consummation" for "consumption" wherever it appears. This is why no one ever undertook to prove that consumption is the "end" for which all the rest is carried on. The distinction of "consumption" from "production" is synonymous with the distinction of "end" from "means."

So deeply is this distinction embedded in the thinking of the community that even avowed revolutionaries have been unable to eradicate it. No other revolutionary slogan has been more widely used and none has made a more effective appeal than the formula, "Production for use." To most people these words seem to appeal to simple common sense. Nevertheless they are in fact a transliteration into economic terminology of Kant's "categorical imperative," and their appeal is to metaphysical tradition. In proposing that we should "treat every man as an end and never as a means,"

Kant assumed "man" to be a spiritual entity. He did so on the basis of the immemorial tradition according to which it has been believed throughout the ages that every man has direct intuitive knowledge of himself as a spiritual entity. For all their anticlericalism it is to this essentially religious belief that modern revolutionaries appeal when they advocate "production for use," and it is this belief alone which sustains the conviction that machines, economic processes, and human life itself can have significance only in terms of the "end" to which all else is a "means."

What is the evidence by which man knows himself "intuitively" to be a "mind" or "spirit"? It is "intuitive" in the sense that this is "inner" knowledge, "inner" in the sense that it is not based on the evidence of the senses. The "knowledge" of primitive man was derived from the evidence of dreams, the departure of "life" with a dying gasp, and the like. But for all these phenomena modern science has other explanations, explanations which cover not only the actual phenomena of dreams, respiration, and the like but also the social processes of legend creation and transmission by virtue of which these phenomena have been so persistently misconceived, with the result that no evidence remains; and in destroying the last remaining vestige of supposed evidence of direct, intuitive, inner, self-knowledge of spiritual "reality," modern science has precipitated an intellectual revolution far more momentous than the one effected by Copernicus.

For what is at issue now is the "common sense" of the community. Copernican astronomy and Newtonian physics claimed the whole physical universe as the domain of science; but through the efforts of Descartes and his successors, of whom Kant was perhaps the greatest, an armistice was arranged between science and metaphysics. A boundary was established between the "outer" world of science and the "inner" world of metaphysics. According to the terms of this armistice the validity of the findings of science was conceded, subject only to this reservation. Such an arrangement was of course extremely favorable to science. Not only did it bring an end to the long struggle in which scientists had been engaged, permitting them to explore the moons of Jupiter and even the organs of the human body without further opposition; it also permitted scientists to be scientists and still to be men, retaining with regard to the "inner" and "real" world the beliefs with which they no less than all their neighbors had been indoctrinated "at their mothers' knees."

The relief was more than personal. Many a troublesome problem could be solved by judicious application of the Cartesian compromise. Thus it was that classical political economy solved the troublesome problems of value and progress. Price is a physical phenomenon, a feature of the "outer" world, and therefore subject to scientific analysis. But the valuations which this mechanism of the market assembles and summarizes are the private experiences of individual souls and are therefore real and valid within the purview of Cartesian and Kantian metaphysics. The mechanism of production and the pecuniary organization of society is the "means" to which the satisfaction of the inner aspirations (wants) of mankind is the consummatory "end." In theory these two worlds are linked by price, which is both a physical mechanism and a register of spiritual experience.

This happy compromise was upset by the Darwinian revolution. It was of course science which violated the terms of the Cartesian armistice, and not in the field of biology alone. The demonstration of the continuity of the human species with all other species was of climactic importance, but archeological evidence of the continuity of present civilization with extreme antiquity, increasing knowledge of comparative cultures, analysis of social mechanisms in terms of "collective representations," "folkways," and "mores," greatly increased knowledge of the physical mechanisms of behavior and of the processes by which behavior patterns are formed in individual and social experience, all contributed to the elimination of the last frontier between knowledge and belief. As a result of all these developments science no longer respects the frontier by which the universe was once thought to be divided into "outer" and "inner" worlds, and no longer credits the supposed "immediate" knowledge of "inner" spiritual reality or recognizes the so-called "individual" wants and satisfactions as having any unique validity or as being in any sense "consummatory."

The disrepute into which the idea of progress has fallen in recent years is a further consequence of the collapse of metaphysical dualism and a phase of the general moral nihilism of the times. As such it is historically explicable. Just as the identification of the mores, the recognition of the traditional character of the "eternal verities," has given rise to the assumption that there are no verities, so the nullification of the "inner" world of consummatory spiritual experience has given rise to the assumption that consummation is meaningless; and since progress itself is supposedly meaningless except in terms of such attainment, the idea of progress itself has fallen into disrepute.

But however explicable, this situation is a paradox. It is the validity of science which has supposedly destroyed the values of the modern world, and it is the progress of science which has rendered the idea of progress itself supposedly untenable. Clearly there is more here than meets the eye. Why do we say that machines must be "for" use? The meaning "use" is implicit in the meaning "machine." We know that every paradise is a projection of some community's actual social arrangements into infinity. For South Sea Island dwellers it is the Ultimate Atoll, for Eskimos the Infinite Snowbank, in each case ruled by the Perfect Chief, and so on. Such projections, we know, are without validity. Yet we still insist that progress must be conceived in this way or not at all. Why? What principle of logic, or of common sense, presents our thinking with this absolute disjunction: either progress must be traditionally conceived and therefore without general validity, or it cannot be conceived at all? Such a disjunction can be sustained by definition. We can agree to limit the use of the word "progress" to "progress-as-it-has-been-traditionally-conceived," and by doing so we can assert with confidence that progress-so-defined can be conceived only as-progress-has-been-traditionally-conceived. But this is only a restatement of the initial agreement. The question still remains, Why should we subject our thinking to such limits in the first place? Doubtless it would only add to the confusion if we were to agree to throw the meaning of the word "progress" wide open by making it synonymous with "change." On the basis of such a preconceived definition we might then declare that a chemical reaction is progress; but that would certainly not increase our understanding of social development. Surely there is some meaning which all the "collective representations" of human societies have had in common. What is it? What have they all been trying to do?

All human behavior exhibits a certain continuity of a technological, instrumental, or cause-and-effect character. It is with reference to these observed and instrumentally "controlled" continuities that we use such terms as "value" and "progress" in common speech. In speaking of his "progress" down the page a writer is thinking in terms of the instrumental continuity of each written line with the line which precedes and the line which is to follow it. Such continuities are clearly more significant the further they extend. Progress "toward" the "completion" of an essay is an extension of this character. Here also what the mind is grappling with is not a preconception of the finished essay but a continuity which exists in any given sentence or paragraph and extends to the paragraph, the sentence, and the final word to which this continuity extends. Meanings such as this are capable of a considerable degree of extension without confusion. Thus we speak quite easily of "the progress of science." It is the paradox of our present state of mind that in spite of the disrepute into which the whole conception of progress has fallen we do actually continue to employ such phrases as this quite without embarrassment. When a scientist speaks of the progress of science other scientists do not leap up to reproach him with having uttered nonsense, for the phrase "the progress of science" is not nonsense. Neither does it depend for its meaning on any preconceived idea of what "the total realization of all scientific knowledge" might be. The meaning to which such a phrase refers is not that of a quantity of knowledge—not a finite quantity any more than infinity. It is that of a process which is now going on and which may quite reasonably be conceived as continuing.

It is this meaning of process-continuity which has given rise to the conception of progress as a metaphysical projection. In the effort to extend our understanding of the continuities in which we are engaged we have inevitably raised even such extensive continuities as that of science to a larger scale. The question then becomes, in what fashion is science continuous with human activity generally? At this point, however, the imagination of mankind is liable to that peculiar sort of stimulation which we have recently identified as "ceremonial." We become excited, and we begin to think in capital letters. The everyday thinking which has sufficed for an understanding of common continuities now gives way to our inveterate propensity for myth-making; group loyalties become obsessive; and so we find ourselves insisting that the progress of science is but a "means" to the far more sublime "end" which is the eventual triumph of the Republican Party, or something of the sort. Does this mean that human behavior is wholly without significance? Or does it mean that our problem is one of decontamination?

Is there no point of which we can say, "This is the point at which we went astray. Up to this point our thinking was sound; beyond this point it was unsound; and consequently it is to this point that we must return and renew the attempt to carry on from here by the same sound methods which had been employed hitherto"? Those who declare that the concept of progress "must" have reference to metaphysical ultimates, that metaphysical ultimates are without significance, and therefore that the concept of progress is itself without significance, seem to deny the existence of any such point. In doing so they seem to be making the same mistake into which we have been misled by the principle of "mores," that of asserting that all judgments are conventional observances and nothing more. Said the Cretan, all Cretans are liars. Since the effort to extend our understanding of the continuities of human behavior has resulted in metaphysical fatuities, they seem to say, all intellectual efforts must be of this character.

It is the progress of science which belies this judgment, and it does so not only by example but by precept. Not only is the progress of science and technology itself a significant reality; its inevitable extension to the study of human behavior has given us the means of distinguishing between technological and ceremonial activities. This is the point at which scientific generalization is securely tied to the everyday judgments of which common existence is composed. Speaking of the progress of science, for example, we can say with certainty that it is continuous with the technological practices in which men have engaged as far back as our knowledge goes, as it is also continuous with all present tool-using activities of the commonest and humblest sort. It is also continuous with all the "creative" activities which we designate as the arts.

This total activity, as we know, has undergone progressive development throughout human experience. All that we can now do is done by virtue of that progressive development. Progress is the continuation of this process. We speak with certainty of the progress of aviation, meaning that better planes are built now than formerly—better in the sense of larger, faster, stronger, lighter per horsepower, and so forth. This judgment is valid quite without reference to the "ends" for which planes may be used. The fact that some people are using planes to kill other people is quite as irrelevant as it would be for a hardware merchant to inquire whether a hammer is to be used to bash in someone's skull before venturing an opinion which is the better of two hammers. In the same sense the judgment that the progress of aviation is a part of general progress is a valid judgment. The continuity it asserts is between plane-building and building in general. Since the building of better planes is in fact contingent upon and contributory to better building generally, it is a part of a general process, coextensive with human existence, by virtue of which the human race has risen above the brutes and gives every indication of rising far higher than anyone can now foresee.

The fact of war is by no means irrelevant to this judgment. We sometimes hear it said that the only result of the invention, for example, of airplanes is that people are killing each other on a larger scale than ever before. If such a proposition were true, it would indeed nullify the technological conception of progress; for if people are indeed being killed on a larger scale than ever before, this circumstance must eventually operate to the disadvantage of further airplane building and of technological development generally. But is it true? To say that killing is the "only" result of the technical development of the airplane is patently false, but this is perhaps a rhetorical exaggeration. The essential question is whether advancing technology creates disorder, and whether the disorders so created are in fact increasing by a cumulative process such as might be conceived to nullify the progress of the arts and sciences.

There is a sense in which technological development might be said to give rise to disorder. It has been recognized all along that technological development alters the physical habitat of a community in such a way that a shift in the institutional balance of power becomes inevitable. This shift may well be accompanied by disorder. In this sense the perfection of the airplane may be said to have brought on the present war; since, if the supposed supremacy of the French army and the British navy had not been a technological illusion, doubtless the present war would not have occurred. Does this mean that German (and Italian and Japanese) aggression had no part in bringing on the conflict? To say so would be equivalent to attributing the increase of kidnapping in recent decades solely to the development of the automobile without any reference to pre-existing organized crime (especially of the prohibition era) or to police corruption and inefficiency, the confusion of legal jurisdictions from which law enforcement has always suffered in America, etc., etc. Doubtless it was the development of automobiles and motor highways which gave to crime this particular direction, and doubtless it was a change in the technology of war which gave international conflict this particular direction; but the forces of conflict are in every case institutional.

Even so, the question still remains whether conflict and disorder are in fact becoming more general and catastrophic. If they are, progress is nullified irrespective of the distinction between causes and directions. But on this point the evidence is conclusive. Current pessimism to the contrary notwithstanding, population has increased tremendously throughout modern times. To be sure, this is no positive guarantee that it will continue to do so throughout the indefinite future, but neither is there any conclusive evidence that it will cease to do so. If the present disorders were unique, the situation would be rather more terrifying than it is. The very fact that they are not unique suggests that we must judge future probabilities in terms of an experience in which disorders such as the present ones have nevertheless been accompanied by continuing increase of population. It has been said that wars have been increasing in frequency throughout modern times, but in that case they must have been decreasing in violence—appearances to the contrary notwithstanding—since throughout the same period population has unquestionably increased. If later wars had brought the same devastation throughout the areas involved which the Hundred Years' War and the Thirty Years' War brought to the areas most seriously affected, the situation would be quite different. But such is not the case. To recognize these facts is not to condone war, nor even to accept it as "inevitable." The only question at issue is whether the current evidence shows that disorders are in fact increasing catastrophically; and the answer is that the evidence shows nothing of the sort—or rather, just the contrary.

What the evidence shows is that humbug, cruelty, and squalor have been decreasing for the population as a whole throughout modern times as they have been decreasing throughout the history of the race. No one seriously advocates turning back the clock to the day when Plato dispensed sweet wisdom to a few disciples while all the rest of the world lived in fear of evil spirits, or to the day when theology was most angelic and the clergy lived in open concubinage, lords enjoyed first night rights with every bride, and no man was safe from violent molestation or from smallpox, typhus, and starvation. In spite of all sentimentality and all the intellectual scruples of scientific caution, we are all committed by the whole continuous series of everyday judgments and activities to carrying on those achievements of tool and instrument, hand and brain, the genuineness of which no one really doubts.

It is from the pattern of this continuing activity that the idea of progress derives its meaning. Nevertheless this meaning can be projected into the future. If the progressive advance of technology means a similarly cumulative diminution of the extent and importance in the affairs of the community of superstition and ceremonial investiture, then the projection of this process into the infinitely remote future would seem to reveal an "ultimate" condition of complete enlightenment and efficiency wholly devoid of mystic potencies. Such a state of affairs is perhaps difficult to imagine, and yet these phrases have a familiar sound. This would be in effect a classless society, one in which as a consequence of the withering away of the state (that is, the whole institutional scheme of rank and privilege) all prerogatives of status would have disappeared. It would be a society in which men and women would go about their concerns with the simple innocence of little children, one in which the lion and the lamb would lie down together in common amity.

These are poetic expressions. They lack the precision and detail of scientific formulas. What they express is perhaps vision rather than analysis. Nevertheless, as scholars have often remarked, the visions of the great spiritual leaders, the visions by which mankind has been most profoundly moved, exhibit striking similarities. It has often been remarked that the teachings of Jesus and Buddha were both characterized by a gentleness, an abhorrence of every manifestation of coercion, which is more than a mere quality of temperament. For both the injunction to turn the other cheek is accompanied by an equally fundamental abhorrence of Phariseeism, of the mores of conformity, and of the institutionalization of human behavior. These ideas, or attitudes, are also found in the teachings of lesser men such as Marx and even Condorcet. Perhaps it is impious to couple the name of Condorcet with that of Gautama Buddha, but Condorcet's aversion to Phariseeism and his conviction that emancipation comes only by enlightenment are singularly reminiscent of the teachings of Buddha. Scholars are still uncertain as to what "nirvana" meant to Buddha himself (as distinguished from the institutionalization of Buddhism in later centuries), and therefore we may perhaps be allowed to conjecture that the "nothingness" by the attainment of which man was to free himself from spiritual slavery was less metaphysical and more sociological than the priestcraft of organized Buddhism has supposed and was not altogether unrelated to the Marxian nothingness of the classless society which follows the withering away of the state. It is also worthy of remark that all these seers viewed the use of tools, the ordinary act of the common artisan, as a function of the profoundest import. The fact that Voltaire closed *Candide* by retiring to cultivate his garden means more than a mere shrug of ironic shoulders; it imputes a reality to the act of cultivation which is absent from the institutionalized humbug of the world of affairs. We must not overinterpret these poetical expressions. Certainly we must not impute to the teachers of the past—in some cases of many centuries past—all the analytical clarity which our generation owes to the sum of the scientific achievements of the race. But perhaps the difference is more one of terminology than of substance. Perhaps the knowledge we have attained by laborious analysis may be essentially the same as the insights of poetic vision, the vision of a world in which enlightenment would have replaced superstition, and efficiently organized teamwork institutional coercion.

But even such a vision is a projection of the current process into the indefinite future, not an independently conceived "end" by which present process is to be judged and guided. What it represents is insight into the current realities of human life. It is these current realities of which the vision is a poetical expression and from which it derives its meaning, not the other way about. In this sense perfection may be conceived to have an operational meaning like the mathematical concept of infinity. Doubtless mankind will achieve perfection only at infinity. Doubtless technological progress is an asymptotic function. There is no finite moment in the past at which human behavior is known to have been wholly ceremonial. As far back as our knowledge goes rudimentary tool-activities have been going on; and our knowledge of the present situation does not encourage any expectation of the total disappearance of superstition, status, and institutional coercion within the foreseeable future. This does not mean that our interpretation of current process as one of progressive enlightenment and efficiency is incorrect. It means that the reality of progress is implicit in the finite process of which visions of infinity are a projection, just as mathematical infinity is a projection of finite series.

Within the limits of current process it is true that mankind needs superstition and coercion. This fact is often cited as the climactic nullification of the "illusion" of progress. But such an interpretation is an expression of the metaphysical misconception of the idea of progress. To whatever degree superstition and institutionalized status may prevail at any given time, the habituation of the race to those forms of behavior does constitute a need, just as a cripple needs a crutch. But the fact that a person is habituated to the use of crutches does not establish that crutches are good in themselves or that the attainment of crutchless health is a fatuous illusion. Needs conceived in weakness are not a sound criterion of possible achievement, for individuals or for societies. The supposition that the prevalence of institutionalized humbug and coercion at any given time proves the impossibility of progress is a special case of the paradox of Zeno. It was precisely by this method that Zeno was supposed to have "proved" that a moving object does not move, since at any given moment it is at a given point. This fact, as we have long since assured ourselves, does not prevent an object from passing through an infinite series of points during an infinite series of moments; and in the same sense the deplorable conditions which prevail in any community at any given time do not constitute a proof that such conditions must continue to prevail. Doubtless the immediate future will be not wholly different from the immediate past; but the fact that a given difference is infinitesimal does not mean that it is not profoundly significant.

The changes which have accompanied industrial revolution have been felt to be significant by the whole community throughout modern times. It is this judgment which has given rise to the idea of progress, an idea which is one of the most characteristic features of modern Western civilization.[3] The idea has of course been institutionalized. When dynastic power was paramount, that was the force to which the progress of opulence was prospectively attributed. When money power superseded dynasties, the attribution was to "Capital the Creator." Throughout both these periods the nature of the process was but dimly apprehended. It is much clearer now. But the identification of technological process and its dissociation from institutional obsessions has been at the expense of the idea of progress. What we now have to do is to de-institutionalize that idea itself—to recognize as a misconception the idea of progress as movement toward the attainment of some previsioned "end," and to reconstitute the criterion of progress in terms of the continuity of technological development. If we can do this—if we can now see that the path of progress is the advancement of the arts and sciences, tools, instruments, and the machine process, and not the apotheosis of any legendary power-system—we shall have consummated the revolution to which the Copernican revolution was a preliminary skirmish.

[3] J. B. Bury, *The Idea of Progress* (London, 1920).

Chapter XII

THE STRATEGY OF PROGRESS

TWO MAJOR PROBLEMS confront every attempt to conceive a strategy of economic progress. One is the logical problem of the meaning of value. The other is the methodological problem posed by the magnitude and complexity of the industrial economy. Both seemed to have been solved at one stroke by the classical formula with an apparent nicety to which that way of thinking owes its charm. For if price is the measure of value, then price equilibrium is the criterion of economic welfare; and if price equilibrium is what obtains in the absence of unnatural restraints, then we are at once provided with a clear definition of the strategic objective. The tactical difficulties involved in the removal of restraints and impediments may still be considerable, but such difficulties are practical and administrative. The supposition is that both of the really formidable intellectual problems have been solved.

It is this supposition which makes students of economics so resistant to criticism of the price theory of value and so reluctant to attempt any other solution of their problems. For even if it be supposed that a solution to the logical problem of the criterion of value can be found in terms of the continuous advancement of the arts and sciences, tools, instruments, and the machine process, the methodological problem still remains. How can such technical advancement be insured and accelerated? How can institutional obstacles be weakened or removed? Not, obviously, by letting things alone! To suppose that in any given area or period technology must inevitably prevail is contrary both to the instrumental logic and to all that we know of history. It depends entirely upon our efforts whether the economic progress already achieved by Western civilization is to be continued and accelerated, or whether it is to be extinguished. The question is, what efforts?

In squaring off to face this question we can at least take comfort from the fact that Western civilization still exists. Fortunately our task is not Utopian. For it can be said without disparagement of the great literary monuments of the past that they are literary. As such—as intellectual stimulants—they have been among our most precious possessions. But no Utopia has ever been realized, or can ever be, for the obvious reason that a work of art is not the equivalent of reality. No man has ever drawn a complete "blueprint" of a society, or can ever do so, any more than a scientist can draw a complete blueprint of the human body. Even the architect, whose efforts are suggested by the blueprint metaphor, takes for granted most of the materials, tools, and "know-how" by use of which his building is to be constructed. In effect the new building will only reproduce others already in existence with certain specified alterations and, perhaps, improvements. Surgeons do not hesitate to improve the human body, although to do so they must be presented with a living organism, actually existing as a going concern. Society also is a going concern. Even Western civilization, for all the loud knocking and other signs of faulty lubrication, is still going. The problem is not one of conjuring a culture out of nothing. For better or worse we are "stuck with" the existing civilization of the Western world. Our problem is to make it work, better if possible.

The impression is quite general today that Western society is breaking down, or at least threatening to break down, and everyone agrees that it is not working as a sound mechanism should. Furthermore everybody agrees that whatever may be the cause of our present trouble, it is not due to a failure of technology. Some people do blame science and technology for all our troubles, but they fear what they regard as overdevelopment. What they challenge is not the fact of technological development but its meaning. They deplore the "materialism" of the age, as the devotees of ancient sanctities have always done, looking back to some earlier day when (as their kind always think) men lived "simply" and communed with Truth. In short their value judgments derive from the institutional traditions of the past and they abhor technological progress because it has led the modern world to break with those traditions. Unfortunately, but inevitably, it has not been a clean break. The neo-medievalists think we have too much science, and even too much "material" comfort, for our spiritual good. We think the trouble lies altogether on the other side. But with regard to the present and prospective vigor of science and technology all agree.

The tenacity of institutional traditions is likewise a generally admitted fact. But it is one thing to reach the logical conclusion that institutional atavisms are the seat of all our trouble and quite another to determine methodologically what to do about it. The immediate and complete abrogation of the institutional structure is both impossible and inconceivable. We may deplore the organization of society along the lines of coercive power with its penumbra of legend and mysticism; but the immediate alternative would be a void. Since it is beyond our powers to conjure a new social order from a void, we have no alternative but to carry on. This means that, in spite of anything we may be able to do within the predictable future, coercion, injustice, inequality, ignorance and superstition will certainly persist. Progress will consist in pushing back their boundaries here and there; and the question is, where? Where and how can the present confusions be most effectively relieved?

In part "the sickness of acquisitive society" is a police problem. Mr. Tawney himself has attributed the disease to the moral deliquescence of the age, but this etiology is extremely dubious. One cannot indict a civilization. What we know of medieval culture—not the high principles of leading churchmen, which we also could match with the writings of Mr. Tawney and many other high-minded contemporaries, but the actual behavior of ordinary people of high and low degree—scarcely leads us to believe that sin is a modern invention. Indeed, what makes the iniquity of modern business stand out in bold relief is the comparatively high standard of public administration which modern governments have been able to achieve in contrast to those of medieval times. Furthermore it is doubtful if any general condition can be properly attributed to the moral tone of the community. What then determines that moral tone? If the streets of modern cities are safer than those of medieval towns, that is due in the main to the modern development of street lighting. Crime flourishes in the dark. Any system of general illumination makes crime more difficult and therefore scarcer, and so brings about a general rise in the moral tone of the community. No such change ever originates in moral attitudes nor even in the more conscientious application of the existing machinery of law-enforcement. Even conceived as a police problem what the general delinquency of acquisitive society plainly calls for is the business equivalent of street lighting.[1]

[1] This will be recognized as an application of one of Dewey's most significant educational and ethical principles to the field of economics.

Obviously the need is greatest in the domain of big business. This is true not because one class of business men is more conscienceless than another but because big rascals are by definition more troublesome than little rascals. Students of economics have traditionally conceived this problem in terms of monopoly. They have done so in part because the classical way of thinking has represented competition as natural and wholesome and so has automatically identified unwholesomeness with deviations into monopoly, but also in part because business crimes are committed in the dark. As Adam Smith remarked, business men seldom dine together without entering into criminal conspiracies; but since the privacy of the dinner table is inviolable, "Gary dinners" are exceedingly difficult to proceed against. Even a stenographic report of the conversation may reveal no single word or phrase which can be made to prove criminal intent. Mr. Gary has let drop a few bits of information, and that is all. The real conspiracy is tacit. The only proof is the astonishing coincidence of the subsequent price quotations of the several diners. But since no specific act of collusion can be established by such evidence, the charge is necessarily limited to that of monopoly, that is, deviation from common competitive practice. Thus monopoly has come to head the calendar of economic crimes and to be the chief concern of many students.

Admitting the importance of the problem, we may still question the strategy and tactics of the attack on monopoly. However probable it may be that firms which have the power to dominate a market will do so and in doing so will commit a great variety of acts which would be judged criminal if they could be proved, courts hesitate to proceed on wholly or largely inferential evidence or to condemn "mere size" on the ground of deviation from a competitive norm which in the circumstances must be wholly or largely theoretical. Mr. Thurman Arnold has demonstrated that much can be accomplished by vigorous enforcement even of the anti-trust laws; but his successes were achieved in considerable part by using the "nuisance value" of threatened prosecution as a club to compel suspected firms to sign consent decrees agreeing to abandon various supposedly criminal practices, and this has already provoked a violent reaction against what is called "governmental blackmail." Apparently the attack on monopoly cannot be made permanently effective.

The plain lesson of this failure seems to be that we need another strategy. As Mr. Arnold himself wrote, before he became assistant attorney general, the condemnation of monopoly is itself part of the folklore of capitalism. The real evil is not size nor even power, unless all power and all bigness are to be condemned—and society is far from ready to take this stand. The real evil is the whole congeries of common crimes, suspected but unprovable, which big and little business men commit, the swindles and defalcations and embezzlements which Mr. Tawney attributes to the spiritual bankruptcy of capitalism. As our public life reveals, such things are a function of concealment. It is one of the ironies of capitalist culture that the practices which all good citizens condemn in government—bribery and graft, nepotism, the multiplication of unneeded offices solely in the interest of their incumbents—are not merely common but universal in business. The very considerable degree of purification which has been effected in government in spite of continual reinfection from the much larger area in which business standards still prevail is a testimonial not to the superior character of public servants but to the effectiveness of public scrutiny under which, to a steadily increasing degree, the affairs of government are conducted.

In part this is a matter of organizational technique. Business men themselves have been leaders in devising techniques to insure the honesty of their subordinates. It is such things as the cash register and the filing system that make large business organizations possible. What we need, obviously, is a system of cash registers for managing directors of the same sort as they impose on their subordinates. But this raises a larger question, the question of the "inalienable right" to privacy. In spite of the fact that business men deny any such pretensions on the part of their subordinates, not to mention "public servants," they are ferociously indignant at any suggestion that their own much-touted consecration to the service of the public carries any obligation to submit their acts to public scrutiny.

But obviously they have no case. It is ridiculous to suppose that opening the accounts of great corporations to public inspection is a violation of the personal privacy for which free men fought. Any free man can still have as much privacy as he likes by the simple expedient of not being a corporation executive, just as any man who objects to having his physical disabilities listed on his driver's license may retain his privacy by the simple expedient of not driving a car. At this point the contrast of the present situation with that of medieval times carries weight, but it is not the weight of other-worldly scruples. The simple intimacy of medieval life meant that in spite of all attempts at "privacy," business was conducted under the direct and knowing gaze of customers and competitors. What is required by the modern world is a system of grade-labeling and public supervision of accounts which will restore the checks and balances which were provided by the common acquaintance of the medieval town.

Business men and their hired spokesmen constantly protest that any procedure of this sort will inevitably impose on them an intolerable burden of "paper work." This is obvious nonsense, as thin as it is disingenuous. A business man who complains that for him to be required to declare on the label that his "Extra-Super-Fine" canned peas are in fact "Government Grade 4" would impose on him a terrible burden of inspection is in effect alleging that he buys his cans from local canners without specifications or inspection. If this is true, he deserves to fail; and if it is not true, his protest is a lie. The supposition that his peas are too subtle to be subjected to simple grading (*e.g.*, of the proportion of peas to water in the can) is similarly disingenuous. This is the protest which is urged with greatest vehemence against the supervision of accounts. Business accounts, it seems, are tremendously complicated, far too complicated to be submitted to the naïve scrutiny of public officials; but they are so, of course, because business men make them so, and business men make them so for this very purpose. It is often said that many large corporations are already "obliged" to keep three distinct sets of books: one for their own cost accounting, one for local property tax authorities with their physical properties valued low, and one for income tax purposes (and rate regulation, if they are subject to it) with their properties valued high. But that sort of thing is precisely what ails the modern world. If all business men could be obliged to tell the simple truth about their investments and their equities and their intercompany charges for "services" (usually the "service" of relieving a subsidiary of its earnings), the bookkeeping difficulties of the business world might be greatly reduced.

No doubt the task of policing business is one of great magnitude. But it is certainly not impossible. On the contrary, many steps have already been taken in that direction, steps which any student of economics could enumerate. Food and drug regulation broke trail in one direction, and in another, railway regulation. As was demonstrated many years ago, it is not impossible to standardize the accounting system of so complex an enterprise as a railroad. What we require is more of the same until the coverage is complete—not necessarily of regulation but of standardized accounts fully open to public scrutiny as, for example, the accounts of banks are published. Thus all income tax returns should of course be open to inspection and even locally displayed. Argument to the contrary is in effect disparagement of lighted streets. No honest man can possibly object to walking openly before his neighbors.

The principal reason for our failure to proceed farther in this direction is not the difficulty of the task nor the strength of the opposition but preoccupation with other things. Revolutionaries have been too preoccupied with attacking the foundations of plutocratic power to see what a very great difference full publicity would make in the exercise of that power, and business men have been too busy combatting this attack to see how very greatly their legitimate position would be strengthened by a strategic withdrawal from their present illegitimate and indefensible position.[2] But most of all, preoccupation with the classical way of thinking has confined the whole discussion to the alternatives of monopoly versus competition and bigness versus littleness. Since financial bigness is in large measure (though by no means altogether) a consequence of the steadily increasing technological scale of machine production (including transportation and communication) we have been forced to make terms with it; but even so the terms we have made for the regulation of great financial power have attempted only to simulate competitive conditions. But the evils of bigness have their origins in competitive littleness. As Mr. Tawney rightly insists, the moral decay is general. It can be arrested only by an equally general alteration in the physical habitat of capitalist business. To remove the smoke screen of concealment behind which business is conducted is therefore one of the strategic objectives of a technologically sound program of economic progress.

But it is only one. The larger problem still remains. This

[2] There are, of course conspicuous exceptions. For example, E. A. Filene, H. S. Dennison.

is the problem of equilibrium. In some sense or other all social philosophers have realized the strategic importance of maintaining some sort of balance between the various activities and interests of the community. A great deal of present-day discussion centers in the disequilibrium which has resulted from the rapid technological development of recent decades and even centuries. The common supposition is that institutional development has "lagged" behind the machine process and that our institutions need to be brought "up to date" and the equilibrium of institutions and technology thus re-established. As we have already noted, this view of the matter misconceives the nature of technology and institutions; but the conception of equilibrium is nevertheless sound. Perfection is beyond the power of social theory. The alterations which any single generation can make in the existing social structure must be very slight. This means that their effectiveness will depend on their success in restoring the whole structure to efficient functioning.

Their perception of this truth was the greatest achievement of the founders of the science of political economy. As such it will continue to command respect after all the misconceptions of classical tradition have been clearly recognized and discounted. Because price seemed to provide an intellectual vehicle for understanding the forces at work in modern economic life as well as an effective mechanism for the control of those forces, the vehicle has very largely displaced the "pay load" in the apprehension of economists and the whole problem has been conceived as that of price equilibrium. But the larger realities have never altogether disappeared from view. For the mercantilists no less than Adam Smith, for Professor Pigou no less than Thorstein Veblen, the basic economic problem is that of increasing the "national dividend." All considerations relating to the distribution of the product of industry are of secondary importance; for when the volume of production per head of population is increasing sooner or later every member of the community, even slaves and untouchables, will eventually benefit, whereas in a community in which the volume of production per head of population is decreasing the assignment of a larger share of community income to any given individual, group, or class will not save these beneficiaries from sharing the eventual ruin of the whole community. Production and distribution are related. If there were no relationship between these two sets of concerns, economic activities would not constitute an economy but only a patternless heterogeneity of acts and interests. What by contrast does constitute an economy is a continuous relationship between these two sets of concerns so that the volume of the national dividend is indeed conditioned by the fashion in which it is distributed, while at the same time distribution is conditioned by the social pattern of production.

It is the task of the economy to effect two sets of adjustments, one between the rich and the poor, and another between "alternative uses" of the instruments and materials of production; and these two adjustments must be adjusted to each other so as to maximize the national dividend. This is what price equilibrium has been traditionally supposed to achieve. The particular form which this pattern took in the classical theory of the economy was of course dictated by the existing structure of society. The founders of economic science lived in a world in which a very extreme degree of inequality already prevailed. It was also a world in which the national dividend was plainly on the increase. Economists have not been more callous to the cruelties of the prevailing system than most of their contemporaries, but their attention has been quite properly focused on the growth of the national dividend. In early modern times they were also deeply impressed by the change which the form or mechanism of inequality had undergone simultaneously with this sudden growth of the national dividend, the change by which money power had been substituted for feudal rank as the basis of the social system. It was the simultaneity of these changes which gave rise to the belief in a causal relationship between them. This conviction was nourished by the institutional apparatus and ideology of capitalism and so eventuated in the theory that the growth of the national dividend is contingent upon a social structure in which inequality results in saving, saving in the growth of capital, and the growth of capital in the increase of the national dividend; and it was this central idea that economic inequality is a condition by which all members of the community are eventually blessed which inaugurated and still sustains the policy of laissez faire, the fundamental strategy of which is that the existing structure of society must at all costs be let alone.

The chief strength of this policy and of the system of ideas by which it is sustained lies in the dynamic relationship between distribution and production which it presumes to establish and sustain. Price equilibrium is only the outward and visible sign of a real balance of forces in the economy. Doubt on this point is fatal to the whole theory, and that is why the doubts which have been multiplying in recent years even among the faithful are so disconcerting. They have taken many forms, but all have the same consequence. One is that of a reservation with regard to income distribution. It has become increasingly common for economists to insist, with an air of superior sophistication, that price equilibrium effects optimum efficiency in the use of the factors of production only for a given schedule of income distribution. This leaves the way open for the advocacy of a deliberate policy of reducing the extremities of inequality, but in doing so it reduces the whole theory to nonsense. Nowadays some economists even talk of a community's having to choose between a greater degree of distributive justice at the cost of a lowered national dividend and a greater national dividend at the cost of a greater degree of distributive injustice. Quite apart from the fact that it seems to imply that slavery is the most efficient, and equality the least efficient, productive arrangement, this formula represents the complete abandonment of the classical theory. This is even more obviously true of "pure" equilibrium theory and the theory of monopolistic competition. To old-fashioned orthodoxy competitive price equilibrium meant *both* the maximization of satisfactions and the optimum use of the factors of production, not the dubious achievement of one at the expense of the other, and certainly not a mere meaningless balance of prices by which neither maximum satisfaction nor optimum efficiency is guaranteed. The net result of the logical sophistication of contemporary price theory is the complete elimination from its neat array of simultaneous equations of all the larger realities for which price was originally conceived to stand.

Meantime direct scrutiny of those realities has raised a more insistent question. The classical supposition that the growth of the national dividend is enhanced by inequality raises an inescapable issue of fact. The question is what social forces are in fact chiefly responsible for the productive achievements of industrial society. The weakness of the classical theory at this (by its own reckoning) crucial point would be apparent if the issue had not always been obscured by the complex apparatus of price theory. For nothing is more obvious than its total lack of any realistic study of the actual processes of production or analysis of the actual history of industrial society. It has long been notorious that the supposed "factors of production" with which classical economists have been so much concerned from the eighteenth century to the present day are in fact distributive categories the very identity of which emerges from the analysis not of physical production but of the division of money income among its typical recipients. The whole effort of this analysis has been to show *how* industrial production is "made possible" by the accumulation of capital funds. At no time has economic orthodoxy ever approached the concrete reality of the industrial world with the intent to ascertain without previous commitment *whether* such is the case. From the very beginning the representation of the real balance of forces in the modern economy in terms of price equilibrium has owed its amazing plausibility to antecedent conviction with regard to the central issue of fact—the conviction, shared by the whole bourgeois community, that the exercise of financial power *must* be accompanied by the exercise of creative powers, a state of mind which owes nothing to fact and prevails among us as such beliefs do among all communities as a reflection simply of the acquiescence of the community in the prevailing social structure.

But the exact opposite is no less conceivable. That is, it is conceivable that the productive powers of industrial society have grown not because of the institutions of capitalism but in spite of them; that the chief, and catastrophically serious, obstacle to the full utilization and continued growth of those powers is precisely the distributive system which perennially baulks industrial production by failing to provide the consumer purchasing power which is essential to the absorption of the product of industry; and that the welfare of the whole community—the rich no less than the poor—is contingent upon the successful prosecution of a policy of income redistribution by which this deficiency of consumer purchasing power will be corrected. This policy also, and the system of ideas by which it is sustained, have their origin in the fundamental relationship between distribution and production by which an economy is constituted. No less than the classical theory of capital accumulation and policy of laissez faire, the theory of purchasing power deficiency and the policy of income redistribution center upon the growth of the national dividend to which all distributive arrangements are ancillary.

The question upon which the strategic issue of policy thus turns is whether the national dividend is enhanced or inhibited by inequality. It is with regard to this primary issue of fact that the analysis of the industrial process in terms of the technological and institutional factors which condition it presents the strongest contrast to the classical way of thinking. In attributing the extraordinary growth of the national dividend in recent centuries to the equally extraordinary development of tools and machines and scientific "know-how," this way of thinking establishes the continuity of recent developments with age-old process, a point at which the failure of economic orthodoxy is most striking. Such a way of thinking violates popular belief, but it coincides exactly with the findings of the other sciences. Indeed, the role of science in the transformation of modern life is now quite generally regarded as an established fact, even by people whose economic convictions flatly contradict it. For however plausible the theory may be which attributes the growth of industrial tools to the investment of capital funds, nobody [3] supposes that the intellectual achievements of modern science are attributable to financial benevolence alone. This contradiction has become so obvious in recent years that many economists have felt themselves compelled to take cognizance of it to the extent of declaring that although the development of science and technology must be acknowledged to condition the whole industrial process, it does so in a "non-economic" way and must therefore be excluded from economic analysis; but such an exclusion in effect brushes aside the basic issue of fact by which the validity of economic analysis must be eventually determined.

That the institutions of modern Western society as well as its technology have prodigiously affected industrial pro-

[3] An exception must be made in favor of Professor J. A. Schumpeter. See, for example, *Capitalism, Socialism and Democracy* (London and New York, 1942), Chapter XI.

duction no one doubts, least of all those who think in terms of technology and institutions. The question is, How? It is one thing to recognize the importance of the release of Western society from feudalism, quite another to attribute the growth of the national dividend to the exercise of financial power. After all, capitalism is only one feature of the modern social structure. It may well be that the progress of technology and the consequent growth of the national dividend owe more to political democracy, the separation of church and state, and the deliquescence of class distinctions than to financial overlordship. Insofar as it can be distinguished from the other features of the institutional scheme the latter may be an unqualified nuisance.

Such a nuisance is no less catastrophic for being indirect and unintended. In a society in which power can be achieved by the accumulation and investment of capital funds, it goes without saying that ambitious men will devote themselves to this activity. To suppose that in doing so they are acting with conscious solicitude for the welfare of posterity is so preposterous that no one has ever ventured to assert it, the idea being rather that in seeking their own gain "they are led as if by an invisible hand to promote an end which is no part of their intention." But it is equally fantastic to suppose, as classical theory has done, that a preference of future for present consumption is the guiding motive, a preference which is therefore thought to be expressed in and guided by the interest rate. This idea contains the antecedent assumption that the accumulation and investment of capital funds is the true essence of industrial growth, which is thus supposed to be automatically adjusted to the "needs" of the community by the rise and fall of the interest rate. But the point is one which has always given trouble, since it is obvious that people of modest circumstances who are "saving for a rainy day" will hardly be moved to desist by a fall of the interest rate, while to people who are engaged in carving empires for themselves out of the commonweal a per cent or two of interest is of no concern whatever.

Granted the existence of the financial power system, the participants, both large and small, in the struggle for economic power will accumulate all they can. If the funds from which such accumulations are made poured from the heavens in a never-ending stream, this exercise might have no effect on the national dividend. But such is not the case. It is the essence of the case as stated by classical economists themselves that saving is alternative to consumption and chiefly to the consumption of the masses; and since consumption is the sole eventual outlet for the product of industry this means that the inevitable effect of the struggle to accumulate financial power is the constriction of industrial output—the precise opposite to what has been conventionally supposed.

Here the basic issue of fact is posed again. Is there any evidence of any such constriction? Up to a few years ago the evidence on this point was still obsure, but the past thirteen years have provided as clear a demonstration as the most exacting experimentalist could wish. According to judgments expressed at the time, the functioning of the capitalist economy during the 1920's was as near perfection as it has ever attained. This was, indeed, the "New Era" of prosperity. But this era was followed by the greatest depression of modern times in the course of which the following facts emerged with unmistakable clarity. Most conspicuous, perhaps, was unemployment, that is the severance of many millions of families from their sole source of income and the consequent curtailment (virtual cessation) of their consumption. This was accompanied by widespread and very considerable restriction of production, that is, shrinkage of the national dividend, either by outright suspension of production or by the destruction or sequestration of huge segments of the national dividend after it had been produced. Nothing could have been clearer than the fact that the national dividend was suffering not from the inability of the community's industrial plant to maintain output but rather from the inability of the community to absorb that output. To complete the demonstration, it was no less conspicuous that a vast surplus of idle funds existed, funds which had been accumulated and were continuing to accumulate for which no "investment outlets" could be found.

Here was in fact the very condition the impossibility of which has always been a major premise of economy orthodoxy, and the demonstration still continued. Beginning in 1933 a new national administration inaugurated a series of efforts to put consumer purchasing power into circulation, with the result that conditions improved steadily if slowly, leaving the winter of 1932-33 as the trough of the depression. In 1936 these efforts reached their peak and the soldiers' bonus was pyramided on top of them, with the recovery of 1936-37 as the unmistakable consequence. Since the bonus was a single incident, and since the first sign of recovery brought a great outcry for "balancing the budget," as many economists had long ago predicted that it would, this brief respite was followed by a slackening of recovery which was still continuing when the effects of the present war began to be felt.

The fact that it is war and not economic "experimentation" which has finally ended the great depression of the 1930's is frequently cited as though to discredit all efforts to stimulate consumption by the expansion of mass consumer purchasing power. But such a reading of the facts overlooks the most conspicuous features of the present situation. War is in effect a public-works program which absorbs immense quantities of materials and puts millions of men directly on the public pay roll thereby increasing consumption not only to the limit of the slack occasioned by depression but far beyond it, with the result that consumer demand far exceeds the current output of industry. No responsible student would argue that the present situation is an economically wholesome one. In the long run consumption by destruction is bound to be suicidal, and a catastrophic price inflation is bound to be the effect of the simultaneous expansion of purchasing power and curtailment of *civilian* production unless extreme measures—price control, rationing, and the recapture of purchasing power—are taken to prevent it. But however excessive the answer, it is scarcely possible to doubt, in view of this demonstration, that a depression can be completely obliterated, full employment achieved, and industry exerted to its uttermost limits, by governmental stimulation of consumption.

As many writers have pointed out, none of these facts is new. Every feature of this demonstration has been enacted before, indeed many times before. It is therefore necessary to inquire why such facts have not been perceived before. The first answer to such an inquiry must be that they have been perceived before, both perceived and to a considerable degree understood. The so-called "underconsumption fallacy" has been in circulation at least since the seventeenth century.[4] To scotch it was the object of "Say's law," the dogma that under capitalism there can be no such thing as general overproduction (or underconsumption), a law in which its first great codifier sought to epitomize classical doctrine. This issue was the focal point of a long and lively controversy between Malthus and Ricardo, and it runs through virtually the whole literature of socialism.[5] To be sure, the identification of "the underconsumption fallacy" with what Mr. Keynes has called "the underworld" of eco-

[4] *E.g.*, Hazel V. Roberts, *Boisguilbert, Economist of the Reign of Louis XIV* (New York, 1935), Chapter X, esp. pp. 206-7.

[5] The most complete and satisfactory analysis of this controversy is contained in the unpublished doctoral dissertation of Professor George H. Hildebrand, Jr., "The Theory of Markets and the Problem of Economic Crises, from Quesnay to Marx" (1942), available only in the library of Cornell University.

nomics can scarcely be said to have added to its fame. Discussion of "the flaw in the price system" [6] went under ground with Sismondi and there it remained until the upheaval of the 1930's. Long before this time, as Mr. Keynes admitted handsomely in 1936, a few isolated but able individuals of complete respectability were deeply troubled by their discovery of this fundamental defect in the capitalist system, notably Silvio Gesell, A. F. Mummery, and J. A. Hobson. But their publications were greeted by what can only be called a conspiracy of silence.[7] They were joined in later years, especially during the New Era of the 1920's by other mavericks, such as Martin in England and Foster and Catchings in the United States; and during the 1930's there was of course an eruption of "underconsumptionism." Even then the discussion of the deficiency of purchasing power was clouded by social credit schemes of varying degrees of monetary wildness; but for the first time since Malthus the idea was seriously discussed, in large part under the leadership of Mr. Keynes (now Lord Keynes).

But "the underconsumption fallacy" still remains the orphan child of economics, partly for lack of the parenthood which only a general theory of economic progress could afford, and partly because of the asperity of its foster parents. If capitalism suffers from a fatal defect, it would be greatly to the advantage of the people who have the biggest stake in the present order of things to recognize and remedy that defect. A few have indeed tried to do so. Thus Gesell, Mummery, and Catchings were successful business men. But capitalists generally have not, largely no doubt because they considered the very thought socialistic—as indeed it was, at least by adoption. Meantime the socialists, who were quite undismayed by the perception of a fatal deficiency in the

[6] P. W. Martin, *The Flaw in the Price System* (London, 1924).

[7] Vividly described by Mr. Hobson in his "Confessions of an Economic Heretic," quoted by Mr. Keynes, *General Theory*, pp. 365 ff.

capitalistic system, were on that account all the more eager to pull the whole thing down. The strategy of reducing the extremes of inequality in the present distribution of income with a view to restoring the balance of the present social order is equally unpalatable to people who regard it as only a prelude to the destruction of that order and to people who regard it as a subterfuge for retaining the capitalist system.

It is to this situation that the unwillingness of the community to face the fact of a strategic deficiency of consumer purchasing power has been chiefly due. The hostility of socialists to "mere amelioration" has contributed to the neglect of underconsumption; but the effective opposition has been that of the respectable nine-tenths of the community, and it has been motivated by fear. Some of these fears are justified, and some are not. Conservative economists do not refute "the underconsumption fallacy," they brush it aside with a single footnote reference; and they do so because they rightly fear that admission even of the possibility of such a thing would endanger the whole structure of their argument. In like manner conservative citizens—and they are by no means limited to the very rich—fear to admit that expansion of consumer purchasing power by reduction of accumulation is an economic possibility lest that be a prelude to general confiscation. The rich have good reason to be afraid; and there is also good reason for the widespread aversion to indiscriminate confiscation, but it is not the reason which capitalist orthodoxy has given.

As far back as the record runs, long before the time of the Hebrew prophets, the rich have been the objects of impassioned denunciation. Their position has of course been extremely vulnerable to such attack. Some of the rich have always made hogs of themselves. Some have found no better use for wealth than to flaunt it in the faces of the poor, and "pecuniary canons of taste," as Veblen called them, have enforced quite unnecessarily invidious distinctions throughout the community. But it is nevertheless true that some people of wealth and many in comfortable circumstances have lived exemplary lives, avoiding ostentation insofar as it was possible for them to do so within the limits of modes of behavior of which they were the victims along with all the rest of the community, and using their wealth to foster beauty and learning. It is not necessary to argue that they have been ideal patrons of science and the arts, or to suppose that it is patronage which makes creative achievement possible. The point is that given a social structure which produces extremes of wealth and poverty, a great many people of good fortune have behaved as well as might have been expected under the circumstances. To denounce all the beneficiaries of an admittedly vicious system is to condemn the innocent along with the guilty—if the corruption of the rich by their riches can be regarded as guilt any more than the corruption of the poor by their poverty.

The injustice of such a condemnation has always been strongly felt by a large part of the community, and it has been accentuated by the extravagance of the claims which represent the whole national dividend as belonging "by right" to the poor. It is one thing to recognize that extremes of wealth and poverty are deplorable and quite another to denounce everybody above the level of the "proletariat" as by that fact alone a scoundrel who is engaged in robbing and otherwise exploiting the unfortunate. For if it is untrue that the rich enjoy their wealth by divine appointment, it is equally untrue that any other section of the community has any a priori warrant to the whole of the national dividend or for that matter any special part of it.

The supposition that a distinction can be drawn between the "productive" and the supposedly "unproductive" members of the community by which the claim of the former can be established and that of the latter nullified is without any merit whatsoever. In recent years that claim has been advanced on the basis of the supposed distinction between income from labor and income from property. This claim is of course a perversion of the classical doctrine of productivity by which the creation of "value" was imputed to the supposed "factors of production." That argument had as its object the validation of the claims of capital, as spokesmen for the "proletariat" have easily established. But in applying the same reasoning to establish the claim of labor to what is supposed to be its exclusive product the advocates of revolution have committed the very error to which they so cogently object when it is committed in the interest of "capital." The supposed distinction between the productive and the unproductive parts of the community is based not on the actualities of the industrial process but on the exigencies of the existing distributive system. Productive labor is identified by receipt of wages; unproductive "idleness" is identified by receipt of income from property or at least in some other manner.

Such a distinction can be made in no other way. Revolutionists have rough and ready tests by which they purport to distinguish friend from foe, for example by examination of their hands. But a surgeon or a composer may have hands as devoid of callouses as those of any millionaire, while a rich yachtsman's hands may be as rough as those of any fisherman. Is the surgeon therefore a drone, and the yachtsman a useful citizen? Housewives receive no wages and are therefore classified by the Bureau of the Census as not "gainfully employed." Are they therefore members of the idle rich class? It may be supposed that allowance can be made for the social connections of these members of the community. But if a rich polo player is idle however assiduous a player he may be, are his hostlers members of the leisure class? What is the difference between shoeing a farmer's horses and shoeing polo ponies? And if a blacksmith passes from one clientele to the other, what is his status? If the "hangers-on" are infected with the idleness of their principal, what about the miners and smelterers who produce the iron that is used to shoe polo ponies?

The truth of the matter is that the national dividend is the product of the community. It is conditioned both positively and negatively by every member of it, and in ways so complex and recondite as to make the attribution of credit and discredit, responsibility and blame, the most difficult of judgments—one which is indeed traditionally reserved to God. To make the distribution of income contingent upon such a judgment is to render the whole problem utterly insoluble. Everybody is to some extent aware of this difficulty, however strongly he may feel that his own contribution is undervalued, as the aphorism which reserves judgment to God plainly indicates; and this is one of the principal reasons why, in spite of all the misery and squalor of inequality, the community continues to look coldly upon proposals for a sweeping redistribution of income.

But none of these issues is germane to the strategy of the industrial economy. If it is true that under capitalism industrial society suffers from a chronic deficiency of mass consumer purchasing power and a corresponding surfeit of funds accumulated for investment, then it seems clear that the object of economic strategy must be a redistribution of income calculated to relieve industrial society from the burden of excess funds and to swell the mass of consumer purchasing power to the point at which it absorbs the whole product of industry under full employment of men and machines. To this strategy it makes no difference what the social sanctions are by virtue of which excessive incomes have come into existence. The danger of overaccumulation is just as great in the case of an income derived from landed estates inherited from the time of William the Conqueror as in that of a like income derived from speculation or from bootlegging. Each gluts the investment market no less than any other, and each represents the same degree of diminution of mass purchasing power.

Nor is there any question of checking the extravagances of the rich. Insofar as the rich spend their incomes they are providing an outlet for industrial production, as economists have known at least since the time of Bernard Mandeville. Some such outlets may seem less praiseworthy than others; but this is true of the poor no less than the rich, and is not at issue in any case. If the industrial system can be made to work, society can easily afford even the wildest extravagances of the rich. As economists have often pointed out with reference to proposals for a division of the good things of life such that everyone may have his "fair share," the rich are by definition not very numerous and a division of their perquisites among the many millions of the poor would still leave each individual share disappointingly meager. The only hope for substantial betterment of the lot of the whole community is by the increase of the national dividend on a scale such as that of the increase which in spite of everything has actually been realized during the past five centuries or even on a far greater scale. It is not the spending of the rich which prevents the realization of such an increase but the accumulation which results from their inability to spend their entire incomes and from their pursuit of power by accumulation and investment.

There remains the objection that the volume of funds which could be diverted from accumulation would be inadequate to create a volume of consumer purchasing power commensurate to the present supposed deficiency. This objection has no basis whatever, for it contravenes two principles on which all economists agree. One is the principle of "the multiplier." If the entire future increase of consumer purchasing power had of necessity to be taken from present accumulation, the objection would of course be valid. But obviously such is not the case. All economists agree that such adjustments are cumulative. They are so because expansion of consumption brings about expansion of production which in turn means an expansion of employment and so a further expansion of mass purchasing power. So sensitive are the construction, or capital goods, industries to such movements that many students, including Mr. Keynes, look to them as the key to the whole problem. If the interest rate and the prices of capital goods could be brought low enough, so they argue, real investment would increase and the resulting multiplication of the flow of purchasing power would be sufficient to balance the economy. With regard to the multiplication which such expansion effects, they are of course right. The sole defect of their argument is its neglect of the present flow of purchasing power as the vital limiting factor. How cheap must capital be in order to induce a producer to expand who sees no immediate prospect of selling more goods? The economy may create its own market (or may be made to do so), but no single producer does. What is necessary in order to put Mr. Keynes' multiplier to work is first of all to set in motion an expansion of consumer purchasing power; but once the expanding is under way, the multiplier of course does all the rest.

The supposition that such "pump-priming" involves a sacrifice of capital funds that are essential to real investment is a contradiction of the holiest of the sacred cows of orthodox theory, "Say's law of markets." Economists would have been forced to realize this long ago but for the fact that there is no criterion by which real investment can be distinguished from spurious investment. That is, in the inflation of capital values by virtue of which the investment market absorbs excess funds there is no point at which the funds which arrive early in a rising market and might therefore be judged to have been used for the actual purchase of capital equipment can be distinguished from funds which arrive late and might be judged to have contributed nothing but inflation to the industrial process. Even the time factor is irrelevant, since stock-watering goes on early as well as late in any given period, and in any such period later accumulation would not have been excessive had not the earlier preceded it. Consequently there is no distinct fund or stratum of investment which is clearly chargeable with the economic crime of superfluity. The absence of any such clearly marked distinction must have contributed mightily to the failure of the classical economists to recognize even the possibility of excess accumulation. Certainly it is responsible for the confusion which has attended all recent efforts to determine statistically the amount of real investment for comparison with the total amount of accumulated funds.

This means that the amount of funds to be diverted from accumulation to consumption cannot be determined by any qualitative test. The problem is wholly quantitative. Under conditions of depression the magnitude of excess bank reserves and of sums withdrawn from circulation by outright hoarding might be taken as an index to the magnitude of required transfer, not of those particular funds, but of sums in like amount to be diverted from the accumulating function as a whole. But at other times even this index would be lacking, and it is with such other times that we are most concerned since the whole idea is to prevent anything resembling depression from occurring at any time.

Fortunately the other side of the equation is much less obscure. Output and employment are physical facts, susceptible to physical measurement. The two do not exactly coincide. As a result of technological development, physical output might remain stationary or even show some increase in combination with increasing disemployment of men. Doubtless something of this kind was going on during the twenties, although as the Brookings study of "America's Capacity to Produce" seems to have shown, output was far short of the possible maximum even then. But if disemployment be taken as the basic guide, it would hardly be possible to go wrong. To increase the diversion of funds from accumulation to mass purchasing power proportionately to the increase of disemployment, decreasing the diversion with the decrease of unemployment, would make the punishment precisely fit the crime both qualitatively and quantitatively. The levy would be upon accumulation as such without reference to any other consideration, and it would be directly proportional to the failure of accumulation to achieve in fact the one social consequence by which it is presumed to be justified and necessary.

Do funds exist in sufficient quantity for such an operation? This is one question to which classical price theory provides an answer. For a century and a half it has been a commonplace of economics that the creation of pecuniary values in production cannot be less than the sale value of what is produced. If the total amount of income so created somehow fails to flow into the market, obviously something must have happened to it. Under conditions of depression it may have been destroyed. In that event the re-creation of money-values by deficit financing up to the amount of purchasing power necessary to absorb the product of industry at full employment would only be a salvage of purchasing power already lost by its former owners and so to the whole community. It is this circumstance which has led to the recognition of deficit financing by many respectable economists in recent years as a maneuver calculated to implement Say's law. Indeed there is no good reason why such a program should not take the form of the outright issue of currency in the amount so indicated.[8] Insofar as the deficiency of funds at any given moment were the result of sequestration

[8] This proposal has been made most clearly and forcibly by Professor E. E. Hale, of the University of Texas, unfortunately never in print.

rather than destruction, such action might be inflationary; but objection on this ground is itself a sufficient answer to the question whether funds exist. Insofar as they do exist, the question is answered. Indeed, at the first sign of an inflationary movement energetic measures to recapture and reactivate sequestered funds might well be undertaken in complete assurance that the funds sought do in fact exist and in a form in which they do nobody—neither their owners nor the community—any good whatsoever.

On the basis of our meager experience it would be extremely difficult if not impossible to compute in advance how much income would need to be diverted from accumulation to consumer purchasing power in order to bring about full employment at any given time. But one thing we can know: real investment, whether by private or public agency, would suffer not at all from any such diversion. This is true for a number of reasons. In the first place, as the classical economists have been reiterating, lo, these many years, real investment is consumption. Furthermore, as we know, it is a form of consumption which is self-multiplying, since investment in productive equipment releases purchasing power to those who fabricate that equipment, who in turn become consumers of the products which the whole economy turns out, thereby further stimulating expansion of the productive mechanism. Real investment therefore works with consumer purchasing power to stimulate total production, not against it. It is also very significant that funds available for investment are uniquely elastic. Some economists have even argued that industrial expansion creates its own funds through the action of the banking system with the assistance of national monetary policy. This is true because real industrial expansion creates values, so that the financing is largely a matter of paper transactions, whether the transactions are by public or private agencies. The decisive factor is the expectation of profits, and it is at this point that the importance of consumer purchasing power is most decisive; for profits can be expected only by virtue of a continued flow of purchasing power. The complete mutual contingency of the productive and distributive aspects of the economy is exemplified by the complete mutual contingency of real investment and sustained consumption.

This, after all, is the central fact. In all the foregoing discussion of the obstacles by which, in the apprehension of many people, the strategy of income redistribution appears to be confronted, and in the attempt to understand how such a strategy and the facts which point to it could have been so generally neglected in the past, no mention has been made of the most important cause of this neglect and opposition. For it is negative. The fatal defect of capitalism has not passed altogether unnoticed. But it has been noted by people whose minds were preoccupied with other things. Malthus was in the main a classicist. Sismondi and Marx were revolutionaries. And even Mr. Hobson, the dean of contemporary "underconsumptionists," has never broken with orthodox price-value theory nor with the legendary history by which that theory is sustained. The "underconsumption fallacy" has never in the past appeared to flow directly from any systematic analysis of the industrial economy of which it was the inescapable conclusion—from any way of thinking of which income redistribution was the characteristic expression. It has been a biological sport, without proper intellectual parentage, and therefore without standing. Even Veblen, whose thinking more than that of any other economist did afford a systematic theoretical foundation for such a strategy, failed to carry through at all from analysis to policy. It was his chief failure, and one that has not yet been rectified.

We have only to contemplate the present scene to realize how serious that failure was. Among the democratic peoples of the world two great crusades are now under way upon which they are in effect staking their hopes of a democratic future: the crusade for peace and the crusade for social security. There is a general feeling that these two movements are related, that world peace is somehow contingent upon world economic order and vice versa, but it is far from clear to the community at large just what this relation is. The real force behind these drives is fear: fear of want and fear of the renewal of total war. In appealing to such fears President Roosevelt has given voice to the common apprehension.

But fear does not solve problems. How is social security to be achieved? Sir William Beveridge and the National Resources Board have devised far-reaching plans for dealing with old age, sickness, unemployment, and kindred evils. As a consequence of the circumstances under which it is undertaken it is inevitable that such an effort should be "first and foremost a plan of how social insurance should be organized," [9] and not a strategy of economic progress. One would never guess, from the Beveridge Report at least,[10] that such an undertaking could be anything but a heavy burden of expense to the community. The whole emphasis of the Beveridge Report is upon the ability of Great Britain to bear so moderate a cost even after the present war, especially since a considerable part of it is to be borne by the wage-earning class itself. As its author remarks:

> Want could have been abolished before the present war by a redistribution of income within the wage-earning classes, without touching any of the wealthier classes. This is said not to suggest that a redistribution of income should be confined to the wage-earning classes; still less is it said to suggest that men should be content with avoidance of want, with subsistence incomes. It is said simply as the most convincing demonstration that abolition of want just before this war was easily within the economic re-

[9] Beveridge Report, *Social Insurance and Allied Services* (Publ. by His Majesty's Stationery Office, London, 1942), p. 103.

[10] The proposals of the National Resources Board had not yet been released to the public at the time of writing.

sources of the community; want was a needless scandal due to not taking the trouble to prevent it.[11]

But how convincing is a demonstration likely to be so long as its tone is one of apology? "Properly designed, controlled and financed," says the famous Report, social insurance "need have no depressing effect on incentive."[12] In short, this great crusade is for as much decency as is compatible with capitalism. But capitalism itself is collapsing, and it is collapsing precisely because of the maldistribution of income for which it is responsible. The great need for such a program of social security is not to correct a public scandal but to restore the balance of the economy. Until this is understood apology and timidity will of course continue to prevail. We will enact enough social security legislation to ease our consciences, but not enough to save the economy, and so we will have more depressions and more wars.

For war is the same problem in another guise. All the talk now is concerned with the permanent organization of the United Nations, with the flow of international trade, and with the regulation of traffic on the sea and in the air. Such talk is not "globaloney." World peace, no less than social security, calls for a plan of organization. But here too the atmosphere is negative. World organization, it seems, will require some sacrifice of national self-interest. The argument is that what sacrifices we may have to make are a small price to pay for security from war. One would never guess that in modern times the international trade and foreign policy of each of the leading industrial nations have become, in the words of Mr. Keynes, "a desperate expedient to maintain employment at home by forcing sales on foreign markets and restricting purchases," a policy "which, if successful, will merely shift the problem of unemployment to the neighbor which is worsted in the struggle" and is therefore the

[11] Pp. 165, 6.
[12] P. 167.

"predominant" cause of war.[13] This means that the present cycle of wars can be brought to an end only by the correction of the deficiency of consumer purchasing power which forces each industrial nation into this "desperate expedient." Until that is done, treaties can be nothing more than the rules of the game under which (at first) the next war will be fought.

Why does the world so obstinately refuse to see what is so apparent to many observers? These two crusades, against want and against war, in fact are one. Neither can be successful except by achievement of the other, and both together depend upon the correction of the distributive balance of the industrial economy. One set of idealists opposes war; another opposes poverty; and meantime the defect of the present economic system which is the cause of both disorders is recognized as such only by still another set of cranks—scornfully known as "underconsumptionists."

Judged by the present scene, our case is hopeless. But such a judgment would not only ignore the possibility of change; more important, it would overlook the process of development which has led to the present situation. Ideas do not originate in vacuum. The abhorrence which intelligent people feel toward war in steadily increasing degree is more than a vague, emotional humanitarianism, and so is the abhorrence of poverty. Both express a deep and growing sense of travesty, a sense still largely inarticulate but none the less genuine on that account that poverty and war are not only shameful but quite unnecessary, that it is only our stupidity which permits poverty and war to flourish in the midst of plenty. We have not yet brought these ideas to full articulacy. As yet they seem to lack theoretical foundations such as the classical economists provided for the policy of laissez faire, and consequently the strategy of income redistribution as yet lacks the force of full conviction. But the

[13] *General Theory*, pp. 381-83.

facts of which such a theory of economic progress would be a formulation are there and are already dimly realized. Sooner or later we shall achieve a theoretical reformulation of the economic life process of which the strategy of income distribution will be the inexorable logical consequence and the prelude to a new age of economic progress.

Chapter XIII

THE POWER OF IDEAS

IS THE FULFILLMENT of these ideas a visionary hope? Have they insufficient roots in the motives which govern the evolution of political society? Are the interests which they will thwart stronger and more obvious than those which they will serve?" These questions cut to the heart of one of the most fateful confusions of contemporary economic thinking. It is most significant that Mr. J. M. Keynes should have asked them and correspondingly unfortunate that he should have postponed them virtually to the last page of his *General Theory* and then stayed not for an answer.

Do ideas have the power to affect the actual course of events merely by virtue of being true? Have we any certainty of an idea being true in such a field as economics until its general adoption proves its effectivenesss in action? And what determines the effective adoption of ideas? Is it not after all a matter of the power of vested interest and the opposing power of revolting masses? Such questions express the spirit of the age. The eighteenth century believed in ideas; the nineteenth century in institutions; the twentieth, apparently, in force. Or perhaps it would be closer to the truth to say that the twentieth century is confused. Later criticism of eighteenth-century ideas has thrown an ironic crosslight on the confidence of that age in its reason. The twentieth century has lost much of the naïveté as well as the complacency of preceding generations.

This is true in part because ours has been a period of extreme violence. Economists after all are singularly modest men. In view of the magnitude of the disturbances which have followed the resort to naked force we hesitate to assert that truth will eventually triumph in spite of dictators. "Eventually" is a rather unsatisfactory word, under the circumstances. To rest content with the "eventual" triumph of the truth seems uncomfortably like letting others do the fighting. For how shall the truth be vindicated if its defenders merely sit and wait? Our sense of the necessity we share with all living things to defend ourselves against attack thus leads us to identify the fulfillment of our ideas with the outcome of the physical struggle.

Even Mr. Keynes succumbs to this confusion. For after saying in effect that the fulfillment of ideas is a function of their validity, he goes on to declare that "the world is ruled by little else . . . both when they are right and when they are wrong," thereby in effect giving away the ground on which his confidence in the vindication of his own ideas was based; and in doing so he exemplifies another major source of our confusion. The eighteenth century could avow a naïve confidence in the power of ideas because, as Professor Becker has demonstrated, the philosophers of that age still lived in a heavenly city in which truth was absolute. But the twentieth century is relative. The present climate of opinion is that of a debased, or rather an immature, sort of "pragmatism." Ideas are now quite generally held to be true only if they "work." How they "work" seems, in our confusion, to be of no consequence. In the easy-going logic of the age of relativism no distinction is made between different kinds of "work," with the result that we have become more and more committed to ways of thinking which assume that a social theory "works" if it leads to any sort of action. In this spirit even Mr. Keynes remarks that "madmen in authority, who hear voices in the air, are distilling their frenzy from some academic scribbler of a few years back." Is this evidence of the power of ideas? If so the effect is to put the distinguished work of Mr. J. M. Keynes on precisely the same plane as that of any other academic scribbler, whether right or wrong, and so to make the madmen in authority the final arbiters not only of the fulfillment but therefore even of the truth of our ideas.

There is even some justification in social theory for doing so. The scepticism of which the pragmatic logic was one fruit has also taken note of the linkage between ideas and the communities which entertain them. Apparently every community has its climate of ideas, and so it would seem that every idea does but give voice to some community. So striking is this phenomenon that it has threatened to dominate all our social thinking. Since, as we know, social scientists live in climates of opinion, there seems to be no basis for a distinction between their theories and the group ideologies which they so suspiciously resemble. Thus we find ourselves thinking, more or less explicitly, that the ideas of economists prevail only through the agency of organized communities, and so that of their more or less phrenetic leaders, and finally through the triumph of that leadership over others in the struggle for coercive power, a struggle in which force supplements and qualifies "ideas."

The upshot of this way of thinking in all its forms is not only that one community is very like another but even that one idea is very like another. This is of course a highly unsatisfactory conclusion, and it has therefore provoked a reaction by which our confusion has been twice confounded, the neo-medievalism which not only denounces "pragmatism" as the cause of our cultural disease but proposes to cure it by a return to the simple faith of other days.[1] It might be remarked that a plea for faith as a restorative of social health is itself pragmatic in the worst sense; but such a retort, however satisfying, would miss the point at issue. The point is that the confusion of our day is itself an index of intellectual and social progress. Obviously the clock can no more be turned back from the twentieth to the thirteenth century than organic evolution can be reversed, nor would such a reversion be desirable. In spite of the pains which still attend it, our intellectual growth has been genuine. It has been incomplete, and therefore unsatisfactory. But growth is still going on. Implicit in the dilemma of pragmatism and sociological relativism is the distinction between technological and institutional processes, a distinction by which that dilemma and all the confusion to which it has given rise may be entirely resolved.

It is only in terms of this distinction that the power of ideas can be understood. Ideas, powers, and "work" are all of two kinds. That is, ideas must be distinguished from ideologies, power conceived as the flow of cause and effect must be distinguished from authority conceived as a function of the "causes" for which men fight, and the tool-efficiency with which an idea "works" as part of the instrumental process (in the laboratory or the shop) must be distinguished from the efficacy with which an ideology "works" upon the memories and sentiments of a community. The power of

[1] *E.g.*, John U. Nef, *The United States and Civilization* (Chicago, 1942), p. 405: "The moral and intellectual crisis of Western civilization, which has accompanied the material crisis, is common to all the Western nations. Far from escaping it, the United States has been to a considerable extent a leader in those movements (such as pragmatism) which, in spite of the intelligence and character of some of the leaders, have helped to produce a decline in the integrity and the freedom of the mind and spirit during the last fifty years. It is ironical that, up to the present, the one conspicuous sphere in which we should have taken the lead in connection with thought should be in the undermining of it."

ideas of the first order is a function of their truth, which in this case is a tool function. Thus the determination of the truth of such an idea as that of the binomial theorem is a definition of its power: it has the power to solve certain equations, this being the only sense in which it works. It does not have the power to move communities of men to action. That power is exercised by ideas of quite another type, the ideologies of which it is futile to inquire whether or not they are "true" in the scientific sense because however efficacious they may be as shibboleths they are not tools and do not work at all in the fashion that tools work.

Both sorts of ideas find their way into the pages of academic scribblers, since even the most academic writer is still a social animal. But the ones from which madmen in authority distill their frenzy are the expressions of belief and sentiment which even writers share with their communities. Such ideological figments may indeed derive added authority from their association with scientific truths in the pages of savants, since in our community the name of science is something to conjure with—and this is very significant. But it does not mean that an expression such as "Aryan supremacy" derives its (institutional) power from its supposed (scientific) truth.

If any particular social conflict be assumed as "given" and viewed, so to speak, as "a going concern," it has in effect been defined as a shock of opposing forces the outcomes of which will be determined solely by the strength of those particular forces. In such a situation it is indeed entrenchment, physical and ideological, that counts and not the power which (in quite another setting) accrues to ideas because they are right. Thus Mr. Keynes was very right indeed in his judgment of the economic consequences of the Treaty of Versailles, as subsequent events have demonstrated, and his ideas on that subject have therefore won virtually complete acceptance among economists and political philosophers;

but in the struggle for power at Versailles as he described it in his justly celebrated book those ideas were quite without effect.

If this were the whole story—that is, if history consisted only of a series of conflicts, each wholly self-contained and unaffected by anything save perhaps the outcome of the conflict immediately preceding—then no case could be made for the power which ideas might be presumed to exercise by virtue of being right. Every party to every conflict might still boast its favorite social philosophers and economists, but they would be honored not because they were right but only because they were on the right side. Thoughtful men have sometimes wondered whether such is not indeed the case. But to recognize this as the condition which prevails within the limits of any particular struggle in which opposing forces already exist and are even dug in and firing at will, amounts only to saying that ideas are ineffective within the limits of situations in which by definition ideas are ineffective. Anybody can define such a situation. A traveler who is waylaid by a thug (who may have mistaken him for somebody else) is for the moment in such a case, and so is a nation which is waylaid by another nation (led, perhaps, by madmen in authority). It has often been said that although the political and economic ideas of the Danes and the Norwegians were among the most advanced in the world, they were of no effect in saving those peoples from conquest. Once the Nazi *Wehrmacht* had begun to roll, a frame of reference existed to which all ideas were irrelevant.

But institutional conflict is not the whole story. Nobody seriously and consistently supposes that it is. Historians sometimes talk as though they did, but no historian denies the long-run effect, for example, of the development of science upon modern civilization, although science has never been a participant in any battle nor even the "cause" for which any participant has ever engaged in any struggle. The most obvious weakness of dialectical materialism which interprets history as an unbroken series of class struggles is the supposed consummation of the process. Marx wrote as though the outcome of the final struggle would be determined by the logic of force; but he also wrote as though the analytical correctness of the proletarian case could be established in advance, and his conviction that the bourgeoisie would have occasion to remember his carbuncles was based on the supposition that in his case the (instrumental) logic of (scientific) ideas would prevail over capitalist ideology and entrenched privilege. Thus in effect Marx's own work constituted a denial of dialectical materialism.

What is involved here is not only the distinction of the technological from the institutional aspects of the social pattern but the difference between an instantaneous cross-section and the long-run process of social change. In the former, virtually by definition, institutionally and ideologically entrenched authority prevails. It is in the long run that technologically correct ideas get in their work, in modern Western society so effectively that our world is indeed ruled by little else, as Mr. Keynes clearly implied by speaking of their "gradual encroachment." The power which ideas exert by virtue of being correct is a function not of mind over matter but of technology over institutions in the long-run process of social change.

As the experience of Western society demonstrates, this power is manifested in two ways: by the changes which technological development effects in the physical medium with resulting institutional obsolescence and eventual change, and by changes which scientific enlightenment effects directly in the ways of thinking by which institutions are ideologically sustained.

The former is the more obvious because it is the more spectacular. This is what people have in mind when they say that social problems are never solved, only forgotten.

Perhaps the most tragic irony of institutional conflict is the fact that neither party to any social struggle can possibly prevail unchanged, since the struggle is itself a symptom of ensuing change. The present world struggle is clearly of this character on both its fronts. These disorders are due to the strain to which the institutional framework of Western society has been subjected by the industrial revolution. For several centuries past the process of industrialization has been increasing the scale of industrial operations until it has become virtually world-wide, with the result that a very extreme contrast has developed between the physical range of machine technology and the parochialism of certain institutions.

These are, of course, the state and property. To some degree the entire institutional pattern is involved in any general change; but such an institution as the family is less vitally affected than others by the present crisis because machine technology has long since passed the confines of the family, leaving it quite different from what it was but still more or less intact as a residential rather than an industrial unit. But no such easy transition has been possible in the case of the state and property because although both have already undergone profound modifications, both still retain organizational structures which offer the sharpest possible contrast to the global scale of industry. Great as the difference is between the national state and the feudal principality, the former still retains something of the latter. It is still in essence limited in area, a jurisdictional subdivision of a technologically integrated world. Property also has undergone profound modification. The remark has often been made in recent decades that while statecraft remains parochial finance has become international. But the internationalism even of finance is subject to sharp limitations which correspond to those of the national state. Even the most far-flung financial operations rest on a foundation of ownership, and since ownership assumes political sovereignty it is still national in scale. Furthermore ownership is still a limiting conception. It draws a line between one owner (or set of owners) and another, and also between owners and non-owners, and in these respects it contrasts with the universal pervasiveness of technology.

The strain to which these two institutions are thus subjected is one continuous strain. It is this circumstance which has led to the general recognition of the present war as revolutionary in character. As a great many people already see, neither property nor the national state is going to emerge from the present convulsion quite unchanged; and this is true irrespective of the immediate outcome of the struggle since it is a consequence not of the declared intentions of any party to the struggle but rather of conditions to which all industrial communities are subject.

Most conspicuous are the revolutionary changes which are imposed by military necessity in the conduct of the war. Many instances have come to light of trade agreements, patent restrictions, and even of control of essential materials, by which favorably placed firms have limited production especially on the part of actual or potential competitors. Indeed, the solution of this problem has obviously been far from complete. There are many indications, such as the concentration of war orders among the largest firms, which even suggest that war accentuates the concentration of control of industry. But war necessarily imposes limitations upon business autonomy of even the largest corporations. In principle at least the rights of property are suspended wherever they conflict with military necessity, including the necessities which result from drastic curtailment of the production of civilian consumers' goods.

These changes are sufficiently marked to elicit anguished cries for the restoration of such property rights immediately following the conclusion of the war; but the problem which war thus throws into sharp relief exists at all times. For many years it has been apparent to all students of economics, government, history, and related fields, that the growth of financial power had come to constitute a challenge to the state itself. Even in the field of foreign relations, presumably the exclusive domain of government, great corporations and international cartels have drawn boundaries, allocated spheres of interest, and generally divided the world among themselves, sometimes with the assistance of departments of state which they have been able to call upon to do their bidding, and sometimes in defiance of the contrary policies even of their own governments, not to mention the political establishments of the lesser "sovereign states" which they have traded back and forth like business assets. In war the military requirements of distant strategic materials and of defense of lines of approach inevitably supersede the bargains of the business men, but war only reveals the fashion in which technological development has set property and government at cross purposes at all times.

Furthermore the problem is by no means limited to matters of jurisdiction or even of the conflict of special interests with the national interest. It has been a commonplace for many decades that all the wars of modern times have been economic in origin. This has sometimes been said of all conflict throughout the whole course of history; but whereas the latter generalization refers only to the supposition that it is always food for which men fight, it is the economic organization of capitalist society which has activated the wars of modern times. The struggle is no longer for food or even for "room." On the contrary, it is a struggle for markets. As such it is a consequence of the fundamental defect of the capitalist system: deficiency of consumer purchasing power. The failure of capitalism to distribute enough purchasing power to absorb the product of industry at full employment subjects every industrial nation to the continual threat of "overproduction." Since the export trade offers an immediate relief to this artificial surfeit, the industrial powers have all sought foreign markets. Their efforts in this regard have been competitive and have inevitably brought them into conflict. Indeed it is in this sense alone—with reference to their "access to foreign markets"—that any industrial nation has had any real ground for complaining of being "hemmed in," as all neutral commentators now agree. Furthermore the purchasing power problem is no less acute in foreign than in domestic trade. Not only is the purchasing power of non-industrial peoples even less than that of industrial communities; the maintenance of an export balance (by historic fallacy known as "favorable") obliges the exporting powers perpetually to refuse payment (lest foreign goods compete with domestic production). Thus it turns out in the end that the exports have been largely given away (at the expense, of course, not of the exporters but of the purchasers of foreign bonds). These exigencies also lead inevitably to trouble.

The present cycle of wars is the consequence of all these troubles, and its termination is contingent upon the correction of the unbalance between industrial capacity and the distribution of consumer purchasing power for which the capitalist system is responsible. A realization of this truth is now gradually dawning upon Western society. That the wars of modern times have been actuated by a struggle for markets is now recognized as a fact by a great many people who do not yet appreciate the significance of this fact, and its significance is fully recognized by the smaller number who have begun to understand the chronic deficiency of purchasing power which has resulted from the obsession of Western society with the accumulation of "capital," and who are therefore unanimous in their conviction that the indefinite prolongation of the present cycle of wars can be prevented only by a solution of this problem. Nevertheless it is not with the power of these ideas that the present analysis is concerned. What is now under discussion is the power of the scientific and technological ideas from which the industrial process itself results. The point is that the world crisis is itself a manifestation of the power of ideas, inasmuch as it is a consequence of industrial development.

Not only have science and technology subjected the institutions of Western society to intolerable strain; it is industrial necessity which likewise defines the conditions under which alone the strain can be relieved. This does not mean that much (indeed, most) of the institutional content of the past will not be retained in the future. Such has always been the case and doubtless will continue to be. It does not even mean that science and technology will necessarily prevail. Perhaps the world will "choose" authority rather than plenty. But it does mean that if institutions are retained under which industry cannot operate, industrial technology will be destroyed. This seems unlikely. More than ever during the period of strain the world seems to be committed to the truth of science and the efficiency of the machine. War itself employs technical expedients and reinforces the power of scientific ideas while loosening the ties of ancient institutions. The probability is that these ideas will prevail in the end, and when they do the future world-state and economy of abundance will reveal their pattern.

Meantime the power of ideas is exerted in quite another way. Whereas changes in the physical setting which result from technological development might be said to have a negative effect upon institutional situations as a result of which issues are not so much solved as forgotten, such a development as the growing recognition of the market-seeking character of capitalist imperialism exemplifies the positive effect of movements of thought upon the ways of thinking of which community action is an expression. The expansion of knowledge is itself an aspect of the technological process, and as such it is subject to certain rules or "laws" of which all technical development is a manifestation. One is that it proceeds at a self-determined rate. While the advancement of knowledge, or of technology generally, can be impeded locally or momentarily, what determines the rate of its over-all development is its own substance. Another closely related principle is that of inexorable growth. Granted a given state of knowledge, no other power can prevent the developments from taking place which are implicit in that state. As Galileo understood, no institutional power, political or ecclesiastical, could long prevent the world in which Copernicus and Lippershey had done their work from identifying the moons of Jupiter.

It is these principles which impose narrow limits upon all the undertakings of the propagandists. Any idea can be successfully disseminated, and its propagation will be an instrument of power, only so long as it is not susceptible to verification. In the case of matters of fact, such as the outcome of military campaigns, the limits are narrow. In other cases the propaganda itself consists of folklore rather than matters of fact. Such ideas have indeed persisted over vast periods of time. But on this account the present strength of folk belief derives from immemorial tradition, not from the machinations of any propaganda bureau. Bureaus of public enlightenment create and disseminate quasi-folklore such as belief in the quasi-divine character of an "inspired" leader; but the effectiveness of such concoctions is limited by the body of genuine tradition with which they inevitably collide at various points and by eventual verification which may be all the more disastrous by virtue of the revulsion of feeling which results when a community discovers that it has been duped.

The power of propaganda is greatly exaggerated, especially by its opponents. Citizens of democratic countries, knowing the use that is made of propaganda by totalitarian regimes, are therefore prone to attribute the whole body of public sentiment by which those regimes are sustained to the success of their campaigns of organized deceit. In similar fashion opponents of capitalism, knowing that newspapers suppress information harmful to their advertisers, therefore attribute the very existence of the capitalist system to "the kept press"; and in the same spirit men of substance commonly attribute an "upsurge" of economic and political reform to the demogogic cajolery of some politician who has not scrupled to "set class against class" in furtherance of personal ambition. But in every case it is not the power of propaganda which is responsible for these momentous consequences but rather an underlying truth, in each case one which the commentator finds so unpalatable that he seeks to represent it—to himself and if possible to others—as a villainous creation of scheming propagandists. Certainly the democratic "upsurge" of the 1930's was a public reaction to the fact of economic collapse. What has baulked the growth of radicalism in America has been the high standard of living which has prevailed, hitherto at least, and in comparison with other countries. And as the German people well know, the intolerable conditions by which they were afflicted (for whatever cause) during the 1920's and early '30's were not the product of the imagination of any propaganda bureau.

The dependence of successful propaganda upon underlying truth leads to the recognition of a third principle. The advancement of knowledge follows certain more or less clearly marked channels. Veblen emphasized the importance of the flow of scientific thinking from mathematics and astronomy through physics and chemistry to the biological sciences and so eventually to the moral and social sciences,[2]

[2] "Why Is Economics Not an Evolutionary Science", *Quarterly Journal of Ecomonics,* XII (1898), republished in *Place of Science in Modern Civilization* (New York, 1919), pp. 80, 81; *Instinct of Workmanship,* pp. 323 ff., and elsewhere.

as of course many others had already done. Immanuel Kant, writing under the influence of Rousseau, predicted a Copernican revolution which, he thought, was the certain outcome of the incidence of science; and however much his conception of the nature of this revolution may have been distorted by his metaphysics, there can be no doubt that he was right both about the general direction and about the magnitude of the expected change.

Various reasons can be given for the direction which the advancement of science has followed. To some degree, no doubt, scientific investigation (and technological development generally) has followed the line of least institutional resistance. The logical abstractions of mathematics and the motions of the stars and planets have been permitted subjects long before the human body. But it is also true that technological pressure has been exerted along the same lines. As Dewey has pointed out, the "retarded and immature state of social subjects" is explained by the fact that "only recently has there been sufficient understanding of physical relations (including the biological under this caption) to provide the necessary intellectual instrumentalities for effective intellectual attack upon social phenomena."[3] Since the instrumentalities of science are genetically indissociable from the tools and expedients of the industrial arts, this means that scientific ways of thinking have gradually pervaded the whole field of human interest and inquiry just as machine technology has pervaded all the activities of life; and this fact also can be stated as a principle. By virtue of the fashion in which it moves from one field to another making use of one technical instrumentality after another, science gradually pervades every department of life and all the strata of society.[4]

[3] *Logic, the Theory of Inquiry* (New York, 1938), p. 492.

[4] This conception of "the cultural incidence of the machine process" upon the whole community is the point of departure of a recent study

In conformity to this general process, the economic thinking of Western society has undergone profound modification. The change is much greater than is yet realized by many professional economists. Concepts such as "utility" and "productivity" which only half a century ago circulated freely and were generally regarded as sound intellectual currency are now just as generally viewed with extreme suspicion. The virtual identity of saving with investment is now universally admitted not to be an identity at all. Furthermore, changes such as these are not expressions of any special interest the growing ascendancy of which they might be thought to register. Just as truly as any mathematical demonstration or physical discovery they are the consequences of a genuinely intellectual process of conceptual clarification and of recognition of matters of fact. The criticism to which the conceptuology of economics has

---

of the development of collective enterprise. Detailed examination of developments in a wide variety of fields has showed that the dynamic force making for social change is not occupational habits of thought or even special interests but is rather the changing thought-patterns of the whole community functioning as the consumers of the industrial economy. The consuming function is significant not as the distinction between receipt of income and its expenditure, and certainly not as the distinction between occupational activities conceived in the light of economic orthodoxy as "means" to the attainment of consummatory values regarded as "ends," but only in terms of the extent of the two disciplinary areas in which people produce and consume. Their employment seldom occupies more than a third of the time of the gainfully employed who are themselves considerably less than half the community and are dispersed among a great variety of occupations; while the consuming function occupies the greater part of the time of all members of the community and in spite of great differences of volume of consumption exposes all to very much the same kind of disciplinary influences. Hence the consumer interest is virtually synonymous with the public interest as that interest has found expression in the actual process of "collectivization."—Seba Eldridge and twenty-nine associates (among them, the present writer), *Development of Collective Enterprise: Dynamics of an Emergent Economy* (Lawrence, Kansas, 1943).

responded has been scientific criticism; and the recognition of such a fact as the non-identity of saving and investment, though it has been brought about very largely by the cogent demonstrations of Mr. J. M. Keynes, does not on that account owe its truth to his personal ascendancy—certainly not to the ascendancy of any class or special interest which he might be conceived to represent.

Nor is the impact of such ideas concentrated upon any particular community or class. The issues by which communities and classes seem to be divided are not resolved by either side winning complete ascendancy over the other. No idea will endure such treatment.

So general and pervasive is the process by which ideas are subjected to the transforming touch of science and technology that the issues by which people are divided are themselves transformed even while the struggle is going on. Neither side is immune to the infection. On both sides the ideological dogmas are undergoing a continuous shift of emphasis and the ideological symbols continuous redefinition, with the result that issues and even alignments themselves are continuously shifting; and since the changes on both sides constitute responses to the common and pervasive influence of scientific and technological development, the process is one in which opposites are perpetually converging. As George Soule has pointed out,[5] all revolution is counter-revolution. In the same sense all wars are fought for causes which are already lost. Thus the present war is a bid for empire, or even world dominance, made at a time when empires are already obsolete and the idea of dominance is fast giving way to the idea of unity and common interest. No issue is ever drawn so sharply as a dead issue. The most violent altercations always occur between Tweedledee and Tweedledum. Economic controversy now seems to be rising to a higher pitch of violence than ever before. Many people

[5] In *The Coming American Revolution* (New York, 1934).

now concede the possibility that capitalism may be giving way to some sort of socialism, or that we may be entering a period of struggle—a struggle that may be indefinitely prolonged and marked by violence going far beyond anything we have experienced as yet—by which the issue will be finally determined. Whereas the economic controversies of the past have been concerned with such trivial issues as the tariff and free silver, it is nothing less than the merits of the capitalist system that are now at issue. But how are those merits stated?

A century and a half ago during the debate over the Constitution the right of property owners to direct the affairs of the community was openly and clearly asserted, and men of substance did not hesitate to advertise their contempt of the propertyless mob. But nothing of that sort is ever heard today. In theory the right to income from investment is perpetual, but in actual practice nobody defends the rights of heirs to be endowed in perpetuity. Even men of the greatest wealth publicly deplore the indefinite perpetuation of their own estates. The principle of estate taxation is universally accepted, and even the eventual extinction of inherited wealth by rates that ultimately become confiscatory has no open opponents. The right to income itself—once an absolute of virtually feudal rigidity—is now qualified by common consent.

Judging by the controversial literature, the vital issues of the present day are those of "free enterprise" and "the profit motive." These principles are indeed hotly defended, and always with the implication that these phrases designate institutions, or aspects of existing institutions, which are in gravest danger of extinction. But do they? The expression "free private enterprise" has been in general use among economists for many years to refer the competitive economy to the analysis of which classical theory has been addressed. Whether any such actuality ever existed is perhaps an open question; but there is no question that the economic actuality of our time has long since been quite different from the free private enterprise of theory. Even those who believe most stoutly that such an economy once existed now mourn its demise.[6]

Nevertheless there is a sense in which free enterprise exists and is worth defending, and it is this actuality which gives plausibility and force to all the pleas for its preservation. Modern industrial society has offered to its subjects a wider range of choices among occupations and greater freedom in the exercise of such a choice than people have ever enjoyed before. The spirit of enterprise which this freedom fosters is very real and very precious, and equally so to all social ranks. The children of industrial society do not find themselves bound to follow the occupations of their fathers. Avenues exist by which they can enter other occupations and even aspire to the professions. The whole community has learned to cherish free enterprise in this sense, and it is on this account that free enterprise affords the best of all possible grounds on which to defend the economic oligarchy under which we live.

But against what threat does this real economic freedom need to be defended? There is much talk of "regimentation," by which the opponents of social change mean to stigmatize everything to which they are opposed. It is good tactics to give a dog a bad name before kicking him, but the name must be made to stick. The trouble with this characterization is its obvious insincerity. Traffic signals are regimentation; bank examiners are regimentation; the pure food laws are regimentation: all bitterly resented by food adulteraters, embezzling cashiers, and escaping convicts. Regimentation may be defined as overorganization. But this is a universal defect of human character by no means confined to government. Corporations secrete red tape no less copiously than

[6] For example, Schumpeter, *Capitalism, Socialism, and Democracy.*

government bureaus.[7] Annoying as overorganization certainly may be, it is not the nemesis of free enterprise. What is implied by the representation of free enterprise and regimentation as opposites is that economic freedom is freedom from supervision. But such is clearly not the case. No freedom of occupational choice exists in a culture in which there is but one occupation, and by contraries the greatest freedom is a function of the widest variety of possible activities. It is of course industrial technology which has broadened the choice of occupation in the modern Western world, not only by creating an immense range of occupations but also by enlarging the facilities of communication and transportation by which actual mobility is continually increased.

So long as technological development continues, no amount of "regimentation" can prevent the emergence of new occupations and the consequent enlargement of the occupational opportunities open to the community. Obviously the organizational pattern will affect the distribution of those opportunities. If we want to know who it is that is most fearful of the threat of "regimentation" to the future of his opportunities, we have only to identify the people who are most concerned about the fate of free enterprise. On this showing it is the discretionary heads of the enterprises collectively known as Big Business who are most fearful for their freedom, perhaps with good cause. No doubt they are very strongly entrenched. They may indeed be able to

[7] *E.g.*, the recently reported case of the extension of the official lunch hour of a certain bureau from thirty-five to thirty-six minutes. The *New Yorker*, Jan. 9, 1943, p. 9. The *New Yorker* speculates on the editorial agitation which would have resulted had this been done by a government bureau, and concludes that since it was in fact done by the Metropolitan Life Insurance Company, "it was done by hard-headed businessmen who obviously had a good reason for it, even if it isn't plain to the layman. Our reflection on this is merely that the adjective 'bureaucratic,' though it springs up like a sturdy weed in the editorials, is really a delicate little plant; transplant it from Washington, it dies."

defend their position successfully. But it is most significant that they should not do so openly.

What is true of free enterprise is also true of the profit motive. When economists, speaking carefully, refer to profits, they mean not the gross earnings of a business but certain net returns which are by no means universal and are not even a sign of general economic health or even of the acumen of their particular recipient but are rather a consequence of the uncertainties and even unpredictabilities of business life. It is not such gamblers' gains that people have in mind when they speak fondly of the profit motive. We may be a race of inveterate gamblers, but it is at least in terms of a game of skill that we idealize the gamble of life. What makes the profit motive precious to the whole community is a much more general conception of profits as the reward of energy and skill, knowledge and judgment. Such qualities are very frequently rewarded, and everybody believes that they should be—hence the effectiveness of the appeal.

The profit motive is a controversial issue only on the supposition that virtue is rewarded only in a capitalistic society, that under "socialism" (in any of its forms) vigor and acumen must go unrewarded while a bureaucratic state takes from each according to his ability and gives to each according to his need with a consequent down-grading of all distinction to the common level. This is nonsense, of course. There is a not-to-be-gainsaid technological linkage between abilities and needs by which the needs of musicians, generals, and commissars are occupationally determined. It is their occupation, not their agony of soul, which requires that violinists be relieved from heavy manual labor and that professors have access to books; and since the achievement of any sort of occupational or professional competence requires some industry and some brains, it would seem that no community can possibly "eliminate the profit motive" altogether and survive. Certainly no community has ever done so, and no leader of any influence in the modern world advocates doing so.

As in the case of free enterprise, advocacy of the profit motive is disingenuous. The activities in behalf of which the principle of just reward is most commonly invoked quite uniformly turn out on examination to be the most outrageous impositions. Thus it is argued at the present time that owners of plants upon the use of which the success of the war effort ultimately depends must therefore be satisfactorily rewarded lest they should feel disinclined to coöperate in the war effort. What is at issue in such cases is obviously not profits either in the economic or the popular sense but tribute exacted by threat of sabotage. It is such tribute and the threat and even the actuality of capitalist sabotage that is the object of condemnation in the slogan, "Production for use and not for profit." Since all production is for use, and since a given volume of production will go no farther by reason of the motives which induced it, this slogan is intelligible only on the assumption that what it advocates on the ground of usefulness is production and what it condemns is profit-motivated non-production.

The issue could be clearly drawn if the familiar slogan were phrased something like this: "Production irrespective of profits." There might then be an alternative slogan, "Profits irrespective of production," which would be a clear and succinct statement of the real concern in behalf of which the profit principle is commonly invoked. But no such slogan exists or could be publicly proclaimed in the present state of civilization.

Such is the fashion in which the power of entrenched privilege is circumscribed by the power of ideas. Certainly vested interests do exist and do exact their tribute in their devious ways. But their ways become increasingly devious as the technological realities of the productive process are more and more clearly understood while the ceremonial amenities on the basis of which the lords of heaven and earth once openly asserted their prescriptive rights have been reduced to tawdry subterfuge.

The bifurcation of the institution of property is an instance of this process. The dissociation of the function of management and that of receipt of income which has been so much discussed in recent years should not be interpreted to mean that the institution of property is disappearing. Feudal rank continues to persist in the full flower of industrial society, and patronymics still preserve a vestige of the patriarchal family. Doubtless property will display a corresponding longevity. But on the managerial side nothing is more certain than the continued socialization of the managerial function, and this certainty is no mere historical inference based on the experience of the recent past. It is a matter of idea. Once the exercise of the managerial function has been identified as such and completely dissociated from the mystic potency of inalienable right, it has no ground to stand on save the technical efficiency with which it may be exercised. No doubt the elaboration of corporate devices was the work of financial legerdemain, and the insincerity with which Big Business has intoned the gospel of service has been sufficiently obvious; but the real irony of the situation lies in the fact that corporate structures themselves provide the machinery of regulation while the gospel of service provides the objective.

Meantime the idea by which excessive inequality of income has been sustained throughout modern times is being gradually undermined. With the advancement of science and the proliferation of machinery, it is gradually dawning upon the industrial community that economic progress is a function of technology, and at the same time the pathetic futility of accumulated money-wealth in the face of economic depression and its complete irrelevance to the prodigious expansion of industrial capacity occasioned by the war is relegating the myth of the creative potency of funds to the limbo of legendary fancies. Gradually but inexorably a state of mind is growing in which the continuous efficient operation of industrial machinery will have replaced the accumulation of funds as the object of general concern and the aim of public policy.

Being a state of mind, this change marks the supreme importance of ideas. But such ideas are the work not of individual thinkers in economics or any other science but rather of a whole community, just as the idea of capital of which capitalist institutions and economic theory have been the embodiment was not the creation of any individual economist but a coinage of the acquisitive society which emerged from medieval feudalism.

To recognize this fact is not to excuse ourselves from individual effort, since the social process is only a summation of the growing enlightenment and the persisting stupidity of individuals. Nor is it to depreciate the intellectual leadership of individual economists or other scientists. Their work is to elaborate and codify, to relate and systematize. Without the work of the classical economists, correlating a quasi-empirical conception of value through the instrumentality of the price system with the basic idea of capital, that idea could not have served as the epitome of the economic life of the Western world for something like four centuries. The debt which future centuries may owe to such economists as may arise to elaborate and systematize the economic thinking of our time will be correspondingly great. But the influence of their ideas will be more than personal.

Furthermore, their formulations, like those of the founders of classical political economy, will be notable for their simplicity. In recent decades economic orthodoxy has become increasingly recondite, and professional economists have barricaded themselves from criticism behind the formidable complexities of their trade. "Oversimplification" has become a mortal sin. This is scholasticism, the last stage in the decay of "the obvious and simple system" described by Adam Smith. The progress of science is always in the direction of the simplification of what seemed complex before. As Willard Gibbs used to say, "The whole is simpler than the sum of all its parts." Einstein's general theory of relativity, of which we were once told that not more than twenty masterminds in the whole world understood it, in fact reduces confusions and contradictions which physicists had contemplated with hopeless bewilderment for generations to a neat and simple series of equations and is now presented to college freshmen in the elementary course. Economics is no exception to the laws of thought.

In the simplification which the economic thinking of our time is just about to undergo, most of the esoteric formulas of scholastic orthodoxy will be swept away. The world will continue to be twenty-five thousand miles around, and with the growth of industry the variety of the economic activities of its inhabitants will continue to increase. But the meaning of those activities may still be essentially simple and comprehensible once they are stripped of the half-truths of the past and the humbug of the present. And as that meaning emerges, no power can prevent it from effecting a like clarification and simplification of the actuality. Already the possibility of abundance is beginning to haunt the economic thinking of our time as a corollary to the meaning of industrial technology. Once that idea has become clear, the actuality will be on the way.

Index